The UN Security Cou
Politics of Internatior.

The relationship between the United Nations Security Council and member countries constrains and empowers both the UN and its member states. While the UN has often provided crucial legitimacy for collective action by the international community, individual countries have also sought to increase their influence by drawing from the authority of the Council. The interaction between the Council and governments helps to define the Council's authority and also the rules of sovereignty, intervention, and power politics.

As countries strive to use and redefine the Council's authority within the international community, this volume examines the politics and law that follows. In doing so, the book observes how the growth of the political authority of the Council challenges the basic idea that states have legal autonomy over their domestic affairs. The individual essays survey the implications that flow from these developments in the crucial policy areas of:

- Terrorism
- Economic sanctions
- The prosecution of war crimes
- Human rights
- Humanitarian intervention
- The use of force.

In each of these areas, the evidence shows a complex and fluid relation between state sovereignty, the power of the United Nations, and the politics of international legitimation. Demonstrating how world politics has come to accommodate the contradictory institutions of international authority and international anarchy, this book makes an important contribution to how we understand and study international organizations and international law.

Written by leading experts in the field, this volume will be of strong interest to students and scholars of international relations, international organizations, international law, and global governance.

Bruce Cronin is Associate Professor of Political Science and Director of the Master's Program in International Relations at the City College of New York, U.S.A. He is the author of *Institutions for the Common Good: International Protection Regimes in International Society* and *Community Under Anarchy: Transnational Identity and the Evolution of Cooperation*.

Ian Hurd is Assistant Professor of Political Science at Northwestern University, U.S.A. He is the author of *After Anarchy: Legitimacy and Power in the UN Security Council*.

Security and Governance Series
Edited by Fiona B. Adamson
School of Oriental and African Studies, University of London
Roland Paris
University of Ottawa
Stefan Wolff
University of Nottingham

Editorial Board:
Mohammed Ayoob, Michigan State University
Richard Caplan, University of Oxford
Neta Crawford, Boston University
Stuart Croft, University of Birmingham
Donatella della Porta, European University Institute
Michael Doyle, Columbia University
Lynn Eden, Stanford University
Takashi Inoguchi, University of Tokyo
Elizabeth Kier, University of Washington
Keith Krause, Graduate Institute of International Studies, Geneva
Bruce Russett, Yale University
Timothy Sisk, University of Denver
Janice Gross Stein, University of Toronto
Stephen Stedman, Stanford University
Mark Zacher, University of British Columbia

This series reflects the broadening conceptions of security and the growing nexus between the study of governance issues and security issues. The topics covered in the series range from issues relating to the management of terrorism and political violence, non-state actors, transnational security threats, migration, borders, and "homeland security" to questions surrounding weak and failing states, post-conflict reconstruction, the evolution of regional and international security institutions, energy and environmental security, and the proliferation of WMD. Particular emphasis is placed on publishing theoretically informed scholarship that elucidates the governance mechanisms, actors, and processes available for managing issues in the new security environment.

Rethinking Japanese Security
Peter J. Katzenstein

State building and International Intervention in Bosnia
Roberto Belloni

The UN Security Council and the Politics of International Authority
Edited by Bruce Cronin and Ian Hurd

The UN Security Council and the Politics of International Authority

Edited by Bruce Cronin and Ian Hurd

LONDON AND NEW YORK

First published 2008
by Routledge
2 Park Square, Milton Park, Abingdon, Oxon OX14 4RN

Simultaneously published in the USA and Canada
by Routledge
711 Third Avenue, New York, NY 10017

Transferred to Digital Printing 2008

*Routledge is an imprint of the Taylor & Francis Group,
an informa business*

Typeset in Times New Roman by
RefineCatch Limited, Bungay, Suffolk

British Library Cataloguing in Publication Data
A catalogue record for this book is available from the British Library

Library of Congress Cataloging in Publication Data
The UN Security Council and the politics of international authority /
edited by Bruce Cronin and Ian Hurd.
    p. cm. – (Security and governance series ; 3)
  Includes bibliographical references and index.
1. Intervention (International law) 2. United Nations. Security
Council. 3. Security, International. I. Cronin, Bruce, 1957–
II. Hurd, Ian.
  KZ6368.U5 2008
  341.23′23 – dc22
                                                2007035829

ISBN10: 0–415–77527–2 (hbk)
ISBN10: 0–415–77528–0 (pbk)
ISBN10: 0–203–93330–3 (ebk)

ISBN13: 978–0–415–77527–4 (hbk)
ISBN13: 978–0–415–77528–1 (pbk)
ISBN13: 978–0–203–93330–5 (ebk)

Contents

Illustrations

Figure

Tables

Contributors

George J. Andreopoulos is Professor of Political Science and Director of the Center for International Human Rights at John Jay College and serves on the Editorial Board of *Human Rights Review*. He is the co-author of *Human Rights Education for the Twenty-First Century*, editor of *Genocide: The Conceptual and Historical Dimensions* (1994), and co-editor of *Non-State Actors in the Human Rights Universe* (2006).

Bruce Cronin is Associate Professor of Political Science and Director of the Master's Program in International Relations at the City College of New York. He is the author of *Institutions for the Common Good: International Protection Regimes in International Society* (2003) and *Community Under Anarchy: Transnational Identity and the Evolution of Cooperation* (1999).

Mitushi Das is a Public Information Analyst at the Strategic Partnerships and Communications section of the United Nations Development Fund for Women (UNIFEM). She has worked as a Program Intern in different parts of the United Nations system and for several non-governmental organizations in the field of women's rights and international development.

Jonathan Graubart is Associate Professor of Political Science at San Diego State College and holds both a Ph.D. in Political Science and a J.D. in Law. He specializes in the areas of international relations, international law, and transnational activism. He is the author of *Legalizing Politics, Politicizing Law: Enlivening NAFTA's Citizen-Petition Mechanisms* (2007).

Ian Hurd is Assistant Professor of Political Science at Northwestern University. His book, *After Anarchy: Legitimacy and Power in the UN Security Council*, examines legitimation and delegitimation of international organizations. His articles on international relations theory and international organization have appeared in a wide variety of academic journals.

Ian Johnstone is Associate Professor of International Law at the Fletcher School, Tufts University. Dr. Johnstone has served as an aide in the Office of the Secretary-General, the Department of Peace-keeping Operations, and the Office of Legal Affairs at the United Nations. He is the author of *Rights and Reconciliation: UN Strategies in El Salvador* (1995) and *Aftermath of the Gulf War: An Assessment of UN Action* (1994).

Jean Krasno is a Distinguished Fellow at International Security Studies, Yale University; adjunct professor of International Relations at City College of New York; and Director of Multilateralism and International Organization Initiative at the Colin Powell Center for Policy Study. Her publications include *The United Nations: Confronting the Challenges of a Global Society*, editor, (2004); and *The United Nations and Iraq: Defanging the Viper*, coauthored with James Sutterlin (2003).

Wayne Sandholtz is Professor of Political Science at the University of California, Irvine. He is the author of *High-Tech Europe: The Politics of International Cooperation* and co-author of *The Highest Stakes: The Economic Foundations of the Next Security System*. He is also the co-editor of a pair of books on European integration: *European Integration and Supranational Governance* and *The Institutionalization of Europe*. His forthcoming book is titled *Prohibiting Plunder*.

Erik Voeten is the Peter F. Krogh Assistant Professor of Global Justice and Geopolitics, Edmund A. Walsh School of Foreign Service and Government Department, Georgetown University. He has authored a number of articles on the United Nations that appear in *International Organization*, *International Studies Quarterly*, *The Journal of Politics*, the *Journal of Conflict Research*, the *American Journal of Political Science*, and the *American Political Science Review*.

Part I

Concepts

1 Introduction

Bruce Cronin and Ian Hurd

The United Nations Security Council is the most powerful international institution in the history of the nation-state system. As a body comprising the world's most dominant and influential states—as well as representatives from each of the world's regions—it has the means to establish and implement a wide range of policies regarding international peace and security broadly defined. When its members pool their military and economic resources, it represents the strongest combination of states in modern times. Yet it is not the mobilization of military or economic power alone that makes the Security Council such a formidable body. Despite their overwhelming resources, the five permanent members of the Security Council (P5) often cannot enforce their resolutions without cooperation from the less powerful states. Thus, for example, economic sanctions, arms embargoes, peacekeeping operations, nation-building, the prosecution of war criminals, and the resolution of civil wars require widespread support from even small states that may otherwise not be considered major players in international affairs. As recent events suggest, even a powerful "coalition of the willing" cannot impose stability in a chaotic region without the active participation of less-powerful countries such as Pakistan, Turkey, and India. These events also indicate that such cooperation can no longer be obtained entirely through coercion or diplomatic inducements; it often requires a widespread acceptance by governments and their populations of the Security Council's legitimate authority to act.

The United Nations Charter invests considerable political and legal authority in the Security Council, and the requirements of UN membership imposes a substantial level of obligation on the states to follow Security Council mandates. In practice, the success of the Security Council often depends less on its capacity to employ its collective military or economic strength than on its ability to gain recognition as the body with the legitimate authority to take a particular action on a particular matter. It is this authority that enables the Security Council to act on behalf of the international community, rather than simply the self-interest of its members.[1] The Council is therefore qualitatively different from previous associations of powerful states such as the nineteenth-century Concert of Europe (which was self-appointed), the League of Nations Council (which lacked credibility) or alliances such as NATO (which represent only a self-selected faction of states).

This volume seeks to explain the sources, effects, and implications of the international authority vested in the Security Council. This approach represents a shift from the traditional ways most scholars in the field have conceptualized international organizations in general and the United Nations in particular. The idea that an intergovernmental body like the Security Council could represent a form of centralized authority challenges our notions of how global governance operates within an anarchical system. Indeed it raises significant theoretical questions about the state of scholarship in the field, and more importantly, about the nature of international relations itself. While the contributors to this volume disagree with each other over whether a radical transformation of the international system is underway, they present important evidence that at least in some areas of international politics, international authority and international anarchy do coexist.

This suggestion requires the support of a volume-sized study. The dominant paradigms in contemporary International Relations (IR) theory either rule out or deny the possibility that any form of centralized authority could exist in an anarchical international system. In fact the very concept of anarchy as commonly understood in the field precludes this possibility by definition. For all the recent talk of "global governance," the serious study of the institutionalization of global authority has not yet begun. Rather, most approaches to this question view global governance as the management and/or coordination of various aspects of global politics, economics, and environmental policy by international and regional organizations (Held and McGrew 2002; Hewson and Sinclair 1999; Vayrynen 1999; Wilkinson and Hughes 2002). If authority implies a right to decide and an obligation to follow, then the concept has been effectively marginalized in mainstream international relations theory. Instead, realists see a system governed by the drive for hegemony and material power (Gruber 2000; Gilpin 1981); institutionalists by cooperation and collaboration under anarchy (Keohane 2002); English school theorists by commonly accepted regulatory rules (Bull 1977; Hurrell 1993; Buzan, Jones, and Little 1993); and constructivists by constitutive rules (Wendt 1992). Despite wide differences concerning the implications of international anarchy cooperation, stability, and security, most theorists agree that in an anarchic system based on the principle of sovereignty, authority rests exclusively within the nation-state itself.

At the same time, a number of scholars have recently challenged the notion that the international system is an "authority-free zone," opening important empirical and conceptual spaces for new research. Some critics, for example, charge that the absence of authority from the international system is, for most IR theorists, a matter of assumption rather than one of empirical proof (Milner 1991). IR theorists have been content to assume that it does not exist and then work out the logical implications of that absence. Theorists representing different paradigms may come to different conclusions concerning these implications, but most readily accept Kenneth Waltz's distinction between international anarchy and domestic authority/hierarchy. At no point is that fundamental distinction put to the empirical test.

While direct tests have not been done, there is a growing literature on substantive problems in IR that uses the language of authority to resolve empirical puzzles. It is now increasingly common for scholars to refer to the authority of the United Nations (Russett and Oneal 2001), of international firms (Sinclair 1994; Hall and Biersteker 2002), of international law (Franck 2003), and of international institutions in general (Buchanan 2003). In particular, the literature on global governance paints a picture of a world that is increasingly organized and coordinated by a complex set of institutions, rules, and norms. Yet with all of this research, the concept of authority is rarely developed theoretically, and its relationship to power politics, state sovereignty, and international law remains unexplored.[2] For this reason, we believe that many studies of the Security Council have drifted away from the theoretical moorings.

This volume aims to connect and extend the literatures on Security Council power and on authority, in the belief that this enriches both. Many students of the Council claim that its authority has been increasing in recent years (Malone 2004). Yet there has been little research examining precisely what this means for the organization of international relations and its relation to the political structure of the international system. The Council appears as an anomaly in the theory of international politics. It does not easily fit our conventional models of an international institution; it is more than a security regime but less than a world governing body. It is comprised of delegates representing the interests of their governments, yet it also acts on behalf of the world association of states. It simultaneously reflects both the principles of intergovernmentalism (Moravcsik 1993: 481) and global governance (Wilkinson 2005; Wilkinson and Hughes 2002). The unwillingness of most scholars to conceptualize the Council beyond traditional notions of a sovereign–state association has led them to define it primarily in terms of their preconceived paradigms. Thus, for example, realists tend to view the Council as a forum for the great powers to act out their competition and conflicts, institutionalists as a mechanism for these powers to collectively manage an increasingly complex and interdependent system, and international law scholars as a legally constituted decision-making body designed to enforce the rules of the United Nations.

This book tries to expand these notions by examining—from a theoretical perspective—the degree to which the Security Council may be evolving into a loosely centralized international authority with the legitimate power to act on behalf of the international community on a wide range of global issues. It does so by placing the examination of the Council's role in international affairs within the broader theoretical context of global governance and the nature of "international authority." It builds upon theoretical advances in understanding political authority and international legitimacy, and employs legal, constructivist, and rationalist approaches to explain the evolution of Council authority. In this sense, The book seeks to contribute to a growing debate within the field of International Relations about the nature of international authority, the power of legitimacy, and the role of international organizations in world politics by examining the most visible and contested source of international authority in the modern world, the UN Security Council.

In a broader sense, we also raise questions concerning what, if anything, an increase in the Council's authority implies about the power of nation-states. If there is a zero-sum relationship between the authority of governments and that of international organizations, then there is a tension between the authority of the Council and the power of states. This would suggest that we may need to rethink our common understanding of the institution of sovereignty. On the other hand, it may be that the trade-off model might not be the most appropriate way to conceive of the relationship: in some cases, power and authority at the Council may *enhance* state power, as when a peace-building mission rebuilds central governments in post-civil-war societies or when the Council endorses a member's "coalition of the willing."

Legitimacy, power, and authority

We must be clear what we mean when we speak of the "authority" of the Council. We define authority as a relation among actors within a hierarchy in which one group is recognized as having both the right and the competence to make binding decisions for the rest of the community (this is articulated in detail in Chapter 2). Authority is therefore a form of power, but a special case of the more general phenomenon. As Hall and Biersteker argue, what differentiates authority from power is the place of legitimacy in establishing claims of authority (Hall and Biersteker 2002: 4). Authority is legitimized power, or as John Ruggie puts it, authority is "a fusion of power and legitimate social purpose" (Ruggie 1983: 198). It is this social purpose (as opposed to purely private gain) that facilitates recognition and legitimacy by the members of a community.

Wayne Sandholtz describes this in Chapter 6 as the "purposive" legitimacy of an organization, a concept similar to one employed by Barnett and Finnemore (1999). Legitimation is possible when an organization is identified with purposes and goals that are consistent with the broader norms and values of its society—some consistency between the organization and social values is essential for legitimation. When this exists, there are at least three mechanisms by which the behavior and practices of the organization might contribute to its legitimation (or delegitimation). These are deliberation, proceduralism, and effectiveness. We discuss these next in order to show some of the complexity in the *sources* of legitimation. Our discussion draws on the categorizations provided by psychologists and sociologists, and in IR settings by Zelditch (2001), Tyler (2001), Barnett and Finnemore (2004: 5), Sandholtz (Chapter 7, this volume), and others.[3] The first mechanism refers to the legitimating effect of deliberation within an organization. As Johnstone shows in Chapter 5, legitimacy can be established through the use of argumentation, justification, and appeals to reasons that reach beyond narrow self-interest in the course of making decisions. The second suggests a type of legitimation that flows from following the correct procedures of the organization—in particular, the terms by which the organization was vested with authority. The third corresponds with "performance" legitimation as described in Chapter 7 by Sandholtz. This envisions legitimacy based on positive results, in particular, the accomplishment of the organization's goals. Given a socially sanctioned social purpose for the organization, these practices can contribute to the belief in the audience in its legitimacy and therefore transform its influence into authority.

It is widely observed that the opportunity for deliberation in an institution increases its legitimacy by encouraging group affinity among the participants (Gambetta 1998). The legitimating effect of deliberation appears to exist even when the outcome of the deliberative process goes against the individual's interests, and it also appears to exist if the individual declines to exercise the right of deliberation. It appears to be the case that the opportunity to deliberate, separate from the act of participating in deliberation or the outcome, is legitimating in itself (Tyler 2001).

Jon Elster and others who theorize about deliberation suggest that it is important because it can change the positions that people take and so may change the outcome of decisions. In his defense of UN "gabfests" Shashi Tharoor (2003) says "talk is the necessary precursor for action. Nothing can change unless the world agrees, through talk, upon change." For Tharoor, deliberation matters because it can lead to different (and presumably better) outcomes from decisions. We could add as well the possibility that deliberation might matter even where it is unlikely to affect the present decision—it might also be significant to the extent that it can alter outcomes or perceptions *for the future*.

There is disagreement regarding *how* and *why* deliberation affects decision-making. For some, deliberation is important because it increases the amount of information available to those making decisions. It helps to equalize asymmetries of information and to reveal the preferences of others. New information revealed through deliberation feeds into the decision calculus of players and causes them to strategize differently than they otherwise would (Fearon 1998). For others such as Charles Taylor and Jürgen Habermas, deliberation matters because the act of participating in deliberation changes the actors themselves. It can alter the preferences of players by changing their identities and therefore their perceptions of their interests. Deliberation requires a vocabulary of shared meaning and values—without these discussion is impossible—and this common vocabulary produces a sense of community. According to Charles Taylor (1979, cited in Adler and Barnett 1998: 31), such "intersubjective meaning gives people a common language to talk about social reality and a common understanding of certain norms." Similarly, Chong (2000: 78) suggests that "Group membership leads to identifying with the group and to developing attitudes, traits, and skills that serve the individual in that environment." Once the deliberators have created these common meanings, they are then able to talk to each other in substantive terms that all will understand. However, at the same time, they have themselves been changed by participating in this process. Says Taylor (1979), "common meanings are the basis of community" and the new sense of community shifts the terms of the negotiation (Albin 2001). Deliberation might bring a community into being among participants and thus legitimize to themselves their collective endeavors. This logic is at the heart of the new "security communities" project in International Relations (Adler and Barnett 1998).

For our purposes here we do not need to resolve the differences between deliberative theories, and can conclude simply that *deliberation—understood as the opportunity for participation and voice according to known procedures—legitimizes outcomes.*[4] Being allowed to participate in a procedure of collective decision-making increases the likelihood that one will accept the outcome as legitimate. Deliberation, however, must take place within the context of established procedures, and these rules can have a powerful impact on outcomes. Proceduralism, or procedural correctness, is a further important mechanism in institutional legitimation.

The Council's legitimacy is therefore in part a function of it following the internal procedures of the United Nations itself. One could argue that in signing the UN Charter, states have not only accepted a set of legally binding principles; they have also recognized the legitimacy of a legally binding political *process*. The Council is primarily a deliberative body that not only vests the power to decide in the great powers—the P5—but also representatives elected from each region in the world—commonly called the E10.[5] In this sense the Council's authority is of the "rational-legal" type described by Max Weber. That is, its foundation is anchored in impersonal rules that have been legally enacted and contractually established by the UN membership. Thus, the expansion of the "breach of the peace" clause to encompass areas that were never envisioned by the framers (such as nation-building and humanitarian intervention) may have been possible because it was done according to the accepted procedures of the Council understood as an international authority with broad powers for international peace and security (see Chapter 4). Through ongoing and often contentious efforts to deal with discrete problems, the Council has been able to expand its authority on a case-by-case basis precisely because the UN membership believed that it was following proper procedures in making these decisions.

Actors strive to legitimize their behavior by showing that it conforms to important rules, norms, or laws accepted as appropriate (Hurd 2005). Unlike a pure power relationship—in which coercion or the threat of coercion is the resource that induces compliance—authority is a relationship which is based on rules. These rules may be procedural or substantive, and they may favor one group over another, but in order for them to be *authoritative* in our sense they require recognition and legitimation by the broader political community.[6] For example, even though the former Soviet Union had the military resources to impose control over the foreign policies of its border states in Eastern Europe, it still sought the legal sanction of the Warsaw Treaty in order to legitimize its domination.[7] Rule-following (i.e. proceduralism) is an important legitimating force.

According to the proceduralist view of legitimation, the procedures the organization follows need not be fair or just in themselves, but they must be *applied* fairly and consistently for maximum legitimation effect. Procedural correctness means fairly following the known rules, not fair procedures as such. (This distinction accounts for avoiding the more familiar terms of "procedural fairness" and "procedural justice.") For the Security Council, this means adhering to the procedures set out in the Charter and in the *Provisional Rules of Procedure* of the Council (S/96/Rev.7 and Bailey and Daws 1998). For other international bodies and conferences there also exist formalized rules of procedure and protocol (for instance, Sabel 1997). The level of detail and specificity in these documents is revealing of the importance placed on procedures: they are explicit precisely because it is important that the rules for deliberation be known to all from the start.

The rules of procedure are defined by the organization and its setting. This means that what counts as "correct procedure" will vary among organizations, and also that the procedural rules of any organization can (and probably will) be biased by the power of strong members in the organization in their favor. This creates a significant opening for the operation of power in the manipulation of procedures and thus in the process of legitimation. Strong actors can alter the procedures in such a way that outcomes are biased in their favor. But the proceduralist hypothesis is that legitimation depends more on perceptions of following correct procedures than on self-interested outcomes, and so bias in outcomes is not antithetical to legitimation (Tyler 2001). What matters most is that the procedures for deliberation were followed correctly, even in the presence of hidden structures of power in the procedures themselves. In fact, many have noted the potentially troubling facts that proper procedures are often used to legitimize what objectively look like unjust or even offensive outcomes, and that, once created, legitimacy might sustain highly unequal outcomes. There is much to worry about in the fact that "people who on some objective grounds 'ought' to view the system as unfair often accept social justifications [legitimation] for the system and feel an obligation to accept its rules and obey its authorities, as do those who are objectively benefited by the system" (Tyler 2001: 425).

Deliberation and procedural correctness are not sufficient for legitimation. If they were, then the most legitimate institutions would be those with the most deliberation and most faithful proceduralism, and this is certainly not the case. The International Labour Organization, for instance, employs elegant and broad procedures of deliberation when considering new international standards for work, and it reaches more deeply into domestic civil society for these discussions than do any other intergovernmental organizations. Yet this does not automatically translate into high legitimacy for its conventions. Similarly, the deliberations of the UN General Assembly do not directly produce legitimacy for its resolutions. As has been learned by the theorists of participatory democracy, endless deliberation cannot itself be the end product of a political system. At some point deliberation must give way to decision-making, and at that point the content of the decision becomes relevant for legitimation.

The third necessary element for legitimation is some degree of effectiveness of the organization in achieving its goals. An organization that is seen as successful (measured according to its own standards of success) will tend to be seen as legitimate. Conversely, an organization that consistently fails to meet its goals will lose legitimacy, and decisions that fail to contribute to the organization's goals will speed that loss of legitimacy. "Effectiveness" here is defined according to criteria which the organization sets for itself, based on its own definitions of what constitute the purposes of, and success for, the organization.

While this does not mean that the organization's goals themselves must necessarily be seen as legitimate or normatively right, Sandholtz in Chapter 7 rightly emphasizes that the "social purpose" of the organization may itself contribute to its legitimacy. To the extent that the substantive objectives of international organizations match legitimated social purposes in the international community—for example, human rights or development assistance—the institution may gain legitimacy and thus the relation of authority may emerge. In the case of the Security Council, the members of the United Nations accept the right of the Council to make binding decisions for the larger community of states at least in part because they also accept the social mission of that body (to provide for international peace, stability, and security) as legitimate and worthwhile. Thus, so long as Council actions reflect the broadly accepted norms and principles of the United Nations, the membership will accord it a measure of legitimacy, and this gives the organization some latitude within which to reinterpret its own mission without provoking a backlash of delegitimation.

With the concept of effectiveness we aim to capture the sense among an audience that the organization has the right and the ability to act in its domain, and this is an important legitimating force independent of the substantive goals of the organization. Possessing the *ability* to act is important in creating a sense of the *right* to act and so in creating legitimacy, and the ability of the Council to act is measured by its past effectiveness.

Effectiveness is hard to operationalize, in the UN and elsewhere. Jean-Marc Coicaud (2001: 296, fn.40) has said generally that "the high expectations of the United Nations then [in the early 1990s] indicated a view that the United Nations had a real role to play and responsibilities to fulfill, and that it was thus recognized as one of the major, credible, and necessary international actors." We can say that the Council will be seen as legitimate to the extent that it is seen to resolve crises of international peace and security. It is difficut to be more specific since there is no single passage in the Charter which defines how the effectiveness of the Council should be measured. The Charter uses permissive and procedural language to set out the powers of the Council—it says what the Council *may* do and then explains the procedures by which it may do it. For instance, Article 33 says the Council "shall, when it deems necessary, call upon the parties to settle their dispute" by peaceful means, and Article 39 says that it "shall determine the existence of any threat to the peace . . . [and] decide what measures shall be taken . . . to maintain or restore" it. Article 24, which is the key paragraph in defining the power of the Council, is cast in terms of how the membership relates to the Council: UN "members confer on the Security Council the primary responsibility for the maintenance of international peace and security."

Coicaud (2001: 265) surveys the history of peacekeeping missions and finds that these missions "gave a sense of purpose, and thus of legitimacy," to the Council through the cold-war years.[8] Peacekeeping, in the traditional form with impartiality and consent of the parties "became an important part of the legitimacy of the United Nations, signaling its ability to have some positive effect in the field of security." The renaissance of Council activity in the early 1990s created an opportunity for the Council to legitimize itself by the expansion of peacekeeping missions, in a way that was denied to it when the superpowers were more reluctant to authorize ambitious missions. This opportunity, however, was contingent on the effectiveness of the missions, and therefore on the effectiveness of the Council as a whole in succeeding in its general goal of "saving future generations from the scourge of war." Taking the issue further, Barnett (2002), in his chronicle of the Rwanda debacle, notes how fearful were senior UN officials that a poorly executed enforcement mission in Rwanda might fatally harm the legitimacy of the whole organization. From the perspective of these officials, the UN's legitimacy (and thus its power) was directly connected to its performance on peace and security issues. In 1994 they therefore failed to push the UN membership for a mission to halt the genocide, on the grounds that the odds of generating a successful operation were small. In retrospect, their logic appears correct though the policy implication is reversed: the UN's ineffectiveness in Rwanda undermined its legitimacy.

The combination of deliberation, proper procedure, and effectiveness can together contribute to the legitimation of an organization. Effectiveness of the organization means that it cannot be ignored by others in its social field, while its deliberative opportunities and procedural correctness add the normative component of the "rightness" of its power. Taken together, these give the institution the "power plus a social purpose" that Ruggie indicates is characteristic of legitimacy. The relationship among the three factors is complex, and it is rare to find all three pushing strongly in precisely the same direction. When there is divergence between the three forces, this means that space has been opened for competing interpretations of the organization's legitimacy, and at such moments much depends on the skill and power of actors in presenting their preferred interpretations.

These different hypotheses about the origins of legitimation lead to a common causal argument about the connection between legitimation and authority. They share the premise that an institution acquires authority when its power is believed to be legitimate. Authority requires legitimacy and is therefore a product of the shared beliefs about the appropriateness of the organization's proceduralism, mission, and capabilities. It is therefore derived only indirectly from the treaty that formally specifies the legal powers of an international organization. What actors *believe* about the organization's legal power is the crucial mediating influence. They may believe something quite different than the actual text of the treaty. For this reason, the authority of the Security Council is only partly knowable from examining the Charter, and may change even without an amendment to the agreement. The following chapters show some evidence of this: variation in the perceived authority of the Council since 1945 has taken place without any change in the relevant legal provisions in the Charter.

One such development may have taken place in the Council's role in regulating the use of force by states: a legalist would point out that the legal power of the Council over the use of force is quite limited—only when it passes a resolution to either forbid or authorize military action does the Council have any legally binding competence over states' use of force. Without a resolution, states are free to act unilaterally or collectively, as long as they respect the rest of the Charter and other international laws. The Council has no legal power over the use of force in the absence of an active resolution on a given crisis. This appears not to have been the understanding of most states prior to the U.S.–Iraq war in 2003, when both sides in the diplomacy over the war acted as if the *failure* of the Council to agree on a "second resolution" in 2003 meant the Council understood the war to be illegal.[9] What matters for the authority of the Council—and of all organizations for that matter—is how the important players in the audience *perceive* and *interpret* the legal mandate of the institution, rather than the text of the legal mandate itself. Widely shared changes in the accepted interpretation of the Charter can change the authority of the Council even if the text remains the same.

The complexities of the triangular relation between legitimacy, power, and authority are the subject of Chapter 2. Their application and effects in the politics around the Security Council are examined in the subsequent chapters.

The changing nature of Council authority

What does this mean for the future of the Council's authority? Most analysts would agree that since the late 1980s the Council has moved to a central place in world politics, arguably more central than at any time in its previous history. The collapse of the U.S.–Soviet rivalry, and the attendant rise in both small-scale localized wars and in international cooperation to resolve them, brought the Security Council into the mainstream of international security affairs. Thus, in the lead-up to the 2003 U.S.-led invasion of Iraq, the central role for the Council was evident in the importance all sides apparently attached to whether or not the Council would endorse the American plan. This sense of importance was shared both by the Bush administration—who preferred to avoid the restrictions of multilateralism but sought the Council's approval anyway—and many other governments—who did not believe they could support the war without it.

The most obvious case was Turkey, whose government was under intense pressure from the U.S. to allow the use of its territory for a northern invasion. In many ways this is a signature case demonstrating the power that the Council's authority has in influencing state behavior in general and domestic politics in particular. Turkey's government was strongly pro-American and its leaders were eager to please the Bush administration, particularly in gaining their influence for membership in the European Union. Despite this pressure (and the government's desire for a badly needed American economic aid package that was contingent on their support for the war), Turkey's parliament (which was controlled by the ruling party) could not endorse the U.S. plan without an explicit Security Council resolution authorizing it (Filkins 2003: 1). This suggests that states share a general belief that the Council has the authority to make final determinations regarding threats to international peace and security.

While the mandate to intervene to maintain international order has always been key among the Council's powers under the Charter, it was essentially dormant during the cold war years. It is only in recent years that changes in both practice and theory have combined to generate the expectation that the Council is a rightful place to conduct international security deliberations of the highest importance. The change was not in the structure or legal status of the organization, but rather the acceptance of the Council's authority by the membership.

As any student of the Council can attest, its authority has undergone a series of shifts over the years, expanding and contracting under the influence of broader pressures in world politics. This requires an explanation. From its earliest design as a Great Power compact, the Council's authority was quickly narrowed by the cold war rivalry so as to exclude all but the most peripheral conflicts between the two blocs. The Council was used far more often for the "propagandistic" value of "directing attention on the one casting the negative vote" than for substantive conflict resolution (Wallensteen and Johansson 2004: 20). Each side could embarrass the other by drafting resolutions that would provoke a veto. Improved U.S.–Soviet relations facilitated the development of a more activist Council; it thus expanded its role along two dimensions. It deepened its involvement in traditional international security problems by intervening more forcefully in interstate wars, with the Iran–Iraq settlement of 1988 being perhaps the first and most notable (on the Council and Iran–Iraq, see Pérez de Cuéllar 1997). And it broadened its reach by finding that new kinds of problems were to be included in the definition of a "threat to international peace and security." Thus, air terrorism, the status of girls in domestic societies, and individual criminal behavior all came to be interpreted by the Council as within its purview under certain conditions.[10] Both dimensions of expansion have meant a growth in the Council's authority.

There have also been areas of contraction in the Council's authority. Articles 26 and 47 of the Charter, for instance, specify that the Council play the main role in a system of mutual disarmament among states and in a collective military establishment with a command structure and dedicated military units. Neither came to pass in the immediate post-World War II years, and throughout the cold war the Great Powers denied the basic right or authority of the Council over these matters. That the Council might have the legal authority to create either system remains controversial, despite the plain language of the Charter on this point. A few states have worked to resurrect a Council military force but none have suggested that the Council take the lead on global disarmament. More recently, Council authority over grave humanitarian abuses by states, asserted most strongly in the resolutions after the Rwandan genocide of 1994, seems to have retreated in the face of opposition from some Council members to intervention in Sudan.

The activism of the 1990s to today is worth exploring, but we should not overlook the effect of the Council even in the most constrained moments of the cold war. That the rival blocs believed that they could gain status by embarrassing the other with defeat at the Council is a sign that the Council was seen as an important source of legitimation (Claude 1967; Hurd 2002). The main players acted as if they accepted that the Council had the right to make authoritative statements on international security to, and on behalf of, the international community. Even if they couldn't agree on how to use the Council to resolve the main conflicts of the day, they seemed to agree that Council approval and disapproval was a consequential asset in international political competition.

The legitimacy of the Security Council

The issue of the legitimacy of the Council to make authoritative decisions on behalf of the international community is raised both by the history of changes in its structure, procedures, and substance, and by the conceptual focus on "authority." The legitimacy of the Council can be approached in at least three ways: (1) the degree of public support or state response to Council actions, (2) as an empirical question, or (3) as a normative question about justice. The second of these is the subject of this volume.

All three can be illustrated by their role in the debate over the 2003 invasion of Iraq. The first was evident in the transnational opinion polling done by

Pew, Gallup, CCFR, and others (Pew Research Center for the People and the Press 2003). In its "Perceptions 2004" report, the Chicago Council on Foreign Relations found that 66 percent of the U.S. public and 78 percent of U.S. leaders agreed that "when dealing with international problems, the United States should be more willing to make decisions within the United Nations, even if this means that the United States will sometimes have to go along with a policy that is not its first choice" (Chicago Council on Foreign Relations 2004: 3). Majorities in most countries prefer to see international interventions approved by the Security Council, as compared to those done unilaterally or by self-appointed coalitions.

The reasons for this support could be diverse, and include both norm-driven preferences for multilateral over individual action and more instrumental concerns about cost-sharing. Whatever the reason, however, they converge in agreement that the Council, among all international organizations, is the appropriate venue for authorizing collective force. Mass publics around the world appear to believe in the Council's authority to mobilize collective force in international society. Similar effects are found in research on public opinion and legitimacy with respect to the European Union (EU). EU studies have long argued that the authority of the EU is undermined if mass publics do not believe that it is legitimate; this had generated a good deal of EU-centered work on both the causes and the effects of legitimation for international organizations (for instance, Gibson and Caldeira 1998).

As an empirical issue of state behavior, the contributions to this volume take the view that the legitimacy of the Security Council affects how states perceive their interests and measure the costs and benefits of their actions. Around the Iraq 2003 crisis, this was on display in the positions taken by many countries that they would endorse and contribute to the operation only on the condition that the Council approved it first. In light of the pressure offered to these countries by the pro-invasion coalition, these positions appear to be more than cheap talk. In some cases, as suggested above regarding Turkey, it is well documented that the failure to gain Council authorization raised the costs and difficulty of the invasion for the coalition. This view holds that whether or not the Council is legitimate is essentially an empirical question about the beliefs of countries or their leaders. Following Weber's subjective approach, the essence of legitimacy is thus a perception on the part of an audience that the institution should be obeyed (Hurd 1999).

Finally, we might consider the legitimacy of the Council as a normative question of international justice. From this position, advocated by Allen Buchanan (2003) among others, the key issue at stake is whether the Council's procedures and outputs satisfy a set of first principles that define a "just" institution. Buchanan's principles, which he applies to the process of recognizing new states and secessionist movements, emphasize the treatment of civilians: a state is legitimate when it respects certain fundamental human rights. Because international recognition of states provides political power to some over others, it should be governed by explicit considerations of moral

theory and of justice. On Iraq, Buchanan (2003: 105) asks not whether countries or people believed the invasion to be legitimate, but whether it served to
enhance or detract from the exogenously given principle that "all persons
have [a right of] access to institutions that protect their basic human rights."
What is distinctive about this general approach is its definition of legitimacy,
as the quality of "being morally justified in the attempt to make, apply, and
enforce general rules" (Buchanan 2003: 187).

Each of the three approaches to legitimacy addresses important questions,
but they are very different and in some ways incommensurate. The empirical
model can be useful for behaviorists but necessarily disappoints those looking
for a normative basis to the concept of legitimacy. The public opinion
approach produces important data, but its connection to state decision-
making remains unexplored. Normative theory can produce internally consistent proposals for new international institutions that achieve a greater
degree of justice than do existing institutions, but these rely on prior consensus on what values we should be promoting. For the most part in what
follows in this book, the authors take an empirical approach to legitimacy.

Constraints on authority

The Council is embedded within the United Nations—the only truly global
organization with a universal state membership—and this provides it with
unprecedented authority to act on behalf of the entire international community, at least within its areas of competence. Yet to say that the Security
Council possesses international authority is not to claim an unrestrained mandate to rule the world. There are at least two types of constraints that temper
any analysis on the scope of the Council's right to issue binding decisions.

First, nothing in our analysis suggests that the Council has a monopoly of
international authority or legitimacy, nor does the concept of authority itself
require exclusivity. Authority does not even have to be centralized. Political
systems can contain multiple decision-making centers with competing or even
overlapping authorities and the anarchic nature of International Relations
guarantees that this will continue to define world politics at least in the foreseeable future. Although in practice (if not in law) the United Nations remains
the chief intergovernmental organization in the world, there are many other
international organizations that address issues that generally fall outside the
UN's mandate. For example, the UN (and the Council) has virtually no
authority to act on issues of international trade or monetary policy. The
World Trade Organization and the International Monetary Fund hold the
premier positions in these areas. Moreover, the UN coexists with regional
security bodies, each of which possesses a degree of authority within their
particular geographic areas. This has often led to a type of "forum shopping,"
in which states may choose the organization most likely to support their policies or produce the most favorable outcome. This was clearly the case with
the North Atlantic Treaty Organization's intervention in Kosovo.

Even within the United Nations, there are conflicts among the political organs. While Article 24 of the UN Charter grants the Council "primary responsibility" for the maintenance of international peace and security, it does not give it exclusive authority, even in its most important issue area. The General Assembly (GA) can make a claim to be the most representative body (although it lacks enforcement capabilities), and it tends to be far more influential in the development of new international law. In fact, some of the most important multilateral treaties—such as the Genocide Convention and the Statute of the International Criminal Court—were initiated by the GA and its Sixth Committee, not the Council. Moreover, in practice some of the most important missions of the UN—such as nation-building, the care of refugees, and economic development—are coordinated and managed by other organs such as ECOSOC.

Second, implicit in the concept of authority is responsibility. When any organization or agency assumes or is granted primary authority in a particular area, it effectively pre-empts or at least strongly discourages others from doing so. This produces expectations that the authority will act when circumstances require it to do so. For example, as citizens we cede to the police and the courts the right to obtain redress when someone violates our lives or property. Yet in doing so we also expect them to take action when such a violation occurs. Otherwise their legitimacy to act as the guardians of domestic security may be eroded. Similarly, when the Council reserves the ultimate right to restore or protect international peace and security, it presumably must at least give the appearance of acting in response to a threat if it hopes to maintain its legitimacy. Most students of the League of Nations agree that the failure of the League Council to address the Italian invasion of Ethiopia doomed the League as an organization. Certainly this expectation assumes some level of general consensus around the particulars. If no such consensus can be reached, the pressure to act will proportionately be reduced. Thus, for example, when the United States failed to convince the Council that Iraq posed a threat to international security in 2003, many states saw this as evidence that the Council should *not* act in that case. On the other hand, widespread horror over the genocides in Bosnia, Rwanda, and Sudan forced the Council to become directly involved in the issues, even if many consider their actions to have been inadequate.

Questions and hypotheses

The above discussion raises as many questions as it answers, which is why we have undertaken this study. In particular, we believe that the following questions need to be addressed in order for our analysis to be useful:

- Who specifically defines the scope of the Council's authority?
- How does this authority influence the behavior and expectations of states?

- What is the source of this influence?
- Does an increase in the Council's role in international affairs also mean an increase in its authority?

The chapters that follow address each of these questions in some way. In doing so, they examine various aspects of international authority in general and the authority of the Security Council in particular. We begin with the proposition that the power of the Council in international politics is largely a function of its authority, that is, a recognition by states that the Council has the right to make decisions regarding international security, stability, and justice that are binding on all members of the international community. Following from this, we propose the following hypothesis as the foundation for this study: *The scope and depth of the Security Council's authority expands and contracts proportionately with the degree of legitimacy that the membership grants it.*

Organization of the volume

Some of the empirical chapters in this volume explore aspects of the Council's legal, normative, or political mandate, finding or failing to find authority in them. Others examine the terms of the delegation of authority between the Council and other actors. Still others examine change over time in the appearance of authority around the Council. All, however, address areas of involvement that go well beyond the Council's traditional emphasis on challenging aggression and promoting international peace and security, including the following: international criminal justice, humanitarian assistance, human rights, international trusteeship over sovereign territory, and the establishment of "safe havens" to protect populations.

Ian Hurd opens the study by examining the ways that authority has been conceptualized for International Relations, and considers how we might usefully assess in an empirical way whether it exists or not in the Council. The concepts he develops in this chapter underpin the empirical studies of the Security Council that follow in the subsequent chapters. Hurd begins with the premise that authority is a peculiar form of power, and its importance is illustrated by the differences between it and brute material force. To identify international authority in the real world, we must look for evidence of a legitimated hierarchy in the relations among states or between states and international institutions. The methodological difficulties that this poses are great, perhaps even insurmountable, but Hurd argues that we still have much that is worthwhile to gain from thinking through hypothetical tests.

Part II examines the sources of Council authority by focusing on delegation, consensus, deliberation, and legitimacy.

Erik Voeten tries to explain how the Security Council can lack direct control over material resources, yet its decisions still carry a fair measure of authority in the international system. He addresses this puzzle using principal–agent theory. The premise of his analysis is that Council decisions matter because those actors that do control material resources (states) have willingly delegated some authority to the Council. In developing this argument, he evaluates various reasons why states might be inclined to do this and what types of outcomes would make them more reluctant to support this delegation. He suggests that it is not very plausible that states would sustain the Council's authority out of a desire for decisions that are compatible with a body of international law or that are morally satisfactory. Instead, he contends that the delegation helps address a recurring political problem in assessing the legitimacy of uses of force by powerful states. The chapter discusses some of the agency problems that arise in this delegation process, especially those related to the delegation of authority from foreign ministries to permanent representatives at the UN.

Turning to law and authority, Bruce Cronin examines why the Council has been able to expand the scope of its legal authority without the explicit consent of the United Nations membership. He argues that this contradicts the prevailing theory of international law, state consent, inasmuch as states have been required to accept changes in the practical structure of the Council without either a change in the Charter or a resolution from the General Assembly. Rather, he argues that the expansion of Council authority evolved through political consensus among the members of the Council and the acceptance of this consensus by the general membership of the United Nations. He holds that this reflects a shift in the way international law is created, practiced and interpreted in contemporary International Relations. In particular, he claims that in specific and well-defined issue areas, states are increasingly recognizing the authority of international consensus over individual state consent as the foundation of legal obligation. In a system lacking central governance institutions, such a consensus is determined through a generally accepted political process that states accept as legitimate. As the main decision-making body within a universal membership organization, the Security Council has developed the legitimacy to interpret and implement consensus-based international law. Thus, the expansion of the Council's legal authority has been accepted as legitimate, even though there was no formal process of achieving state consent.

Ian Johnstone examines the degree to which the Council may be expanding its authority into the area of "international legislation." He specifically considers the political implications of Council resolution 1373 (on the suppression of financing and support for terrorists acts) and resolution 1540 (designed to prevent weapons of mass destruction from falling into the hands of terrorists). He argues that both are unprecedented acts of law-making by the Council in that they impose binding obligations on all states but are neither directly related to a particular crisis nor limited in time. Rather, they impose general obligations in a broad issue area for an indefinite period, something that is qualitatively different from the Council's normal crisis management role. He draws on the theory of deliberative democracy to assess the legitimacy of the resolutions. If the Security Council is going to get into the business of legislating, is the deliberative process that leads to and follows the adoption of these resolutions adequate? He considers who has a say, to whom those with a say must appeal in their reasoning, what sorts of arguments they typically make, and how public the deliberations are. Johnstone's analysis suggests that, while the Council is far from being an ideal deliberative setting, it is less exclusive and closed than meets the eye. Moreover, it is not hard to imagine a number of politically achievable reforms (short of expanding membership) that would enhance the legitimacy of this new "legislative" function.

Part III shifts to an investigation of political practice by focusing on the exercise of Council authority. Sandholtz opens this part by examining the expansion of the Council's authority into the area of war crimes prosecution. He argues that since the criminal prosecution of individuals responsible for atrocities had, in the fifty years since Nuremberg, been considered "essentially within the domestic jurisdiction" of states, the new international tribunals constitute a dramatic expansion of international authority in the judicial realm. In effect, with the first tribunals (for Yugoslavia and Rwanda) the Security Council was creating authority, which inevitably raises questions of legitimacy. That is, in order to function effectively, the tribunals required far-reaching material support and cooperation from governments, yet governments would only offer that support if they perceive the international courts to be legitimate. Sandholtz examines five international and mixed tribunals in terms of the three types of legitimacy defined in the introduction. He argues that, though new international institutions may begin with a substantial reservoir of legitimacy, that legitimacy can dissipate if the institutions are not seen as effectively achieving their purposes. The basis of international legitimacy inevitably shifts from purposive and procedural legitimacy to performance. The chapter closes with cautionary conclusions for the International Criminal Court (ICC), which also began with substantial purposive and procedural legitimacy.

George Andreopoulos examines what he considers to be one of the most interesting post-cold war developments at the United Nations: the Council's growing tendency to identify human rights and humanitarian law violations as threats to international peace and security. He argues that this "normative overstretch" in expanding the Council's authority was viewed by many not only as a mere reflection of a changing global context, but as a conscious attempt at enhancing the Council's legitimacy. His chapter assesses this development and argues that while it has contributed to, and is reflective of, the growing sensitivity of the Security Council discourse to humane considerations, it has also reinforced hierarchical tendencies within the same discourse. In this context, human rights can be perceived as facilitators to the legitimation of a growing array of coercive practices. These developments have posed a challenge for the Council whose key task is to ensure legitimacy in a milieu marked by competing pressures from above (the widening of power asymmetries), and from below (shared expectations of adherence to communal standards). He then examines the extent to which current UN reform initiatives can address some of the problems that this reinforcement has generated.

Jonathan Graubart's chapter presents a sharp normative critique of Security Council authority and the role played by transnational humanitarian and development NGOs in enabling such authority. In so doing, he highlights two characteristics of expanded Council authority that are commonly neglected in International Relations scholarship. First, Council authority is far from neutral or benign. Rather, it is primarily shaped by the policy-makers of the most powerful states, particularly the United States. Similarly, he argues that the nature of Council authority is largely one-directional; the P5 exercise their authority primarily over weaker states in the southern hemisphere. Second, Graubart demonstrates that a set of prominent transnational humanitarian and development NGOs have played a crucial role in expanding the Council's scope of authority to encompass domestic restructuring, known as "peace-building." Indeed, without the active involvement of such NGOs, Graubart argues that the Council's authority to establish peace-building operations would not be sustainable. Through a focused look at Council-authorized peace-building, Graubart shows how a seemingly neutral, humanitarian Council–NGO partnership in fact furthers a one-sided intervention designed and implemented to advance the interests and values of powerful Western states rather than the local population.

Finally, Mitushi Das and Jean Krasno explore ways in which other United Nations bodies have tried to circumvent the authority of the Council, specifically by invoking the Uniting for Peace Resolution. They posit that the very fact that such actions occur suggests that the members of the UN take the Council's authority very seriously. Yet with all authority comes challenges by those who are subject to its directives. Building from this premise, Das and Krasno examine attempts by the UN General Assembly to assert the organization's authority through other means when the Council fails to maintain a consensus among its members. They do so by tracing the history of Uniting for Peace and discussing how it remains relevant in addressing a number of contemporary issues. Their investigation also evaluates the feasibility of this approach by non-Council members.

In the final chapter, Cronin and Hurd return to the larger questions in light of all of the contributions in the book. This concluding chapter examines the power of the Council to effect change in member states without making recourse to coercion. The resources available to the Council are in part derived from the authority it possesses by virtue of its legitimation. This does not suggest that states will always or automatically comply with the Council, but it does show that the effects of the Council cannot be understood by reading the Charter alone. The emergent effects arising from the relation of authority between states and the Council shape the environment and the incentives that structure the choices states make in world politics.

For invaluable help in preparing this volume, we wish to thank Christopher Swarat, who read and commented on the chapters and also prepared the index, and Duncan Snidal and Alexander Thompson for comments on early versions of the chapters. We also thank the Buffet Center for International and Comparative Studies at Northwestern University for their support in hosting a conference where the contributors met to discuss the chapters.

Notes

1 Following Robert Jackson (1995: 62, 69), we define the international community as a collectivity of internationally recognized political actors who interact according to generally accepted procedural norms and standards of conduct that are specified in the charters of international organizations and public international law. Such actors include diplomats, foreign policy officials, and the leaders of non-governmental organizations involved in the practice of International Relations.

2 For seminal conceptual work on authority in the field of International Relations, see Barnett and Finnemore 2004, Barnett 2001, and Hurd 1999.

3 Barnett and Finnemore and Sandholtz both identify the *substance* of the organization's goals as important legitimating forces. In our discussion here, that concept is subordinate to the effectiveness of the organization, which is our third legitimating force.

4 The legitimizing effect of deliberation is part of the fundamental insight of democracy, at least in democracy's participatory versions. However, democratic decision-rules are quite separate from the process of deliberation, and legitimization must not be mistaken for democracy (for some of the connections see Habermas 1996: ch.7). A democratic procedure includes more than merely the opportunity for deliberation—it also includes a decision-rule that satisfies some theory of democratic values. The sociological evidence shows that legitimation is possible even in the presence of highly undemocratic rules of decision as long as procedures of deliberation are followed (Tyler 1990; and also the essays in Jost and Major 2001). Even for decisions rigged from the outset, deliberation can still be legitimating.

5 A resolution requires the support of at least four of the E10. While it is rare for the majority of E10 states to refuse to adopt a resolution supported by the P5, it is always a possibility and this possibility influences the actions of the P5. Bailey and Daws (1998: 249–250) cite two cases of where the E10 refused to adopt a resolution promoted by the P5, through January 1997.

6 This is similar to Hans Morganthau's distinction between legitimate and illegitimate power. Morganthau argues that legitimate power "can invoke a moral or legal justification for its exercise; [it] is more likely to be more effective than equivalent illegitimate power, which cannot be so justified" (Morgenthau 1993: 32).

7 The Warsaw Treaty not only formalized Soviet hegemony in Europe; it also made the East European regimes at least formally equal in status with the USSR, making the stationing of Soviet troops more acceptable to their respective populations. See Fodor 1990: 28; Wendt and Friedheim 1995.

8 Coicaud uses the term "peacekeeping" in a general way to include even the more "robust" peace-enforcement missions such as UNISOM II.

9 For the two sides see Glennon 2003 and Franck 2003, and for analysis of their shared premises, see Hurd 2006.

10 On air terrorism, see SC Resolution 731 (1992), on the status of girls see Resolution 1325 (2000), on criminal acts see Resolution 1593 (2005).

2 Theories and tests of international authority

Ian Hurd

Susan Strange made a celebrated critique of the regimes literature in the early 1980s, challenging theorists and empiricists to reconsider the conceptual content and historical development of "regimes" for international politics. In her overview, she found the term to be used in a broad array of ways, allowing a false sense of consensus among scholars over the importance of the new approach by concealing great differences in meaning. Empirically, she found that almost any pattern in IR was likely to end up being called a regime. This had the danger of leading to the reification of what were really just transient phenomena produced by strategic state behavior governed by considerations of power. She said "all those international arrangements dignified by the label regime are only too easily upset when either the balance of bargaining power or the perception of national interest (or both together) change among those states who negotiate them" (Strange 1983: 345).

The literature on international authority is today in an analogous position to that of "regimes analysis" in the early 1980s, characterized by a lack of clarity in the definition of the basic concept and an under-attention to careful tests of its existence. A number of scholars are now making claims about the existence and effects of authority in various corners of IR, and the multiplication of definitions and the absence of testable propositions makes comparing, challenging, and eliminating any of them virtually impossible. As a result, the literature on international authority has been expanding, with endless potential for further growth. Without tests or definitions, neither empirical failure nor conceptual boundaries can possibly limit its expansion. For "regimes" in 1982, as for "authority" today, this is an unhealthy condition for IR scholarship. After Strange's attack on regimes analysis, more carefully bounded and empirically testable research programs on regimes were the result, and a smaller but more coherent field of study emerged. Something similar needs to happen to the concept of international authority.

This chapter addresses the question: Is the Security Council in a position of authority over states? Or, more correctly, it addresses how we might go about answering that question. One goal of conceptual thought on authority must be, as Steven Lukes (1990: 204) put it, "to identify relations of authority and distinguish them from others." We want to know whether a particular relation of power counts as an instance of authority or as something else. From this position we might be able to make claims about the existence and effects of authority among international organizations and the implications for the international system as a whole. Can this be done? Do the existing models of authority in IR provide empirically grounded resources with which to separate the effects of authority from other kinds of influence? This chapter examines the meaning of the term "international authority" for the Security Council and considers how its presence or absence might be assessed. It establishes the first steps toward a strategy for answering the question: "Does the Security Council exercise international political authority over states?"

Defining international authority

Authority is a central concept in the study of human society. In a famous essay in political philosophy, Richard Friedman (1990: 57) said that authority "has proved to be an elusive concept, as well as an indispensable one." An equally famous paper in political science argued that explicating "authority patterns" was at the heart of understanding politics, and at the heart of political science itself (Eckstein 1973). And Hannah Arendt (1958: 81, 83–84, 112) declared that "authority has vanished from the modern world" and that by the twentieth century "it is almost impossible to have a genuine experience of what authority is, or rather was." She came to this conclusion having anchored authority in tradition and then noted the "loss of permanence and reliability" that sustained tradition. In International Relations, there has historically been less of an interest in exploring the workings of authority, but indirectly the concept of authority has been central to IR theory. Authority has always been present as the "quiet" half of the anarchy/authority dichotomy. While "anarchy" has received all of the attention, it has always depended on an implicit contrast with authority (Milner 1991; Hurd 1999). By assumption, neorealism and neoliberalism agreed that authority did not exist among states, only within them. The contrast did not need to be made explicit. Clear definitions of authority and tests of its presence were made unnecessary by the assumption of international anarchy. The "anarchy problematique" (Ashley 1998) proved highly productive for IR theory, and yet its foundation on untested premises about the absence of authority remains intellectually unsatisfying. This chapter aims to delineate what tests for international authority might look like.

To look for evidence of international authority we must first know to what the term refers and definitions of authority abound. They tend however to circulate around a central tendency which can be easily identified. Arendt's (1997: 93) formulation stands as well as any as a conventional one: authority is a relation "between the one who commands and the one who obeys" in which what the two "have in common is the hierarchy itself, whose rightness and legitimacy both recognize" (see also Barnett and Finnemore 2004). The crucial elements here are: (1) a *relation between subordinate and superior*, that is (2) *recognized by both* as (3) *legitimate*. These three are found in most conceptions of authority in political theory and International Relations: mutual recognition of a legitimate relation of hierarchy. The result is a form of power distinct from coercion, from rational persuasion, and from instrumental calculations of costs and benefits. Authority is a subset of the category "relations of power" and its defining feature is the existence of a legitimated hierarchy.

From this common starting point, divergence occurs as cross-cutting typologies are developed. For instance, Weber examined three devices by which power might be legitimized: tradition, charisma, and law. Friedman (1990: 60–61) elaborated on the "familiar distinction" between a person who is "in authority" and one who is "an authority," the former being about a formal position with the right to issue commands and the latter a personal identification of expertise. Lukes (1990) argued for seeing authority as fundamentally different depending on one's "perspective" on the society, so that a relation of authority is a different thing from the points of view of the subordinate, of the superior, of the "objective" outside observer, or of the imagined social consensus.[1] Coherence among these is, he argued, impossible. These typologies are, in Elman's (2005: 298) terms, "explanatory" typologies: they use a prior theory to deduce different categories of authority and make predictions about expected outcomes in each category. The prior theories that they employ, however, are not comparable with each other because they approach different versions of authority questions (for instance, "what makes authority?" as opposed to "how do we know if authority exists?") and so the complexity they produce cannot be reduced.

The common tradition that defines authority as legitimated power implies a unique relationship between ruler and ruled. In philosophy, it is common to distinguish the authority relationship from, on the one hand, coercion, and on the other, rational argument (see, for instance, Friedman 1990 and Lukes 1990). To either coerce or to reason with a subordinate are both taken to be signs of the absence of authority. The contrast with coercion is straightforward: the need for or use of coercion implies a lack of authority. Arendt (1997: 93) says "authority precludes the use of external means of coercion; where force is used, authority itself has failed." On the contrast with reasoning: the logic of the authority relation makes reasoning unnecessary, and perhaps even undermining. Authority involves the "surrender of private judgment" so that the audience's critical faculties are irrelevant to the process. Summarizing the long history of this approach, Friedman (1990: 67) says "To defer to authority, then, is to refrain from insisting on a personal examination and acceptance of the thing one is being asked to do (or to believe) as a necessary condition of doing it (or believing it)." An institution with authority carries with it "a very special sort of reason for action" by subordinates (Friedman 1990: 67) but "reason" here is meant in the sense of a causal factor determining compliance (an independent causal variable) not in the sense of a process of autonomous thought. Following an authority is done without thinking; it is a product of socialization, not of consent.

Definitive interpretation of the "true" essence of authority is impossible. Instead, I want to carry forward the conventional core of the concept, as "legitimated power," and examine how that concept has been applied in International Relations. We can then refine the concept through the interplay of the empirical claims made about international authority and more rigorous tests that we might devise for it.

To sum up, international political authority is a social relation where a hierarchical relation in the international sphere is recognized as legitimate. This may occur in a variety of ways, including between two states, between a set of states and an international rule, or between an institution and states. An example of the first is the social relation when Great Powers are accepted by other states as legitimate leaders (Hurd 2007b). The second might exist in the relation between states and some rules of international law, for instance, the deference of states to the norm that behavior should conform to international rules. The last might exist between a formal international organization such as the Security Council and the states that recognize it, and it is this question that motivates what follows in this chapter.

Authority is a social relation that exists between actors and the structures that make up their social setting. It exists when actors believe that the structures embody legitimated power and they act in ways that reinforces it. Studying possible relations of authority between states and international organizations requires that we pay attention to both how states are affected by the existence of legitimated structures and how those international organizations are affected by the behavior of states. In this chapter, I focus on ways we might observe the existence of authority from the behaviors of states. It emphasizes the effects on agents from the presence of authoritative structures in international society. This is not an ontological commitment to agents over structures but rather a result of the pragmatic decision to explore what observable features might follow from states' beliefs in Council authority. Other chapters in this volume open up the agent–structure relationship differently: for instance, Cronin in Chapter 4 examines some structural effects of changing consensus patterns among states and Sandholtz looks at how institutions of authority might be created in the first place. Throughout, however, the contributions in this book operate from the premise that authority exists (when it exists at all) in the interplay between agent and structure. They find different paths into the complex relationship between states and structures but they agree on the importance of looking at what exists in between the two.

The next section begins the empirical search for authority relations in International Relations by looking at instances where recent claims have been made about the existence of international authority. The subsequent section then considers how we might evaluate these claims with falsifiable tests.

Looking for authority

It is common to call the United Nations an "international authority." In noting the weakness of the UN in the early 1980s, Kenneth Thompson (1981: 411) saw evidence of a general pattern that "when international authority proves ineffective, powerful states intervene and confront the weak." Since then, as Michael Matheson (2001: 76) observes, "the United Nations has exercised authority in significant new ways." Adam Roberts (2002: 136) notes that the Council "has exerted a degree of authority over some recalcitrant states" in international society. David Schweigman (2001: 7) looks to the UN Charter to determine the "limits to the Council's authority." Mark Plunkett (2003: 214) identifies peacekeepers in failed states as the bearers of the authority of the UN and international law. On what evidence do these authors found their claims that the Council has authority?

The premise of this volume, as explained in Chapter 1, is that international authority is a sociological concept rather than a purely legal one. In other words, authority exists when actors believe that a rule or hierarchy is *legitimate* and thereby it contributes to their perceptions of their interests. This approach is arguably less prevalent than the alternative legalist view in the IR literature. The distinction between the two is crucial to devising empirical tests for authority.

The legalist understanding of authority uses the term to refer to the legal powers and structures that constitute the organization: in this view, the legal terms of the Charter delimit its (legal) authority. This view sees the Council's authority under the Charter as delegated by member states through the act of consent when they sign the Charter (Barnett 2001: 59), and from there it can be further delegated by the Council to states, other international organizations (IOs), and other parts of the UN organization (Sarooshi 1999). This approach treats the Council as the "agent" to which authority is delegated by member-state "principals"; ambiguities in the delegation contract might then manifest themselves in oversight and control problems later, but the act of delegation is clearly understood by all parties.[2] This approach involves two distinct steps. First, it defines the authority of an international organization in legal terms, tightly coupled to the founding treaty from which the organization springs. Second, it treats authority as a commodity, tradable among actors on terms of exchange known to both parties in a kind of marketplace of legal relations. The legal powers of an organization can be subdivided and "rented out" to other players as necessary as delegated authority. To equate "authority" with the legal structure of an organization allows that authorities can be weak and ineffective yet remain authorities as long as their formal charters sustain them in a legal and corporate sense.

The existence of international authority in this sense is undeniable although not very interesting. States accept the principle that duly ratified international law is a source of binding and legitimate authority and they generally defer to it, even if they often also promote self-serving interpretations of their obligations under the law. The central role played by state consent in international law makes authority of this kind rather banal; as I discuss below, it removes from the concept everything that motivates the debates among philosophers including the tangled relations among agency, choice, power, and law.

The obligations accepted by states in relation to international law are indeed binding on them, but the usefulness of the legalist conception of authority is limited by the fact that states retain the absolute right to choose which instruments to consent to and to re-evaluate their prior consent at any time. States can choose to revoke their consent to international legal obligations and they can choose to violate the law. The legalist view is therefore fundamentally agentic and shows none of the "surrender of private judgment" that the sociological concept of authority implies. Authority that comes with an opt-out clause is not what the philosophers of authority had in mind. There are of course some obligations of international law from which states cannot escape, either of the *erga omnes* or the *jus cogens* varieties.[3] No state objects to the principle of these kinds of obligations, but there is no consensus on their substantive content either, and so they represent a highly uncertain corner of international law (Bassiouni 1996; Tams 2005). It is precisely the tension between sovereignty and consent on one hand and legal obligation on the other that holds back more general agreement on the nature of these obligations. This supports the general conclusion that legal obligations are strong in international law only when backed by active state consent, and this limits the reach of "authority" strictly defined in the international legal realm.

Focusing on consent as the basis of law is congenial for many in IR since it preserves the dominance of state sovereignty and makes other obligations subsidiary to it. It leads to the conclusion that international political authority, at least as defined in Chapter 1, is fundamentally inconceivable. Since consent and delegation are *revocable*, models that are based on them are guaranteed to find that ultimate authority rests only with the state. This is incompatible with the mutually recognized legitimate subordination of the state to an external source of power which I defined as at the heart of international political authority.

The dominant paradigms of international thought of the twentieth century used this legalist understanding of authority to rule out the possibility that authority could exist in international affairs—for neorealists and neoliberals, authority existed only within the nation-state. For them, the distinguishing feature of domestic government is that it creates a system of hierarchical authority in which it is generally accepted that some are in positions of command and others in positions of subordination. Even in democratic domestic systems, where the equality of citizens is a well-established principle, a hierarchy of bureaucratic offices exists leading up in a pyramid to the head of state. No such hierarchy of authority exists in international affairs, and Waltz (Waltz 1986: 111) takes it to be axiomatic that in an anarchy of states no institutions of authority can develop. "National politics is the realm of authority" he says, while "international politics is the realm of power, of struggle." David Laitin (1998) applies a similar sensibility in his response to Eckstein's definition of authority, where he suggests that International Relations is characterized by "exchange between states" rather than relations of authority among them.

Two recent developments in the IR literature pose potential challenges to this neat pairing of domestic with authority, and international with anarchy. These represent the opening of a possibility for the sociological study of authority in IR. The first is an empirical literature studying the growth in UN peace operations in the 1990s.[4] The UN's peace-building missions, as in East Timor and Cambodia, may include direct UN governance of post-conflict territories and societies. These are often highly intrusive and may, in their mandates from the UN Security Council, establish that the mission is the legal holder of state sovereignty for the duration of the "transition" period. In such cases, the missions are often identified as having authority over the state and society. For instance, Caplan (2004: 60) says of the transitional administration of Bosnia and Herzegovina, "in a legal sense, the high representative's authority would seem to be unassailable [since] the parties to the conflict themselves requested the designation of a high representative and agreed to his mandate." Further, the Security Council, "an important legitimating body," endorsed the arrangement. If mutually recognized, this legitimate hierarchy may qualify as authority.

Studies that take this approach tend to *assume*, rather than test, that the international administration of the territory through the UN is legitimate and therefore "authoritative." By virtue of coming through the UN Security Council or other UN structures, the result is assumed to satisfy the criteria for legitimate power. This approach is thus the mirror-image counterpart to how the "anarchy problematique" dismisses authority: each establishes by assumption rather than empirical testing that only half of the anarchy–authority dichotomy need be considered. They disagree on which half is relevant but the logic is the same.

The second cluster of new research that asserts the possibility of international authority comes from international political economy (IPE). The regimes that regulate firms in IPE sometimes demonstrate a capacity for rule-making that is at once authoritative and not dependent on state power. This, many believe, is a source of "market authority" in the international system. In a well-known case study, Timothy Sinclair (1999) showed that certain firms in the financial services industry exercise effective authority in IPE by virtue of the power of the information that they collect and sell. Credit-rating firms such as Moody's and Standard & Poor's centralize information on the creditworthiness of their clients and disseminate it to potential investors. This information is important for avoiding potential market failures, but it also plays a more political role when states are the ones using ratings or being rated. These firms have legitimated power over states by virtue of their place in the market system and the value of the information they sell. This implies that the firms have crossed the line into being institutions of international political authority. Such institutions therefore transcend *two* conventional boundaries—those between the public and private and those between the domestic and the international. Ellen Wood (1981) has argued that the liberal tradition accepts that authority exists only in the domestic-public quadrant of this two-by-two grid, and builds the rest of its edifice on this foundation. The discovery of private *and* international authority would thus have significant consequences for IR (Rosenberg 1994).

This is pathbreaking and significant in many ways, but it is not clear that the IPE literature on private authority really has found evidence to transcend the domestic-international half of this claim. The essays in the Hall and Biersteker (2002) volume, for instance, provide evidence of a transfer of authority from one kind of actor (states) to another (firms), and while both types of actors have international presences and effects, both are also best conceptualized as national or trans-national rather than international. The changes in the distribution of authority that they describe are horizontal, not vertical. For a vertical dimension to exist, we would need to see evidence of *supra*-national actors or rules with authority.

International authority requires this vertical dimension. Hints in this direction are provided by writers on the "retreat of the state" such as David Held and James Rosenau, but this tends to be impressionistic rather than rigorous. James Rosenau (1992: 256) sets out the logic, though not the empirics, in an early article from 1992:

> At the core of the new order are defined criteria of political legitimacy and a relocation of authority that have transformed the capacities of governments and the conduct of public life. Put most succinctly . . . just as legitimacy is increasingly linked to the performance of officials rather than to traditional habits of compliance, so has authority been relocated in the direction of those political entities most able to perform effectively. This relocation has thus evolved in two directions, "upward" toward transnational organizations and "downward" toward subnational groups, with the result that national governments are decreasingly competent to address and resolve major issues confronting their societies.

Setting aside Rosenau's hypothesis that authority is a product of beliefs about the "effectiveness" of officials, we see here the clear implication that international authority has indeed been created by changes in perceptions regarding which institutions have the legitimate power to perform certain governance functions.[5] This opens the possibility for an international version of the kind of authority imagined by Arendt, Lukes, and Friedman above. Rosenau, however, remains vague about which international institutions he thinks have acquired this authority, and how he is going about determining this.

In the context of the UN Security Council, we might then construct the following claim: if it can be established that the Security Council is seen by states as having authority in determining appropriate and legal uses of force, then a vertical relation of authority from IOs down to states would have been established. For empirical research on the question, we could perhaps make use of the behavior of states around the Council in the lead-up to the U.S.–Iraq war in 2003: several states sympathetic to the U.S. said they would support American action only if it was first approved by the UN Security Council, and the U.S. approached the Council seeking to have its preferred policy endorsed. Kofi Annan (2002) reinforced the issue by saying at the time that "when states decide to use force . . . there is no substitute for the unique legitimacy provided by the United Nations Security Council." If this perception is widely shared by states, it would signal that the Security Council is in a position of authority over nation-states in deciding when international force can rightfully be used. This would amount to a substantial change in the organizing principle of the international system that would require revising the conventional wisdom regarding the anarchic nature of the system.[6]

Testing for authority

These questions cannot easily be answered one way or the other. How shall we approach assessing the possibility that authority exists in the Council? And more generally, where is the evidence for international authority, and what are the tests for it? On both questions (tests and evidence) existing claims to have found a vertical dimension to the transfer of authority are weak, or at least weakly founded. Is it possible to develop empirical tests that would establish whether or not there exists a vertical dimension to authority relations in the international system?

We are presumably interested in studying international authority because we have some reason to believe that its presence and nature affect how world politics unfolds. There must, therefore, be a behavioral consequence of authority which is observable. If it is observable, then it should in principle be amenable to tests for its existence. But testable in principle does not mean testable in practice. It may, for many reasons, be impossible to determine by empirical tests that the Council has authority over states or not. It could be, for instance, that the concept is simply not of a type that can be tested for. Because it relies on the psychological belief in legitimacy, and the scientific method cannot accurately measure subjective beliefs, authority might be inherently untestable. A separate problem would be if the concept was undefinable. If each observer constructed a different but equally plausible definition of the concept then any test that we devised might apply to one definition and not others. Attempting to generalize across tests with incommensurate foundations would be futile. A further obstacle to testing is the problem of observational equivalence.[7] Assuming we are able to identify observable behaviors that are consistent with international authority, we must be confident that at least some of these are also *inconsistent* with competing explanations of social order, such as coercion or self-interest. Any of these three problems would be sufficient to make it literally impossible to use positivist methods to answer the question of whether or not the Security Council is in a position of political authority over states.

Empirical testing is not a problem only for scholars studying *international* authority. It is equally challenging for scholars of domestic states: the domestic literature on state authority is not full of successful models of how to test for authority. The problem of observational equivalence between authority and other forms of social control runs deep. This matters for us in two ways: first, it means there are few ready methods from which to borrow as we approach the issue in relation to the Security Council, and second, it may give reason to believe that such tests are fundamentally impossible.

Thinking through hypothetical tests is important even if one suspects that once developed they won't be practical to perform; it is useful still for helping to isolate what are the essential features and observable implications of authority. This might help further refine the conceptualization of the term, and perhaps secondary hypotheses might emerge that could be testable.

Having defined authority above as the internalization of a belief in the legitimacy of the Council, the purpose of this section of the chapter is to ask "what could constitute evidence either for or against a claim that this belief exists?" I present three possibilities and compare their strengths and weaknesses. Each of the three attempts to measure a different behavioral implication of the presence of international authority. They focus on compliance, justification, and unavoidability.

The first approach borrows its method from recent constructivist literature that attempts to measure the influence of legitimated norms by looking at state compliance. The rules from the UN Charter that set out the Council's legal position on the international use of force could be essentially the same as other international norms whose negotiating history and legal status have brought countries to accept them as legitimate. Since the rules appear to give the Council a position of oversight over states' decisions to use force, this would indeed be grounds for considering them, and the Council as their corporate embodiment, authoritative. To test whether or not the rule is seen as authoritative, we could then borrow from the literature on norms their devices for determining what is or is not a legitimate norm. One such approach comes from March and Olsen's (1998) distinction between the logic of appropriateness and the logic of consequences. They expect a pattern of behavior around a legitimate norm that is different than that which associates with other kinds of rules. When actors make decisions under the influence of legitimized norms, they behave in ways that they believe are appropriate for actors of their identity in the given situation. Rather than consider the instrumental payoffs that would follow from different course of action, agents automatically pursue the action that they have been socialized to believe is appropriate under the circumstances; "appropriate action is action that is virtuous" (March and Olsen 1998: 951, 953). At an aggregate level, this creates "a community of rule followers and role players with distinctive . . . intersubjective understandings, and sense of belonging." The decision-making pattern characteristic of the logic of appropriateness is distinctive as compared to that of the logic of consequences: strategic thinking is out, self-motivated compliance is in. While conflicts within the psychology of the actor might force them to sometimes violate one norm in order to comply with another, we should *ceteris paribus* expect to see compliance with legitim-ated rules as the default option.

This could be used to formulate a test of the Council's legitimacy and authority relative to states. Do we indeed observe that compliance with the Council is the default position for states? Or do we observe states making cost-benefit calculations in a strategic manner around their relations with the Council? The former would support the logic of appropriateness and the latter the logic of consequences. A slightly different test might focus on the surrender of private judgment rather than on the act of compliance: Do we observe states making critical judgments about whether or not to comply with the Council based on expected utility?

If the test is cast in this way, the Council would presumably fail to show evidence of authority. The history of the Council reveals little evidence that states comply automatically with its decisions. Despite the legal obligations in the Charter to "accept and carry out the decisions of the Security Council" (Art. 25) and to "join in affording mutual assistance in carrying out the measures decided upon by the Council" (Art. 48), we see nothing like the unthinking acceptance of the Council and its decisions. Further, on the more specific test of the surrender of private judgment we find little in the behavior of states that fits the standard. States continue to act strategically in and around the Council, as they do in all their foreign policies. Their appeals to the Security Council, and the uses to which they put Council past decisions, are inherently political and so can be presumed to have some instrumental calculation behind them. The effect of Council resolutions on state behavior looks nothing like automatic compliance or a surrender of private judgment. While there may be many reasons that compliance takes place, not all of them attributable to the existence of authority (see, for instance, Hurd 1999), the lack of compliance must on this test be seen as decisive evidence *against* authority.

I suspect that this construction of the test is misleading and ultimately an empirical dead-end, not for any reason having to do with the Council itself but rather for conceptual and practical difficulties in the separation of March and Olsen's two logics. It is unreasonable to set strategic thinking and social-ized rule-following as mutually exclusive categories for decision-making. Authority understood in this sense makes for subordinates who are automa-tons (Wrong 1961). There can be no strategic thought around authority, and no resistance. State behavior is rarely understandable as either entirely norm-driven or strategic—instead, most decision situations appear to be affected both by strategic assessments of self-interest and concern for what is appropriate in the community. Reputation, status, and social standing are all derived from appropriateness, and all enter into strategic thinking. Said differently, at no level of compliance, from none to complete, can we say that compliance gives decisive evidence for or against the presence of authority.

The second approach to testing tries to incorporate this insight by examining evidence that actors feel the need to *justify* their behavior to the institution. Evidence of the authority relation might come from these behaviors of justification, rather than from compliance. For the Council, we might look to see if, and how, countries justify their actions to the Council. A demonstrated need by states to justify their actions in terms approved by the Council could be evidence that they have internalized the Council's position of authority, and so support a claim that authority exists. Conversely, the absence of such a need would presumably discount claims of authority. Ian Johnstone (2003) among others, has used this insight in international law by borrowing from Habermas the idea of a justificatory discourse as an instrument of power. States are displaying a relationship of subordination to the Council to the extent that they behave as if they feel required to justify their behaviors to the institution. This approach is not concerned with rates of compliance with the Council's decisions. It looks instead for patterns of justification, accepted by states as appropriate and *required* in the situation. In March and Olsen's terms, this involves both a logic of consequences and of appropriateness: states believe that a legal discourse is appropriate for the venue of the Council, and then scheme to maximize the benefits to them of providing a legal interpretation of their actions. What this displays is not necessarily authority vested in the Council itself, or in the relationship between states and the Council, but, rather, it reveals a belief among states that the legal discourse is authoritative in this setting. This could provide evidence that international law as a practice or an international institution might be authoritative over states.

This relates to the claim earlier that discussion among international lawyers about "legal authority" of the Council is relatively uninteresting since it removes from authority the complications of interest to the philosophers. Focusing on justificatory discourse in international law brings back these debates about what is or is not part of the Council's legal ambit under the Charter, and who wins these arguments matters a great deal for what kinds of state behavior are approved as acceptable. There is practical power in these debates, but it is indirect and premised on a prior understanding that the terms of legal discourse are in themselves authoritative for deciding what is appropriate for states.

The relationship between reason and authority in this approach is subtle.[8] It does not necessarily contradict the notion, suggested above, that authority is antithetical to reason. Justification involves the giving of reasons for behavior, and this could be consistent with the highly socialized view of the individual that underpins the authority relation. States might believe that they are obligated to justify their actions in legal language at the Council, but as long as they are not using independent critical reasoning to decide *whether or not* this obligation exists then we could conclude that they believe that some international institution, either the Council or the legal discourse, has authority over them.

What evidence is there that the Council is treated in this way by states? There is indeed a great deal of effort by states at the Council to justify their positions in international law—some of this is probably genuine, and much of it likely insincere. Is this evidence for the authority of the Council? It certainly would seem to signal that actors see some advantage from finding support at the Council for their policies. This may be evidence of authority, but it is inconclusive. The distinction between genuine and insincere justification is irrelevant to assessing the evidence of authority since what we are looking for is precisely that actors feel the need to frame their behaviors in ways that they believe will bring approval from the institution. Self-serving and insincere justification is all the more evidence of the institution's authoritative standing relative to the actor. If the institution were without authority, then actors would presumably feel no need to justify themselves to it.

A final way we might test for authority at the Council expands on the justificatory approach and looks for signs that the Council has entered into the decision-making calculus of states. It looks for automaticity of the influence of the Council on state decision-making. If states must, whether they want to or not, include the Council and its effects on the world as part of their strategic thinking about international affairs, then perhaps this is evidence that they, or some subset of them, take it as authoritative. Not every state will believe in the legitimacy of the institution, and so not all will experience it as a relation of authority, but when enough of them do then all must take that into account when making their strategic calculations. Max Weber (1978: 312–320) referred to this as the "validity" of the social system: the structural condition that occurs when enough members of society believe in the legitimacy of the social order that all must incorporate it into their decision-making (see also Hurd 2007a: ch.2). What is crucial to this approach is that the element of choice has disappeared: states do not choose whether or not to include the Council in their calculations—the Council is embedded in the fabric of the society so that it is unavoidable to actors. It can be fought against, contradicted, and reinterpreted, but it cannot be ignored. It is constitutive of the international society.

What is the evidence according to this test? The Iraq 2003 case shows that even powerful states were forced to frame their policies around the existence of the Council. Both coalitions of states, pro- and anti-invasion, found themselves unable to avoid arguing about minutiae of Charter clauses. Both accepted that Council approval was a powerful resource for states, and so they fought to either win it or withhold it from the other (Hurd 2006). The Council was therefore made to seem all the more relevant and powerful at the center of the international regime on the use of force. Is this evidence of its authority? Perhaps, but again the verdict is inconclusive: it shows that the Council has some power, in so far as it has the ability to confer or withhold its approval from states, and perhaps the deference shown by the countries that waited for that approval before supporting the war is evidence of its legitimacy to them, but there remain highly contentious unresolved questions: What is the relation between the power of the Council and the states that make it up? Were the deferent countries motivated by beliefs in the legitimacy of the Council or by something else?

More generally, this approach has a real danger of going too far. Defining "unavoidability" as behavioral evidence of authority risks masking a number of other, non-authoritative reasons why an international institution has a prominent place among states. For instance, the Universal Postal Union is unavoidable for countries that hope to participate in international post, and the International Olympic Committee must be dealt with by states hoping to participate in Olympics. Are these two authoritative in their respective fields? They have power over their spheres and face little obvious opposition, so perhaps this equates to legitimated power. By the same token, Iraq's calculations in 2002 could not ignore the likelihood of an American invasion, just as thieves can't ignore the police and pedestrians can't ignore oncoming cars— these external forces don't add up to authority. The necessity of including an institution in one's strategic calculations may be a necessary consequence of the presence of authority but seems unlikely to qualify as sufficient evidence for it.

Conclusions

This chapter has addressed the question of whether it is possible to prove or disprove the claim that the Security Council has political authority over states in some situations. This required first establishing a common meaning for references to "authority" and then considering what evidence, if any, might be decisive in assessing claims about the Council's authority.

The first goal of the chapter was to define the concept of authority so that we are able to distinguish it in the international system from other kinds of power and influence. My definition borrowed from traditions in sociology and political theory where the concept has been most fully explored, and was set in contrast to the prevailing legalist use of the term in IR literatures. The sociological approach to authority identifies three elements, each necessary and together sufficient: authority is a (1) social relation of hierarchy in which the positions of superior and subordinate are (2) mutually recognized as (3) legitimate. A hierarchy (either among states, or between states and a super-ordinate rule or institution) that is recognized as legitimate becomes an institution of authority.

None of these three elements is directly accessible for empirical testing, and yet some kind of test is necessary if we aspire to assess competing claims about the existence or absence of international authority. Scholars have argued both for and against the existence of international authority, generally dividing between adherents of the "anarchy school" (which finds that it is conceptually impossible for authority to exist above sovereign states) and partisans of empirical constructivism (who claim to have evidence of authority). Both camps rely more on assumption than on evidence to found their claims. Recognizing this, this chapter sketched several approaches to testing for international authority at the Security Council. These were all indirect, reflecting the methodological and epistemological problems of accessing the psychological foundations of beliefs about legitimacy (see Hurd 1999). If any of these tests could be shown to be satisfied, we would have reason to conclude that there is at least the possibility that the Security Council is seen by some states as having authority in some areas.

The three pathways for testing each targeted a different implication of authority. These were compliance, justificatory discourse, and "unavoidability." They all share a resistance to positivist methodology, in that they are only weakly measurable and not amenable to strict separation from confounding influences. They all suffer from extreme problems of operationalization to the point that the tests themselves may not produce meaningful results, but the chapter argued that they are worth considering at least for the conceptual clarity that they might contribute to the idea of authority.

Compliance is often used as a proxy for the authority of a rule or institution. In the case of the Council, I argued that its value is very limited because the observable behavior it predicts is identical to that caused by other relations of power. The same act of compliance with the Council might be motivated by, for instance, the fear of physical coercion or incentives offered by other states, and this is not behaviorally distinguishable from acts motivated by a belief in authority. Also, the rate of compliance with Council decisions is both highly problematic to measure and, by the available crude estimates, quite low. At most, we might say that, given the low probability of force by the Council in defense of its decisions, what compliance there is may be better accounted for by a theory of authority than by alternative explanations, but the methodology behind such a conclusion remains weak.

The presence of a justificatory discourse was examined next as possible evidence of authority. The assumption behind this test is that authority may create an internal sense among states that they must justify their behavior in terms approved by the institution. The internal sense is created by the force of legitimation that is integral to authority: legitimation causes actors to believe in the right-ness of the institution and so to see conformity with it as appropriate. For this approach to accurately indicate the presence of authority in the Council, states must genuinely believe in the necessity and appropriateness of the need to justify themselves to the Council. If justificatory behavior is purely strategic, the relation of authority vanishes. As with compliance, knowing the motivations behind behaviors of justification is impossible, but where we are willing to make strong assumptions about both state person-hood and access to their internal motivations we might make tentative conclusions in favor of international authority.

Finally, I considered the test of "unavoidability." Perhaps authority is on display when an international organization becomes an unavoidable part of the strategic calculations of states. This approach shares with the study of justification a recognition that internalization is crucial to the making of beliefs about legitimacy and authority, but looks at the process of strategic decision-making rather than the discourse of states for its evidence. Where actors reveal, through the process of weighing costs and benefits to action, that they consider an institution an unavoidable part of the choice situation, they may be unwittingly providing evidence that they have internalized the authority of the institution. Even if they have not, by taking the institution for granted on the landscape of world politics, they may be revealing that *other* actors have internalized it. This is arguably the result of the Iraq 2003 episode: enough states internalized the rule that Council approval was necessary for the Iraq invasion that the U.S., which had not internalized that rule, needed to take the Council's position into account as it made its strategic decisions.

All three tests struggle against the problem of the observational equivalence of alternative explanations. The behaviors they seek to measure might well be caused by phenomena other than authority, and distinguishing among them hits up against the limits of empirical methodology and epistemology. Asking the question in the form that I used to start this chapter ("Is the Council in a position of authority over states") invites these difficulties, but remains useful as long as they are admitted directly and respected. We may not be able to operationalize these tests, but by designing them we can gain conceptual clarity on both the idea of authority and the power of the Security Council.

This chapter has attempted to reduce some of the excessive pluralism that has grown up around the concept of international authority. As Susan Strange argued with respect to the earlier regimes literature, pluralism unchecked can be a pathology that facilitates empirical emptiness. Clear conceptualizations and an understanding of the limits of the concept are needed to make it empirically useful.

Notes

1 The last two he illustrates with reference to John Rawls and to Michael Walzer respectively.
2 On principal–agent approaches to IR see Voeten's chapter (3) in this volume and the essays in Hawkins, Lake, Nielson, and Tierney 2006.
3 Obligations *erga omnes* are implicit commitments of states owed to the international community as a whole and so their violation by a state is actionable by any other state. See Ragazzi 1997. A *jus cogens* rule is defined by the Vienna Convention on the Law of Treaties as "a norm accepted and recognized by the international community of States as a whole as a norm from which no derogation is permitted." Art. 53 Vienna Convention, United Nations, *Treaty Series*, vol. 1155.

4 See, for instance, the articles in *Global Governance* special issue 2004 10 (1) on "The Politics of International Administration."
5 This is presaged by, among others, Habermas on the "legitimacy crisis." Habermas 1972. I cite Rosenau here as exemplifying this tradition for IR theory, not necessarily for beginning it. My argument is interested in the "upward" movement of authority, to the international-system level. For discussion of the downward direction, see Mason 2005.
6 For historical reviews of other possible changes in "the constitutional authority underlying international relations" see Philpott 1999: 566. Also, Reus-Smit 1999 and Hall 2000.
7 See Weingast and Moran 1983. I am grateful to Alex Thompson for this reference.
8 The place of reason in authority has long preoccupied political philosophers. See, for instance, Hart 1990 and Raz 1990.

Part II
Sources of Council authority

3 Delegation and the nature of Security Council authority [1]

Erik Voeten

This chapter examines the UN Security Council's authority from the perspective of principal–agent theory. Principal–agent theories stipulate that a set of principals (states) delegate a specific task to an agent (the IO) in the expectation that the IO has or will create an advantage in executing the task (Hawkins et al. 2006; Martin 2003; Nielson and Tierney 2003; Pollack 1997. For a critique, see Barnett and Finnemore 1999). Such advantages may include neutrality, expertise, efficiency, or some other asset that states find difficult to achieve in the absence of an IO. It is generally in the interest of states to grant the IO some amount of discretion in how it executes its task. This leaves the principals with a difficult trade-off: on the one hand, they may wish to ensure that the agent (IO) implements decisions that fit the states' objectives; on the other hand, curtailing the agent's independence may negate the potential advantages of delegation.

At first sight, the authority delegated by the larger UN membership to the Council appears formidable. By ratifying the UN Charter, all 191-member states delegate to 5 permanent members and 10 non-permanent members the authority to make decisions regarding collective responses to threats to international peace and security. These decisions, which are generally binding under international law, may include far-reaching measures such as economic sanctions and military interventions. Moreover, there are few, if any, formal institutional mechanisms through which the Security Council can be held accountable for its decisions by the larger UN membership.

This chapter more closely examines the nature of this delegated authority, focusing on the Council's ability to authorize uses of military force. The UNSC is different from many of the IOs analyzed in the principal–agent literature in that it is not a bureaucracy that builds up an informational advantage in an issue area. Instead, the delegation is first and foremost to a decision-making rule. The first part of this chapter, then, builds on economic theories of incomplete contracting to analyze the institutional features of the authority that states have delegated to the Council. I argue that states have delegated some discretion to the Council in deciding on the amount of collective action that should be produced in response to security threats (production of public goods) and, informally, evaluating whether extra-institutional uses of force are appropriate. These two issues pose very different demands from the perspective of institutional design, yet they are inherently intertwined in international politics. This is especially so given that Council decisions are frequently made in the shadow of implicit or explicit threats that outside actors will use military force in the absence of Council authorization. The second part of this chapter thus evaluates how outside power affects the logic of Security Council action. The analysis clarifies how formal institutional power, such as veto rights, does not necessarily confer genuine authority in international politics.

Before proceeding with the analysis, it is useful to point out that this chapter works from a more narrow conception of authority than most of the other chapters in this volume. In the context of delegation, authority is defined as "the right to pick a decision in an allowed set of decisions" (Simon 1947). This can reasonably be seen as a subset of the broader definition offered in Chapter 1: "a relation among actors within a hierarchy in which one group is recognized as having both the right and the competence to make binding decisions for the rest of the community." As explained in Chapter 2, delegation is only one of the possible sources of authority for the Security Council and my claim here is not that delegation is the only source for the Council's authority. Isolating delegation is useful for analytic purposes because it provides an avenue for understanding how the institution fits into the broader strategic and diplomatic scene in which governments operate. Moreover, it reminds us that the authority of the Council ultimately depends on how the governments that are *not* in the P5 perceive the institution. Council decisions must be self-enforcing. That is: non-members must find it in their interest to abide by these decisions and help finance the peacekeeping missions that the Security Council authorizes. If they would not, then veto power in the Security Council would not add to the authority the holders of such formal institutional authority already have outside the UN's institutional environment.

The chapter also works with an instrumental notion of legitimacy. I define legitimacy as the sustained beliefs by actors that Security Council decisions should be obeyed. As I have argued elsewhere, there is little evidence for the notion that states primarily value the Council for its procedural or moral qualities or for its consistent application of international legal rules (Voeten 2005). Instead, I maintain that the legitimacy of the Council (and thereby its authority) is strengthened when it provides benefits to its support coalition and weakened when it does not.

Delegated authority: the Charter as an incomplete contract

Rationalist explanations of how international organizations obtain a measure of authority in the international system build on contract theory: the branch of economic theory concerned with explaining why, when, and how authority relations emerge in a specific type of anarchical environment: markets (see Bolton and Dewatripont 2005). Contract theorists start with the observation that uncertainty, hidden information, or, more broadly, "transaction costs" prevent otherwise beneficial cooperation from occurring. These inefficiencies occur in part because authority relations are not appropriately allocated. In response, actors may construct contracts that define authority relationships and compensation schemes that provide incentives for improved levels of exchange.

Even though the nature of the anarchical environment in international politics differs from that of a market, international relations theorists have long recognized that the existence of transaction costs and asymmetric information provide a compelling raison d'être for international institutions (Martin and Simmons 1998). As such, scholars have used the tools of contract theory to explore if, when, why, and how states delegate authority to IOs (Hawkins et al. 2006; Martin 2003; Nielson and Tierney 2003; Pollack 1997. For a critique, see Barnett and Finnemore 1999). In this framework, the Security Council forms an institutional solution to problems that prevent states from cooperating with regard to the maintenance of international peace and security. It is important to appreciate that the literature on contracts, including principal–agent theory, does not presuppose that institutional solutions are optimally efficient or that the agents always optimally implement the policies desired by their principals. In fact, contract theory is uniquely suited to analyze why inefficiencies occur and why agents can sometimes escape the reigns of their principals.

Especially relevant to this case are insights from the economics literature on incomplete contracts. This literature recognizes that parties to a long-term contract generally cannot anticipate all future states of the world to which the contract may apply and/or cannot agree on a common description of the complete state space. Hence, contract theorists have focused on analyzing how control rights, decision-making rules, discretion, and so on should be distributed among the contracting parties (Tirole 1999 and Bolton and Dewatripont 2004: part IV). When states contemplate how to regulate future uses of force they cannot anticipate all future instances in which the exercise of force may serve the purposes of the contracting parties. The UN Charter explicitly recognizes this. When states sign the Charter, they agree not to use or threaten force "against the territorial integrity or political independence of any state, or in any manner inconsistent with the Purposes of the United Nations" (Article 2/4). The Charter singles out two circumstances under which the use of force does serve the purposes of the UN (the contracting parties): when it is exercised as individual or collective self-defense against armed attacks (Article 51) or when it otherwise constitutes a collective action against the "existence of any threat to the peace, breach of the peace, or act of aggression" (Article 39). To continue the economic analogy, states may use force to produce public goods (peace) and to protect property rights (self-defense).

Both provisions pose interesting contracting difficulties that can be addressed by allocating authority to an IO. The following two subsections discuss the extent to which states have granted the Security Council discretion over both issues. That an international institution can help states resolve collective action problems in the production of public goods is not a new insight. I argue, however, that the Security Council also plays a role in resolving conflicts that may arise over opportunistic claims that unilateral uses of force are in the interest of the international community. Moreover, I will suggest that optimal institutional solutions to these two contracting difficulties are diverse but that they cannot be separated in the international system.

Collective action to preserve the peace

How do states determine that a threat to the peace warrants a collective response? How do they determine the size and nature of that response? Chapter VII of the Charter explicitly grants the Council authority over this. Article 39 states that "The Security Council shall determine the existence of any threat to the peace, breach of the peace, or act of aggression and shall make recommendations, or decide what measures shall be taken in accordance with Articles 41 and 42, to maintain or restore international peace and security."[2] Council decisions can authorize uses of force by regional organizations or "coalitions of the willing"[3] and they can authorize peacekeeping missions executed and financed by the members of the UN.[4] Such missions theoretically deliver public goods, in that they produce something (peace/stability) that is non-excludable and enjoyed by most or all status-quo powers, although some benefit more than others on individual cases (Bennett et al. 1994).

Models of public good provision predict that poor nations will be able to free ride off the contributions of wealthier nations and that the public good will be underprovided because contributors do not take into account the spillover benefits that their support confers to others.[5] The Security Council may help alleviate underprovision and free riding in three ways. First, the fixed burden-sharing mechanism for peacekeeping operations provides an institutional solution that helps reduce risks of bargaining failures and lessens transaction costs.[6] Second, the delegation of decision-making authority to a small number of states may facilitate compromise on the amount of public good that ought to be produced (Martin 1992: 773). Third, the Council helps states pool resources (Abbott and Snidal 1998). The existence of selective incentives induces some states to incur more than their required share of the peacekeeping burden. For example, Kuwait paid two-thirds of the bill for the UN Iraq–Kuwait Observation Mission through voluntary contributions. Australia proved willing to shoulder a disproportionate share of the peacekeeping burden in East Timor. States are more likely to make such contributions when these add to the efforts of others in a predictable manner.

From the perspective of contract theory, the main question of institutional design concerns the decision-making rule that yields the optimal level of public goods. A general result is that some form of (qualified) majority rule is ex ante Pareto efficient (Bolton and DeWatripont 2005). Before knowing precisely what issues will arise, participants have an incentive not to insist on veto rights. Under very general conditions, each actor would be better off occasionally contributing to public goods that the actor would not have approved than to absorb the underprovision of public goods that results from granting each actor veto power. The delegation of authority to an institution governed by (qualified) majority voting rules helps solve the time inconsistency problems that prevent actors from realizing this trade-off.

The ex ante efficiency of majority rule collapses, however, when institutional decisions are not easily enforceable. In the absence of enforcement, any institutional solution to the production of public goods relies on the persistence of a norm: actors must sometimes be willing to shoulder a larger share of the burden than they would with a voluntary (non-institutional) mechanism because they believe that the long-term benefits exceed the short-term benefits of shirking. When powerful actors lack veto power, majoritarian institutions can take decisions that individual actors choose to ignore, thereby undermining the willingness of others to contribute more than they would under a voluntary scheme. In the shadow of enforcement issues, the Pareto efficient solution is to grant veto rights to those with the ability to undermine the institutions' decisions.[7]

Three implications of this are especially relevant. First, this argument implies that a more majoritarian or inclusive institution than the UNSC may not be better at producing public goods. The history of the Uniting for Peace resolution is illustrative. After the return of the USSR to the Security Council ensured deadlock in that institution, the Western powers used their dominance in the General Assembly to grant the UNGA authority to take measures to preserve international peace and security. This procedure was invoked on ten different occasions and allowed the UNGA to step into what is broadly conceived to be the scope of the Council on some notable occasions. For example, after agreement between the United States and the Soviet Union that allowed the initial authorization of peacekeeping forces in the Congo proved short lived, the UNGA took over decisions regarding the reauthorization of the mission as well as financing questions from 1962 until the withdrawal of the force in June 1964.[8] Yet, the institution could no longer be used effectively after the early 1960s, when the U.S. and the West lost their near-automatic majority in the UNGA.

Second, it is important to appreciate that enforcement problems are the key to the limited effectiveness of majoritarian institutions in the international system. As enforcement problems are solved, veto rights could and have been lifted. For example, the European Union has switched from unanimity to qualified majority rule on many issues where strong enforcement procedures of EU decisions have been realized, for instance, through the ECJ, whereas unanimity rule is preserved on those issues where the institution has few enforcement capabilities, most notably issues of immigration and security.[9] The UNGA still passes many resolutions related to security, but they are routinely ignored and produce few public goods. For example, U.S. President Ronald Reagan famously claimed that the 1983 UN General Assembly resolution condemning the United States for its intervention in Grenada "didn't upset his breakfast at all" (cited in Luck 2002: 63). Perhaps more notably, countless UNGA resolutions have been adopted on the "Palestinian question" without producing much in the form of collective action that helps produce peace.

Third, while this argument highlights that authority with regard to collective actions in the interests of international peace and security is best delegated to a small institution that grants veto rights to powerful countries, the precise institutional design of the Security Council contains clear inefficiencies from the perspective of public good production. For example, China has temporarily blocked peacekeeping missions in Guatemala and Macedonia for the simple reason that government officials in those countries had made statements about Taiwan that the Chinese thought inappropriate. From an efficiency standpoint, China should not have the ability to single-handedly block those efforts. Similarly, Japan and Germany, the second and third largest contributors to the peacekeeping budget, should be given more incentives to help produce public goods by granting them greater responsibilities. If the Security Council was truly just about producing public goods, reforms along these lines should not be terribly controversial and could marginally improve institutional performance. However, the determination of whether force can and should be used also deals with considerable distributional conflict over the extent to which the missions are indeed in the public interest or reflect the needs and wants of a set of countries and/or governments. Those issues, discussed in the following sections, complicate matters considerably.

Self-defense

The self-defense exception defined by Article 51 of the Charter[10] is open to ex-post opportunism: states may and frequently do resort to expanded conceptions of self-defense in attempts to justify unilateral uses of force (Schachter 1989). Theoretically, ex-post opportunism could be resolved by assigning an independent institution, such as a court, the task to evaluate the validity of the claims for self-defense. This has not occurred. The International Court of Justice (ICJ) has no real-world authority on this matter and there has not been any impetus in the recent *High-Level Panel Report*[11] or elsewhere to grant the ICJ a greater role in this regard. There is also no realistic attempt to rewrite Article 51 to identify more precisely when uses of self-defense are permitted.[12] Hence, greater legalization appears not to be a practical solution; there are a sufficient number of powerful states that have strong interests not to allocate authority on this matter to a robust independent institution. The reasons for this are self-evident: those states that cannot resort to expanded notions of self-defense have the most interest in restricting its usage whereas states with greater capabilities to act have fewer incentives to tie their hands to a strong independent institution.

Formally, the Security Council also has little authority on this matter. States must report self-defense uses of force to the UN, something that they have not always done (Schachter 1989). The Council is not, however, explicitly assigned the task of assessing the legitimacy of self-defense claims. In practice, however, states do behave "as if" Council authorization makes questionable uses of the self-defense concept more acceptable. For example, the U.S. referred to Resolutions 1368 and 1373, which reaffirmed the right of states to act forcefully in its self-defense against terrorist activities, to legitimize the U.S. military action in Afghanistan.[13] Moreover, the Council has authorized military interventions exercised by (small coalitions of) states that had little to do with either self-defense and were, at the least, stretches as collective responses to genuine threats to international peace and security. The most obvious example is the 1994 intervention in Haiti, when the United States went to great length to ensure Security Council authorization, even though it de facto executed the intervention by itself.[14]

Presumably, governments care about Security Council resolutions authorizing force in the name of self-defense because they are concerned about their general reputation for upholding norms and rules that regulate uses of force. They may do so out of an inherent appreciation for these norms, to please domestic publics, or because they believe that others are more likely to cooperate with states that show a general inclination to comply with rules and norms. One should be aware, however, that the judgment whether a particular use of self-defense is permitted is ultimately a political one and not subject to judicial review.

The Security Council thus imposes some restraint on unilateral uses of force to the extent that states believe that Council authorized uses of force are more legitimate than those that do not receive the Council's blessing. As the cases of Kosovo and the 2003 intervention in Iraq illustrate, this authority is not absolute. Yet, even in those cases it is clear that NATO and the U.S. would have preferred UNSC authorization had they been able to acquire it.

Outside power and the delegated authority of the Security Council

The preceding section claims that states have granted the Council some discretion over two issues: decisions on whether proposed extra-institutional uses of force are appropriate and decisions if and how much collective action to produce in response to threats to international peace and security. From the perspective of optimal institutional design, addressing these tasks with a single institutional solution is far from ideal in that the task of determining the appropriateness of interventions is best delegated to an independent (neutral) institution, such as a court, and the determination of public good production to a majoritarian (political) institution.

In the practice of international politics, however, the two issues are deeply intertwined. The extent to which a military intervention provides public goods (i.e. is in the interest of the international community) or private goods (i.e. primarily satisfies the interests of those interested in executing the intervention) is often a matter of strong contestation. For example, much of the debate surrounding possible UNSC authorization for military action against Iraq in 2003 focused on the question whether the action served the collective interests of the international community in a peaceful Middle East or the private interests of the United States. This is not necessarily an "either or" question. Collective action authorized by the Security Council has often been most extensive and effective when there has been a strong lead state, for example, Australia in East Timor and the United States in the first Persian Gulf War (Fearon and Laitin 2004). The willingness of a state to "go it alone" helps solve the free-rider problem in the production of public goods. Yet, generally, states are only willing to do this if they are granted some leeway in executing the intervention. As such, the Council cannot simultaneously restrict military interventions by outside actors only to uses of self-defense without undermining its effectiveness at maintaining international peace and security.

This points to an important tension underlying the delegated authority of the Security Council. If the Council were to grant a "carte blanche" that would allow powerful states to simply dress their unilateral adventures in multilateral clothing, then the institution would be of little use to the rest of the world and hence its authority would be undermined. If, on the other hand, the Council were to insist on neutrality and refuse to authorize any interventions that serve the interests of the powerful, then those states might ignore the institution and undermine the Security Council's ability to maintain international peace and security. Hence, to maintain its authority, the Council needs to engage in a trade-off: it must maintain some meaningful level of restraint on unilateral uses of force by the powerful while preserving the incentives for cooperation from those same powerful states, especially the United States.

This dilemma arises because, in practice, the Security Council does not have exclusive jurisdiction over the scope of issues it deals with. States can and have acted with regional organizations, in coalitions of the willing, or unilaterally if the Council is unable to reach agreement. These outside options are not distributed equally among states, even among veto powers. In most situations, the U.S. has a greater menu of choices than its counterparts. The asymmetric availability of such outside options has a profound impact on the logic of decision-making inside the Security Council. Perhaps counter-intuitively, it creates opportunities for multilateral actions that would not exist in the absence of unilateral alternatives (Voeten 2001). These multilateral actions may, however, serve not just the global public interest but also the private interests of powerful states. Moreover, the presence of outside options reduces the actual leverage of veto power: a permanent member may veto a resolution but this does not necessarily prevent the intervention from taking place (see Figure 3.1).

Figure 3.1 illustrates these points based on a simple spatial bargaining model.[15] Suppose there are two permanent members (veto powers 1+2 in Figure 3.1) who prefer to act militarily in response to some situation while veto power 3 prefers a milder response, such as sanctions, and veto powers

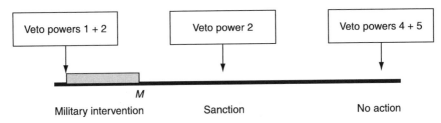

Figure 3.1 Bargaining in the Security Council.

4 and 5 prefer that the UNSC does not act in response to a situation. This roughly describes the basic strategic dilemma that states faced after, for example, Iraq's invasion of Kuwait, the removal of Aristide from power in Haiti, ethnic cleansing in Kosovo, or Iraq's failure to comply with weapons inspections in 2002/2003. If all states strictly voted their preferences, distributional conflict among the veto powers precludes any multilateral agreement. That is: if a UNSC vote were the one and only way to address the situation, veto powers 4 and 5 would get their way and the status quo would prevail.

There are two ways in which veto powers 1 and 2 could still get some multilateral action: they could pay off the other veto players or they could threaten to act outside of the Security Council. I discuss each option in turn.

Vote-buying

If veto powers 1 and 2 cared a great deal about the intervention, they might be able to use side-payments to sway the other veto players to agree on some form of military intervention. This may especially be plausible if veto powers 1 and 2 control assets that have greater relative value to the objecting veto players than to player 1. Examples could be control over World Bank loans or WTO accession. Purchasing votes in this manner may make sense for veto players 1 and 2 to the extent that states that are not Security Council members view the Council decision as a mandate for multilateral cooperation. If this is so, buying relatively few votes in the UNSC could pay for broad-based cooperation.

There is indeed some anecdotal evidence that such assets have been used in this manner. For example, China appears to have been granted U.S. support for a World Bank loan in exchange for China's vote on the Haiti intervention, whereas Russia was extended support for a Georgian peacekeeping mission in exchange for consent on the same vote (Malone 1998). There is also some evidence that non-permanent members were able to increase their aid levels from the United States at times when the Security Council was particularly active (Kuziemko and Werker n.d).

However, equilibrium behavior does not support vote-buying on a grand scale. If multilateral actions were the sole result of vote-buying, non-veto powers would have few reasons to abide by the decisions of the Security Council. This would be true especially if powerful non-members had preferences close to players 3, 4, and 5. In that scenario, the Council would take decisions close to player 1's ideal point, players 3, 4, and 5 would be bought off and the powerful outside members would be left dissatisfied. In the long run, then, such side-payments would undermine the authority of the Council.

There is little evidence that vote-buying occurs on this grand scale. Instead, the evidence suggests that the concerns of powerful non-permanent members are embedded in the decisions of the Security Council (Hurd 1997). Powerful states that lack permanent membership tend to insist as strongly on Council authorization for military actions as do permanent members. India has since 1992 committed to a "pro-active" approach towards UN peacekeeping missions, providing generous troop contributions across the globe to UN-approved missions while refusing to supply to troops for non-UN approved missions (Krishnasamy 2003). New interpretations of Basic Law provisions that restrict German military activity abroad have made exceptions for German participation in UN peacekeeping and peacemaking missions, as well as NATO and WEU operations directed at implementing SC resolutions (see the Bundesverfassungsgericht [Federal Constitutional Court] 90, 286, July 12, 1994). Japan has adopted a law that makes military contributions of most kinds conditional on SC authorization.[16] All of this suggests that the Security Council has sought to keep states that are excluded from a permanent seat on the table on board, an outcome that is not consistent with vote-buying on a grand scale.

Outside options

Suppose that veto powers 1 and 2 from Figure 3.1 have the ability to implement the intervention together with a small coalition of the willing. Thus they could act alone and not bother with a multilateral institution at all. However, veto powers 1 and 2 may have some incentives to sway others to coop-erate. Security Council authorization may encourage burden-sharing, it may decrease the perception among citizens at home and abroad that the military action is threatening or it may in some other way enable the continu-ance of beneficial cooperation (Voeten 2005). Let us assume that veto powers 1 and 2 derive some benefit of Security Council authorization that is equiva-lent in utility terms to a compromise at point M in Figure 3.1.[17] That is: veto powers 1 and 2 are indifferent between the disutility of a compromise at point M and the disutility of failing to obtain Council authorization. This assumption implies that everything else equal, states prefer to have Security Council authorization rather than not have it. In the words of former U.S. Secretary of Defense William Cohen, Council authorization is "desirable, not imperative."[18]

Under these reasonable assumptions, powers 1 and 2 prefer any multilateral action between their ideal points and point M to going it alone. Similarly, veto powers 3, 4, and 5 prefer these multilateral agreements to unilateral action by power 1, which would (from their perspectives) create an undesirable military intervention over which they would have no influence. Thus, the presence of a credible outside option and some incentive for cooperation combine to create a bargaining range where none existed in the absence of the outside option.

This very simple analysis has some relevant implications. First, it points to a straightforward way in which the end of the cold war increased Security Council activity. Two characteristics of the cold war were that there were two veto powers that both had extensive outside options *and* who were reliably on opposite sides of the spectrum (like powers 1 and 5 in Figure 3.1). It is easy to see that in such a scenario, Council action can do little but help maintain a status quo (first generation peacekeeping) even if there were some inherent advantages to multilateralism. Asymmetric outside options, however, create the possibility that the Council can act in the absence of harmony among the five veto powers. Note that this is exactly the opposite conclusion from those who argue that unipolarity has killed the Security Council (Glennon 2003). The bargaining perspective suggests that unipolarity made multilateral actions possible in cases where bipolarity did not. The evidence for the latter view is that the most extensive UN authorizations of force were almost all in cases where the U.S. (and its allies) either implicitly or explicitly threatened to act outside the Council. This is certainly true for the first Gulf War, Somalia, Haiti, Bosnia,[19] Kosovo,[20] and Afghanistan. On the other hand, during the cold war the Council was mostly helping to preserve the status quo by putting neutral forces in between warring parties.

Second, the current Security Council is not just a forum based around great power consent for collective actions, but it has also become an institution that offers states the possibility of imposing some measure of constraint on a superpower. This is a rather different purpose than originally intended by the Charter. The greater the cost a superpower perceives from circumventing the UNSC (M in Figure 3.1), the greater the leverage other states have over proposed unilateral military adventures by a superpower. It should be noted that in the simple model discussed here, the amount of constraint is exogenous (and of size M). In the real world, the cost (in terms of policy compromise) that a superpower is willing to pay in order to have UNSC consent probably has some exogenous features but it may also develop as a consequence of past UNSC actions. For example, if the U.S. public perceives that UNSC authorized missions have generally been more successful and less costly to the U.S. than missions that lacked such authorizations, then the domestic public may insist to a greater degree on authorization for future missions than in the absence of such past successes.

Third, in the simple world of Figure 3.1, states would always be able to achieve a multilateral compromise and avoid unilateral actions. In reality, bargaining failures prevent this from occurring. The argument is essentially identical to rationalist explanations for war (see Fearon 1995). Given that war is costly, there always exists some Pareto improving agreement that does not result in war. Similarly, if unilateralism is costly, then there should be some multilateral solution that benefits all.

Bargaining failures can have many causes. For example, veto powers 1 and 2 may know how much they are willing to compromise in exchange for Security Council authorization but others may not. Powers 1 and 2 will have difficulties credibly communicating their willingness to compromise, given that they have incentives to underreport their willingness to do so.[21] Or, domestic politics may create high (but not precisely known) audience costs for other veto players to agree to a UNSC compromise. For example, the rise of nationalism made it virtually impossible for Russia to publicly agree to the Kosovo intervention. At the same time, they worked hard to avoid an intervention over which they had no say. Russia's foreign minister Igor Ivanov traveled to Belgrade on March 12 to try to persuade Milosevic to accept a peacekeeping force; the same force the Russians had been objecting to so far in the Security Council (*Izvestia* 1999). Some newspaper reports even suggested that Russia effectively participated in the NATO force by allowing its vessels to transport military supplies.[22] A similar story applies to French opposition over the Iraq war. A French general met with General Command staff on December 16, 2002 to discuss the details of a French contribution of 10,000 to 15,000 troops and French President Jacques Chirac told his troops to prepare for action in a speech at the Ecole Militaire on January 7, 2003 (Cantaloube and Vernet 2004; Cogan 2003). Clearly there was room for a compromise, but things changed, apparently at least in part for domestic politics reasons (Cantaloube and Vernet 2004; Cogan 2003).

Conclusion and discussion

This chapter has evaluated the authority of the Security Council by investigating how the institution fits in the broader strategic environment of international politics. The focus has been on two issues: the nature of the delegation of authority by states to the Council and the asymmetric availability of states to realize their objectives outside the context of the Council. As such, the analysis has sought to combine institutionalist arguments about delegation and realist concerns about power asymmetries. Marrying the two is important as institutionalists generally claim that power is "important" but rarely explicitly model its consequences for institutional behavior or design (Voeten 2001). The analysis in this chapter has shown that the UNSC's institutional features are puzzling if we would look at the UNSC as solving various functional problems states have in optimally cooperating to achieve common interests in the maintenance of international peace and security. In order to understand the UNSC's delegated authority, we need to appreciate the fact that the UNSC cannot enforce its decisions without the cooperation of others and does not have exclusive jurisdiction over its issue area. In other words, the power of states outside the institution matters a great deal.

On the other hand, realists tend to pay little attention to international institutions and even less to the UN. Realists tend to argue that the attention paid to the UN by policy-makers is a dangerous (liberal) distraction that will prove to be unwise and short lived (Mearsheimer 1993). Be that as it may, it is difficult to deny that policy-makers have valued UN authorizations since the end of the cold war and thus, as scholars of international relations, we should analyze the consequences of this. Thus, following classical realists such as Inis Claude, I have thought it more useful to analyze how UNSC authority evolves in the context of power politics. For example, the analysis in this chapter explains how the shift from a bi-polar to a uni-polar world affected the kinds of activities the UN could engage in: during the cold war UN actions mainly sought to preserve the status quo whereas the Council has actively sought to alter the status quo in the post-cold war period.

In this focus on realist and institutionalist concerns, the analysis in this chapter differs from most chapters in the volume, which take a predominantly constructivist perspective. I have not directly confronted the extent to which such an analysis would yield different conclusions. For example, constructivists would surely object to the notion that the end of the cold war mattered because it changed the availability of credible outside options to the various veto powers. Rather, they would argue, it represented a shift towards an increasingly liberal world order that puts a premium on multilateralism. I would not deny that ideational change could be an important additional factor. It may, for example, help determine the size of the perceived cost of avoiding UN authorization (the critical variable M in Figure 3.1). Yet, as I have argued elsewhere, if liberal values were the main force behind states' insistence on UN authorization, the illiberal institutional features of the UNSC are puzzling (Voeten 2005). Moreover, common values (norms) have not eliminated disagreement among the world's powerful states about how crises should be resolved. I argue that the UNSC has become a focal point in how to solve these distributional issues (Voeten 2005) As recent events have illustrated, the UN still does not command sole authority on security issues and thus there remains room for a strategic approach to understanding Security Council authority.

Notes

1 Parts of this chapter build on my earlier work in Voeten 2005 and 2007.
2 Article 41 states that: "The Security Council may decide what measures not involving the use of armed force are to be employed to give effect to its decisions, and it may call upon the Members of the United Nations to apply such measures. These may include complete or partial interruption of economic relations and of rail, sea, air, postal, telegraphic, radio, and other means of communication, and the severance of diplomatic relations." Article 42: "Should the Security Council consider that measures provided for in Article 41 would be inadequate or have proved to be inadequate, it may take such action by air, sea, or land forces as may be necessary to maintain or restore international peace and security. Such action may

include demonstrations, blockade, and other operations by air, sea, or land forces of Members of the United Nations."

3 There is some debate as to the legal standing of this. See Blokker 2000.

4 The fixed burden-sharing system for peacekeeping operations was put in place in 1973 (UNGA/Res 1310).

5 This paragraph is adopted from Voeten 2005.

6 A fixed burden-sharing system was put in place in 1973 by General Assembly Resolution 310.

7 For a formal exposition in the context of EU decision-making, see Maggi et al. n.d.

8 The Security Council authorized the mission in July of 1960 and strengthened it in February of 1961 following the assassination of former Prime Minister Patrice Lumumba but could not reach agreement afterwards.

9 I have taken some liberties in interpreting Maggi et al., who argue that the EU uses qualified majority rule on issues that are less "important." I believe that the enforcement interpretation more accurately reflects their formal results and the data.

10 Article 51 reads: "Nothing in the present Charter shall impair the inherent right of individual or collective self-defence if an armed attack occurs against a Member of the United Nations, until the Security Council has taken measures necessary to maintain international peace and security. Measures taken by Members in the exercise of this right of self-defence shall be immediately reported to the Security Council and shall not in any way affect the authority and responsibility of the Security Council under the present Charter to take at any time such action as it deems necessary in order to maintain or restore international peace and security."

11 The International Court of Justice receives one mention, on page 12, acknowledging that "disputes were remedied under the International Court of Justice."

12 The Panel's treatment of the issue (paragraphs 188–192) pertains mostly to the question of whether preventive uses of force could be justified under Article 51, which the Panel rejects. The discussion is a thinly disguised judgment that the U.S. invasion of Iraq was illegal. The Panel is clearly worried about the erosion of a norm ("Allowing one to so act is to allow all") but offers no suggestion for institutional reform other than to point to the necessity of Security Council authorization for such actions.

13 SC Resolutions 1368, September 12, 2001 and 1373, September 28, 2001.

14 See Malone 1998 for an insightful analysis of the bargaining process that led to the relevant UNSC resolutions.

15 The analysis here draws on Voeten 2001.

16 Law Concerning Cooperation for United Nations Peacekeeping Operations and Other Operations (the International Peace Cooperation Law) originally passed in June 1992. For other examples of Japanese insistence on SC authorization see Hurd 1999.

17 We may show how this benefit arises endogenously either from domestic inter-actions or from reputation effects through repeated interactions, but such an analysis would contribute little to the issues at stake here.

18 In Whitney 1998. Remarks were made in the context of the Kosovo intervention.

19 The most forceful UN resolutions were adopted only after the U.S. threatened to unilaterally lift the arms embargo against Bosnian Muslims. See Christopher 1998.

20 The authorization of KFOR occurred after the intervention had taken place. This is a somewhat different case from the others.

21 For a formal analysis of this argument, see Voeten 2001.

22 "Russia is already participating in NATO operations in Balkans," *Izvestia* 1999.

4 International consensus and the changing legal authority of the UN Security Council

Bruce Cronin

The authority of the United Nations Security Council to take action in defense of international peace and security is derived from the UN Charter, a document that has the legal status of a multilateral treaty. Under the prevailing theory of international law—legal positivism—states are obligated to follow the dictates of the Council because they have consented to its authority by signing the Charter.[1] Any changes in the scope of this authority must therefore also emanate from explicit state consent. Yet while the Charter technically limits the Security Council's authority to opposing aggression and responding to threats or breaches of the peace, the Council has rarely acted in this area. Rather, its most effective and significant actions since the 1990s have been in areas that go beyond the powers granted to the Council either by the Charter or by some other means of expressing consent: nation-building (Bosnia, Afghanistan, Somalia, East Timor), prosecuting war crimes (the former Yugoslavia, Rwanda, and Sierra Leone), peacekeeping (57 operations since 1960), dismantling apartheid (South Africa), alleviating serious humanitarian crises (Rwanda, Burundi, East Timor, and Zaire), resolving civil wars (Liberia and Angola) and restoring a democratically elected government (Haiti).

This subtle expansion in the Council's mandate did not involve any legal changes in the scope of the Council's authority. It did not emerge either through amendments to the Charter or through the conclusion of new treaties. It was never debated in the General Assembly, nor was it consciously imposed on the organization by its most powerful members. Rather, it evolved through political consensus among the members of the Council (coupled with the acquiescence of the membership) as they struggled to address various issues that have come before it. While there have been disagreements over the wisdom of specific actions, no state has lodged a formal protest over the fundamental legality of this expansion. If the members of the UN (now including all countries in the world) are legally required to follow Council mandates, the assumption of new legal authority without explicit approval from the membership raises questions concerning the consensual foundation of international law.

This chapter will explain why the Council has been able to expand the scope of its legal authority without the explicit consent of the United Nations membership. It will argue that this change reflects an expansion in the way international law is created, practiced and interpreted in contemporary international relations. Specifically, I argue that in limited but well-defined issue areas, states are increasingly recognizing the authority of international consensus over individual state consent as the foundation of certain legal norms. In a system lacking central governance institutions, such a consensus is determined through a generally accepted political process that states accept as legitimate and authoritative. As the main decision-making body within the world's only universal-membership organization, the Security Council has developed the authority to interpret and implement consensus-based international law. Thus, so long as the Council acts on the basis of generally accepted legal norms, the expansion of the Council's legal authority has been accepted as legitimate, even though there was no formal process of achieving state consent.

My argument is premised on the assumption that the legal authority of the Council is an important factor in determining its ability to develop and implement its policies. Within the field of Political Science, some scholars do not share this assumption. In particular, political realists would argue that the expansion of the Council's authority is simply a function of power and expediency, that is, the ability of the great powers to act when they believe it in their interest to do so without regard to the legal restrictions that may exist. From this perspective, state interest rather than legal obligation guides foreign policy, and thus the legality of Council actions is less important than the internal political dynamics within the Council (Morganthau 1993: ch. 16; Carr 1946: chs 10 and 11; Mearsheimer 1994/5). Following from this, realists could argue that Council action—and the response by the member states—is not guided primarily by an interpretation of their Chapter VII authority, but by the interests of the parties, the balance of power among them, and the necessity of responding to political crises that may affect these interests (Krasno and Sutterlin 2003; Malone 1999). This view is also shared by some international law scholars such as Nigel White, who argues that the "jurisdictional phraseology" of Chapter VII is often "subverted to the need for the Council to react" to events without considering the limits of legal technicalities (White 1997: 41).

As a political scientist, I am also skeptical of taking a strictly legal approach toward explaining Council behavior. The decision by the framers of the Charter not to subject the Council to the precepts of international law suggests that they wanted to avoid entangling the body in legalisms when making decisions regarding international security (see Simma et al. 2002: 52). After all, the founding states created the Council as an intergovernmental body comprised of high-level ambassadors representing each state's chief executive; this makes it a political institution. At the same time, the historical record also shows that from the earliest years of the UN, political leaders paid considerable attention to legal detail in assessing the permissible scope of the Council's authority (Kirgis 1995: 509). This was due in part to a belief by the founding states that the system would only work if most of the UN membership complied with Council directives as much out of obligation as threat of coercion. This is a reflection of the desire by the organization's founders—in particular the great powers—to introduce the rule of law into international relations, at least to the degree possible in an anarchic world. This desire became even stronger as decolonization produced a rapid proliferation of dozens of new independent states, making it that much more difficult to maintain stability and predictability in global politics.

This is further supported by the *empirical* record. In virtually all cases when the Council has acted, the five permanent members (P5) have made extensive efforts to legitimize their actions according to international law and the United Nations Charter. For this reason, virtually all Council resolutions cite specific Charter provisions and make legal arguments drawn from international law to justify their behavior.[2] While some may argue that this is simply a matter of providing a justification for actions that have already been decided upon, it also demonstrates a clear belief by the members of the Council that their actions must at least appear to be consistent with international law. This is especially true if they hope to gain support from the broader United Nations membership for their missions and resolutions. For most states outside the club of great powers, the legitimacy of the Council depends primarily on its legality and its willingness to follow established procedures in making decisions.[3] Even permanent members of the Council have demonstrated that they can be very cognizant of legalities in dealing with issues of peace and security. During NATO's 1999 war against Serbia, for example, France refused to support a blockade of Serbia—even in the midst of NATO's bombing campaign—questioning whether there was a basis under international law to stop and search ships without a new resolution from the Council (Gordon 1999). All of this clearly suggests that the Council is both a political *and* a legal organization.

In fact the trend toward greater legalization in international politics has been rapidly increasing over the past few decades (Goldstein et al. 2000). For example, states have concluded more legally binding multilateral treaties since the 1980s than in the prior 100 years.[4] This suggests that states are becoming more concerned with the rule of law in international relations. Consistent with these expectations, since the 1990s Council actions have not only been based on "findings of fact," as originally envisioned by the Charter's authors, but also on alleged breaches of international law (see Gowlland-Debbas 2000).

Explaining the scope and source of the Council's legal authority

Determining the source and scope of the Security Council's authority is not only important for the internal governance of the United Nations; it concerns the relationship between individual states and the international community as a whole. As the world's only truly universal-membership organization (100 percent of all states are members), the UN can credibly claim to represent the collective will of the international community of states.[5] Since the UN Charter is legally binding on all members, which also means all states, the line between an organizational mandate and general principle of international law is blurred. As the primary decision-making body of this organization (at least in terms of the UN's primary mission, the maintenance of peace and security), the Council possesses considerable legal authority to determine when a violation of international law has occurred, even though it is not technically empowered to either interpret or enforce international law beyond those matters that are specifically contained in the Charter. For this reason, the Council is one of the few international institutions whose decisions carry the weight of a legal obligation under international law.

What, then, is the source and scope of the Council's legal authority and how does it change over time? Traditionally, legal scholars and political scientists have drawn from theories based on state consent in defining the parameters and limits of international law, and more specifically, in defining the scope of the Council's authority. Consent theories hold that states are only obligated to follow those rules that they explicitly and voluntarily adopt, either by ratifying a treaty or adhering to a customary practice (Henkin 1995; Arend 1999: ch. 2). This protects state sovereignty while still providing for general rules that would facilitate cooperation and coexistence. For political realists, consent preserves a state's right to reject any principle or obligation that it does not deem to be in its interest to adopt, and for institutionalists and positivists, it strengthens the international legal system by committing states to adhere to those rules that they themselves have agreed to follow.

In contemporary international law theory, treaties (such as the UN Charter) are the primary source of legal obligation, since they represent the most explicit manifestation of state consent. Treaty commitments are legally binding as long as a state remains a party to the agreement; however, all parties can ultimately opt out, providing they follow the proper procedures for treaty withdrawal. This is because consent theories hold that treaties are not like legislation and therefore do not constitute a source of universal law. They only bind those who specifically ratify them, and their scope cannot go beyond the letter of the text.[6] Since states are not beholden to any higher principle or constitutional law, the text is the ultimate source of legal obligation. In those cases where states consider customary law to be binding, one's obligations are limited to the specific acts of state practice and general recognition over time. This concept is known as "positive law" (Oppenheim 1908). The principle of sovereignty frees states from acknowledging any higher authority, and therefore the interpretation and implementation of international law is usually determined by each state individually, although occasionally the International Court of Justice will make rulings on disputes when the conflicting parties agree to arbitration.[7]

For legal positivists (who comprise the overwhelming majority of international law scholars) and most political scientists, the creation of international organizations such as the United Nations does not fundamentally change this. To the extent that these organizations embody and promote adherence to international law, they do so on the basis of the specific charters that are voluntarily signed by individual states (Bennett 1995: 2–3). From this standpoint, international organizations do not create new independent sources of authority, but simply reflect the overlapping wills of its members (Moravcsik 1993: 481). As such they do not have the power to legislate for the international community as a whole and their decision-making bodies cannot act beyond the specific powers granted to them by their charters. For political scientists in particular, the authority of any international organization is simply that which states delegate to it for the purpose of coordinating their actions and pursuing mutual interests. When it no longer meets these needs, such authority can be withdrawn (Keohane 1992). In this sense, the charters act as legal contract among the member states.

Thus, in signing the UN Charter, the members have delegated specific powers to the Security Council and have explicitly consented to follow the Council's mandates in areas related to international peace and security. The scope of these powers, however, is limited to those specifically defined in Chapters VI and VII of the Charter; any changes in these powers must be formally approved by the membership. Since there is no concept of "inherent" powers within decision-making bodies of international organizations, only those powers that are either specifically enumerated or embedded within the principles of the charters are binding. Moreover, since international law does not acknowledge a hierarchy of organizations, institutions such as the United Nations do not possess any general authority within the international community. Therefore, neither the United Nations nor the Security Council have the authority to enforce international law, create binding legal precedents, or legislate new legal norms.

From this perspective, one can objectively determine the scope and source of the Council's authority either by scrutinizing the text of the Charter and judicial decisions that interpret it (legal approach) or by analyzing exactly what states have consented to (political approach) when they joined the United Nations. In pursuing the former approach, international lawyers examine the role of the Council in international affairs by interpreting the key provisions of the UN Charter and trying to determine precisely what authority the Council possesses in a given situation (Lobel and Ratner 1999). Thus, the international law literature often refers to judgments by international and domestic courts concerning the scope of the Council's authority, particularly those delivered by the International Court of Justice. For consent-based theories of international law, then, the Council can expand its authority in one of three ways: amending the UN Charter, reinterpreting the Council's Chapter VI and VII powers, or evoking customary international law.

Since the United Nations has not expanded the scope of the Security

Council's authority through the amendment process, legal scholars have turned to the latter two approaches. Some have explained the expansion of the Council's legal authority by broadening the definitions of the terms "breach of the peace," "threat to the peace," and "act of aggression," the three key terms authorizing Council action in Article 39 (White 1997: ch. 2; Kooijmans 1993). They do so by (1) developing new understandings of what these terms mean in the light of contemporary circumstances; (2) re-examining the "original intent" of the Charter's framers; and (3) reinterpreting the specific powers within the context of the UN's overall goals (see, for example, Simma et al. 2002: ch. 5; Fassbender 2000). By employing (2) and (3), such scholars discover new authority within the original document. Thus, for example, David Schweigman suggests that the Council's authority is not only articulated in the specific articles that list its powers (Chapters XI and XII), but can also be implied within the text of the preamble and other articles that articulate the purpose of the organization.[8]

Although these efforts to discover new meaning in the breach of the peace clause are innovative and appealing, most of these explanations have a strong *ad hoc* quality to them. Any competent lawyer, political leader or diplomat can construct an argument to show that a particular situation threatens international peace and security, regardless of the specifics. While such scholars and practitioners are generally correct that the Council and the Secretary-General are careful to evoke these phrases to justify actions that may go beyond its Charter authority, this does not explain why non-Council member states have been willing to cede increasing amounts of authority to a body that can impose new legal mandates on them in the future. Certainly diplomats and political leaders realize that any expansion of the Council's authority in one situation can easily establish a precedent for similar action in future situations. Unless the international community of diplomats and political leaders are willing to accept the expansion of the Council's powers in the long term, they are likely to be wary of allowing such precedents to be established, especially if they could potentially be on the receiving end in the future. This is equally true of the P5 states, all of who are acutely aware that their actions will establish precedents that will likely constrain their future behavior.[9] For these reasons, it is in the interest of both P5 and non-P5 states that the Council act according to established standards and procedures in making a determination that a threat to peace and security has occurred.

A second alternative for using consent theories to explain the expansion of Council authority is to evoke customary international law. From the perspective of legal positivists, customary law reflects implied consent inasmuch as it is derived from actual state practice that has not only continued consistently over a sustained period of time, but which has been publicly accepted as a legal obligation by a wide range of states (Byers 1999: 4). This concept of *opinio juris* (an unambiguous belief by state officials that a particular practice is in fact a legal obligation) makes law based on practice a consensual act. This, of course, raises a new set of problems. Some principles—such as the right of free passage on the high seas—have been long accepted as part of international law largely because states have engaged in these practices over several centuries, and a broad range of regime types (monarchies, empires, democracies, theocracies) have acknowledged their legality. Yet recent attempts by international law scholars and diplomats to claim that a particular norm constitutes customary law—for example, the illegality of genocide, states' obligation to protect human rights, and the right to self-determination—involve issues of relatively recent vintage. Most are only a few decades old. More importantly, there is little evidence of consistent state practice in these areas, which is precisely the reason why the Council has been forced to take coercive action when the issues arise. In fact, this problem of defining exactly what constitutes customary law has led states to codify its main principles into international treaties over the course of the late twentieth century.[10] For this reason, customary law—once the main source of international legal obligation—is rapidly decreasing in importance.

Finally, a political scientist could argue that the Council establishes its authority through its practice rather than through a textural interpretation of the Charter. From this perspective, it is the Council itself that determines the scope of its authority and can always reinterpret the text of the Charter when necessary. Thus, the U.S. Department of State held in 1975 that "the language of the Charter permits important evolutionary changes without requiring textural change" (Department of State 1976: 118). Such an explanation is consistent with the argument that the Council is a political body and therefore does not need to be concerned with legalisms. This could explain the willingness of the P5 to act as they see fit in a particular circumstance; however, it does not account for why the non-P5 member states would agree to this interpretation of the scope of the Council's authority. The historical record shows that members of the UN have been very conscious of legalities within the organization, especially in terms of procedure (Blum 1993). While acknowledging that the Council possesses the authority to determine for itself what constitutes a threat to international peace and security, most of the non-P5 states demand that it act on some type of legal basis rather than simply the whim of its most powerful members. In fact, despite their agreement to accept the decisions of the Council in matters related to international peace and security, the non-P5 states have also demonstrated a strong wariness toward any type of hierarchy within the organization. For this reason, most states have indicated a firm interest in discouraging arbitrary action by the P5. Thus, the non-P5 states have considered the procedural safeguards that are both implied and explicit as necessary to prevent the Council from usurping the broader authority of the UN membership. As the representative from Zimbabwe argued in 1992:

> 160 States have placed their security, and possibly their very survival, in the hands of the 15 [members of the Security Council]. This is a solemn and heavy responsibility. . . . It is therefore of crucial importance that

every decision taken by the Security Council be able to withstand the careful scrutiny of the 160 Member States on whose behalf the Council is expected to act. This is only possible if the Council insists on being guided in its decisions and actions by the Charter and other international conventions.

(Quoted in Kirgis 1995: 517)

Political consensus as the source of legal authority

If the members of the United Nations never consented to an expansion in the scope of the Security Council's authority, why has the Council been able to broaden its legal powers to embrace nation-building, war crimes prosecution, safe zones, and humanitarian intervention? I argue that this expansion reflects new developments in international law that—under specific circumstances— allow for collective international consensus to override individual state consent. Under this paradigm, the Council has become a recognized arbiter of what constitutes a legal consensus, and that this has enabled it to expand its mandate to coincide with said consensus.

A theory of consensus-based law holds that under certain conditions, some international legal obligations can be derived from a widespread agreement among the members of the international community over the authority of basic legal principles. Once adopted by the international community of states through a series of legitimately accepted multilateral political processes, such legal norms can become part of general international law applicable to all states, much in the same way that customary law is considered to be universally binding after it has been accepted as such by the international community. Unlike customary law, however, consensus-based norms are not rooted in a long-standing *practice*, nor can states separate themselves from a legal obligation by maintaining a persistent objection. In fact consensus-based international law turns customary law on its head; the norm *precedes* the practice rather than the other way around. Thus consensus-based international law does not *reflect* state practice as much as it *creates* it. This is an important point, because some of the most important consensus-based legal norms are created by political leaders precisely because the practice of states does not conform to the principle. As I will demonstrate below, it is emerging legal norms based on international consensus—not state practice—that the Council evokes when it cites customary law. This is an important point, since it is very difficult to "create" new customary law (inasmuch as it requires time and widespread prior practice), thereby making it difficult for the Council to react quickly to emerging crises.

The source of consensus-based legal norms is neither random nor arbitrary. Political leaders and legal analysts derive them from a combination of the following: peremptory legal norms; multilateral "law-making" treaties; the charters of universal membership organizations; and a consistent pattern of resolutions passed by decision-making bodies of multilateral organizations.

First, legal analysts from a wide variety of states have begun to recognize some fundamental principles—known as peremptory norms—as legally binding on all legal subjects (primarily states) regardless of whether they have specifically consented to them on an individual basis. Peremptory norms (*jus cogens*) are defined as fundamental principles from which no derogation is permitted by any state. Such norms cannot be overridden by individual acts or wills.[11] Thus, norms of *jus cogens* derive their status from deeply embedded principles held by the international community, principles which are at the very core of the community's existence. Violations of such peremptory norms are considered to shock the sensibilities of the international community and therefore bind the members of that community, irrespective of protest, recognition, or acquiescence (Inter-American Commission on Human Rights 2002). For example, all states are bound to respect the universal principle of sovereign equality as fundamental to international relations regardless of whether they have explicitly adopted this principle by signing a treaty. More recently, the principle of national self-determination has emerged as a peremptory norm that most states consider to be universally binding even though no treaty exists that specifically stipulates this. Security Council resolutions frequently draw on such principles in providing a justification for its actions (see below).

In one sense, no community could exist without some types of peremptory norms. At a minimum, they are necessary for defining the conditions of interaction. For example, as J. L. Brierly points out, the fundamental principle of *pacta sunt servanta* (agreements must be observed) cannot itself be subject to consent; otherwise there is no practical way for states to articulate consent at all (Brierly 1936: 54). Without an assumption of *pacta sunt servanta*, consent would be meaningless, since the credibility of one's commitments would be lacking. Increasingly, new principles defining the limits of state action—such as the prohibition of slavery and piracy—have emerged as peremptory. Thus although there is controversy among international legal scholars and practitioners concerning the role of peremptory norms in international law, most political leaders operate on the assumption that at least some exist.

Second, since the mid-twentieth century there has been a growing trend to codify emerging legal norms into a form of universal law through the development of "law-making" treaties. Law-making treaties are multilateral agreements that articulate principles that states consider to be binding on all members of the international community, regardless of whether individual units explicitly consented to them through a formal ratification process. Malcolm Shaw argues that by virtue of their widespread support and acceptance, such treaties have an effect *generally*, rather than *restrictively*. These "law-making treaties" elaborate a common perception of international law in a given topic and establish new rules to guide states in their international conduct (Shaw 1997: 75).

According to Oscar Schachter, in order to be considered to be a lawmaking treaty, an agreement must be intended to regulate a particular kind of behavior that applies universally. In addition, it must articulate a rule formally adopted by an authorized body of an international organization (Schachter 1999: 5). Frederic Kirgis argues that such agreements should also fulfill at least one of the following conditions: (1) it codifies pre-existing customary law; (2) it reflects general principles of law recognized by a wide range of states; (3) it crystallizes "emerging rules of law" (as opposed to simply codifying existing practices); and/or (4) it generates new custom by encouraging new practice (Kirgis 1999: 66). While the first two conditions are consistent with consent-based legal norms, the latter two suggest a broader application that moves beyond individual state consent. I consider those that fulfill the latter two conditions as constituting one piece of evidence for the existence of a universal legal norm based on international consensus. As I argue below, it is not the treaties themselves that bind non-signatories, but, rather, the universal legal principles represented in the treaties. In this sense, law-making treaties provide only one—although an important one—piece of evidence for the existence of a universal legal norm based on international consensus.

The legitimacy of law-making treaties as creating universally binding principles has been strengthened by the existence of a widely accepted process for creating new and/or amending existing international law. Since the 1950s states have developed a practice of holding UN-sponsored conferences to discuss, negotiate, draft, and ultimately sign multilateral conventions and law-making treaties that create new principles of international law. While this does not approach the category of a "legislative body," it does provide a process through which states can develop a general consensus around a particular legal issue. The universality of the UN membership provides the foundation for its legitimacy. Thus, while the United Nations lacks the legal authority to create new international law, it often acts as a vehicle for drafting multilateral treaties and conventions that may do just that. Since these conferences are not provided for in the UN Charter, the multilateral agreements that they produce do not derive their legal authority either from the organization itself or from the obligations that flow from one's membership in it. Rather, it is the legitimacy attached to the world body that enables states to advance claims that certain agreements may be applied universally.

Third, the charters of multilateral universal membership organizations usually contain principles that reflect a consensus around a particular set of political values in international relations.[12] Although these charters are only legally binding on the members of the organization, as states join an increasing number of these multilateral organizations, they begin to accept a common set of principles that are consistently found in each of these institutions. These principles provide one more piece of evidence for a consensus around a particular legal norm. In the case of the United Nations, since all states in the world are members, one may argue that the core principles embedded in the Charter—combined with those found in similar charters of regional bodies—approach the status of universal law.

Similarly, a consistent pattern of unanimous or near-unanimous resolutions passed by decision-making bodies within various multilateral organizations can also provide a source of consensus-based international law. Although—as is the case with the UN General Assembly—such resolutions are legally non-binding, in some cases they represent an international consensus that goes beyond the legal status of the document. Thus it is not the resolutions themselves that states consider to be binding, but, rather, the principles that they articulate. For example, the international legal prohibition against colonialism did not emerge either from a treaty or from customary international law. Rather, it can be traced to a process that culminated in a unanimous resolution passed by the United Nations General Assembly, a body with no legal authority to create new international law. The Assembly's Declaration on the Granting of Independence to Colonial Countries and Peoples (Resolution 1514 (XV)) has been cited many times by a wide range of political leaders and legal analysts as the legal basis of decolonization. It cannot be considered to be part of customary law because at the time of its passage it did not reflect common practice; in fact many of the great powers continued to hold colonies until the late 1960s. Moreover, it emerged over a relatively short period of time (approximately a decade or so after the end of World War II), a period so short that it cannot conceivably be considered to count as evidence of a custom.

Although there is no treaty specifically outlawing the practice, most states have since considered the prohibition of colonial rule to be an obligation. This is because this resolution articulated what has become a fundamental principle in international law, the right of self-determination for all peoples. In fact it was this resolution that provided the justification for the Security Council's 1975 action declaring East Timor to be an independent state and calling on Indonesia to immediately vacate the territory (S/RES/384 1975). It also provided the foundation for the Council's actions against South Africa's possession of Namibia. Similarly, the Security Council and other decision-making bodies constantly evoke other General Assembly resolutions, such as the Declaration on Principles of International Law Concerning Friendly Relations, when providing a legal justification for their actions.

While each of these sources individually may not offer evidence of consensus, in their totality they can demonstrate a consistent pattern of agreement on principles that are generally accepted by members of the international community. In particular, those principles that the members consider to be fundamental to the cohesion and progress of the international community would be binding on all legal entities (states) regardless of whether each state formally consented to specific provisions. With a consensus-based legal norm, then, the power of consent is held collectively by the international community, rather than individually by each state.[13] In these cases, collective agreement can override an individual objection; this is the crucial difference between consent and consensus.

This makes many international law scholars and political scientists uncomfortable. For some, it undermines the foundation of international law by allowing political factors to override legal obligation. Prosper Weil, for example, argues that the concepts such as *jus cogens* make it difficult to define exactly what constitutes a legal obligation and thus international law becomes overcome by political expediency. He holds that only black letter law (treaties) and customary practices can serve as a basis of legal obligation (Weil 1983: 413–442). This is a valid concern. If international law can be created *ad hoc*, then its influence on state behavior would diminish in favor of self-definition based on self-interest.

Similarly, many political scientists and legal positivists would have a problem with legal norms based on consensus, in part because consensus is itself difficult to measure. Unlike other forms of decision-making, consensus is based neither on a numerical majority (which can be counted) nor a specific command issued by a superior authority (which can be identified). In many ways this problem is similar to that of norm identification: how do we know when one exists and how many political actors need to accept it for it to be considered legitimate? Finnemore and Sikkink's efforts to address this question of norms can be helpful in determining the degree to which a consensus may exist around a particular set of principles. They suggest that we examine each norm's particular "lifecycle" by tracing the process through which a critical mass of actors converges around a particular standard. This enables us to determine the "tipping point" after which agreement becomes widespread (see Finnemore and Sikkink 1998). Once this is done, we look for patterns in behavior or discourse to uncover the degree to which states accept the norm. One also investigates any significant and persistent objections. In terms of identifying the norm itself, Finnemore and Sikkink (1998: 892) argue that norms usually leave an extensive trail of communication among actors that we can study. We recognize norm-breaking behavior because it generates disapproval and norm-conforming action because it produces praise.

Similarly, we can identify the evolution of consensus in international law by studying, among other things, the following: (1) the substance of discussion and debate at international conferences where law-making treaties are developed;[14] (2) the discourse that is conducted within the deliberative bodies of formal international organizations such as the UN Security Council, the International Law Commission, and executive councils of regional organizations; and (3) the degree to which states and international organizations make reference to these emerging legal norms when making decisions and articulating policies. After tracing the development of the legal principle underlying a particular rule, one can further investigate how it is put into practice by multilateral bodies such as the General Assembly or Security Council. The most direct way of doing so is to study the resolutions and directives issued by these organizations as they attempt to address specific issues and conflicts that are brought before them. In addition, one can read diplomatic correspondence, rulings by domestic courts, and executive orders issued by governments. In general, the task is to determine whether there is a consistent pattern of agreement over specific obligations within various forums.

This of course leads to an obvious objection: Who gets to decide whether there is in fact a consistent pattern of agreement and when the tipping point I referred to above is reached? Clearly if consensus-based legal norms are universally binding, then this determination cannot legitimately be made either by an individual state or by a self-selected subset of states. Rather, it would have to emerge through a process of deliberation and consultation that is generally accepted by the international community of states. Ian Johnstone (1991 and 2003) argues that such deliberation occurs within what he terms "interpretive communities." He defines such communities as associations of recognized political leaders (usually official delegates from participating states) operating within a multilateral organization that other states believe has the authority and competence to make judgments concerning legal obligation. Johnson argues that the international legal order operates primarily through this process of "justificatory discourse" among key political actors (see Chapter 5). Although Johnstone is primarily concerned with interpretation, his analysis can also be applied to other areas of international law, in this case its formation. In the context of our discussion, an interpretive community would consist of those actors with the expertise, competence, and legitimacy to determine when a particular legal norm has achieved the level of agreement necessary to consider it part of general international law. I will address this more specifically in the next section.

The Security Council and international consensus law

Consensus-based legal norms challenge the volunteerist notion implicit in the concept of sovereignty by requiring states to accept some obligations to which they may not have explicitly agreed. Of course, new states do this all the time; their acceptance of customary law and diplomatic practices is usually required as the price of recognition and their acceptance into the international community of states. It is, however, more difficult to get established entities to agree to such a system, particularly those with the economic and military resources to resist. Thus, the development of a consensus-based legal norm not only requires a deep commitment toward common principles in a specified issue area, it also depends on legitimacy of the process through which the consensus is reached. That is, there must be a widely recognized mechanism with the authority to articulate those legal obligations that have been accepted as universally binding. Until recently, the absence of a central legislative authority has deprived the international community of this type of mechanism, making consensus-based international norms difficult to develop.

The founding of the United Nations was an important step in building the type of legitimate institution capable of articulating universal legal principles. The organization is the first to encompass all recognized states on earth, and the Charter commits states to accept the resolutions made by its decision-making bodies. In this sense, the UN represents the international community.

Thus, although there is technically no hierarchy of organizations under international law, most states clearly view the UN as being the primary mechanism with the legitimacy to take collective action on international issues, particularly those that involve security, stability, and peace.[15] This holds in both a legal and empirical sense. The UN Charter imposes legal obligations on its members; however, of equal importance, the *practice* of states vis-à-vis the organization suggests a broad commitment to the UN process. Certainly states act outside of the UN's mandates, and in its first half century, its effectiveness was hampered by the bifurcation of the international community into two hostile blocs. During the cold war the General Assembly became a forum for acting out the North–South conflict while the East–West competition in the Council rendered the body moribund and unproductive.

At the same time, no state has ever withdrawn its membership from the UN and virtually all have publicly acknowledged the legality of both the Charter and the Council's resolutions. Moreover, most of the problems encountered by the Council have not involved disputes over the legality of its resolutions or the legitimacy of that body to act on behalf of the international community. Rather the deficiencies have been political. The framers of the Charter thought that the five permanent members would act as "security managers," much like the Concert of Europe a century earlier (Hilderbrand 1990: 142). The cold war—which erupted a short time after the development of the UN—made this impossible. The collapse of the East–West and North–South conflicts opened new possibilities for the Council to act as it was originally designed; however, the disparity in power between the United States and the other four permanent members has made it difficult for the other members to play the balancing role originally envisioned by the framers. Despite these problems, however, the Council remains the most legitimately recognized institution for making decisions on a wide range of international issues.

The legitimacy of the Council to articulate principles of consensus-based international norms lies with its internal structure and its relationship to the general UN membership (or in a broader sense, the international community). The Council is primarily a deliberative body, which means it does not act based on automatic "triggers" (the way the League of Nations was designed to do) but, rather, on the basis of political consensus.[16] Decisions reflect the outcome of negotiations among its principle members. For this reason, Council actions will likely always be selective, an important safeguard that provides the flexibility to take into account political factors when they cannot achieve consensus. Sometimes this prevents the Council from acting even when most political leaders believe a violation of the Charter has occurred (Weiss 1996; Barnett 2003); however, this safeguard has ensured that the Council will err on the side of caution. Since the five permanent members represent the most powerful states in the world, a consensus among them provides the means for implementing commonly held standards. The veto—a classic balance of power mechanism—helps to guard against any single state or combination imposing their own interests under the guise of community norms. The diversity of the P5 in terms of interest and worldview ensures that Council decisions will reflect a high degree of broad consensus. Moreover, the rotating members act as a check against a great power cabal, since any binding decision requires that a majority of these smaller states adhere to the consensus, at least in theory. For this reason, the International Court of Justice (ICJ 1971: 16) held that Security Council resolutions that further international law are binding on all states, regardless of whether they are members of the UN or specific parties to a treaty.

Although the Council remains an internally closed body, it has taken steps to strengthen its legitimacy by instituting reforms that increase the transparency of its decision-making process. First and foremost, it has established procedures allowing the participation of those non-member states with an interest in a particular issue before the body. Moreover, it has made its annual report to the General Assembly public and now publishes the Provincial Agenda for its meetings in the official *Journal of the United Nations* (S/26015 1993). Moreover, all draft resolutions are now available to all United Nations delegates, revealing at least one part of the deliberation process that often occurs in private (S/PRST/1994/62 1994).

As a result, in cases where there is widespread agreement within the international community over fundamental principles that underlie legal norms, the Council represents the arbiter of what constitutes a universal legal norm. However, since the Council is a political body rather than a judicial one, it does not issue legal opinions or make rulings. Rather, it articulates its view as to what constitutes a legal obligation through its actions. For example, by creating "safe zones" in Sarajevo to protect civilian populations from gross human rights abuses—without the consent of any state in the Balkans—the Council represented a broad consensus that ethnic cleansing was a violation, regardless of whether Serbia or Croatia were parties to a specific treaty. I argue that the universalization of these types of norms has enabled the Council to expand the scope of its authority beyond that which is specifically granted to it by the Charter of the United Nations and more importantly beyond that which the member states had been originally willing to cede. So long as it is acting within a broad consensus of international law and UN procedure, it can expand the scope of its authority to reflect changing beliefs as to what constitutes a legal obligation.

In the next section, I will briefly examine how the Council has drawn from consensus-based legal norms concerning the use of state violence in expanding the scope of its authority during the 1990s.

Applying consensus-based international law in practice

The maintenance of international security and the prevention of interstate aggression has long been the primary mission of the Security Council. Like most collective security associations, its principal goal has been to protect the territorial integrity and political independence of its member states.[17] Yet since the end of the cold war, the Council has focused as much on containing state *violence* as it has state *aggression*. This is an important distinction. The UN security system was not designed to control violence per se, but, rather, threats to the territory and sovereignty of its member states. However, since the 1980s, the Council's concern with widespread violence has not even been primarily with its effect on territory, sovereignty, or state security, but, rather, with the well-being of civilian populations in such diverse areas as Somalia, the former Yugoslavia, Sierra Leone, and East Timor.

One could argue that this simply reflects changes in contemporary warfare and the concept of threat. Over the past few decades, ethnic conflicts, civil wars, and other forms of internal violence have increased even as large-scale interstate wars have decreased. This has shifted the sources of global instability from great power wars to lower-level internal conflicts. Reflecting this, the motivations behind Council action in the cases cited have not been limited to humanitarian concerns; indeed these have not even been its main concern. The Council has also been guided by a belief that the use of extreme violence by governments against large populations could generate massive refugee flows, illegal arms trafficking, and the rise of paramilitary guerrilla armies, all of which could disrupt neighboring states and regional stability.

At the same time, neither extreme levels of internal violence nor its corresponding effects on neighboring states are new. During the 1970s and 1980s extreme state violence against civilian populations—including genocide and crimes against humanity—occurred widely, in Cambodia, Bangladesh, Uganda, and throughout Africa and Central America. While the instances of ethnic conflict increased with the breakup of the Soviet Union and Yugoslavia in the early 1990s, guerrilla insurgencies and civil wars decreased. All of which suggests that it was not the *level* of violence against civilians per se that has led to a change in international perceptions about the scope of the Council's authority, but, rather, the widespread belief concerning the *basis* upon which the Council could legitimately consider such practices to fall within their Chapter VII powers.

Even during the cold war, a consensus had been slowly building among the members of the international community that certain forms of extreme state violence were, on their face, violations of international law regardless of whether the perpetrators had consensually agreed to ban these practices. The two most important developments in this area were the Genocide Convention and the definition of a new type of international offense—crimes against humanity—that was first introduced at the Nuremberg trials. The Genocide Convention declared, for the first time, that a particular practice would constitute an international crime, not simply a treaty violation (United Nations 1951). Thus the perpetrators would be violating general international law, not simply a contractual treaty obligation to other states. Equally significant, the convention authorized both individual states and international courts to prosecute individual perpetrators *even if they were nationals of states that were not parties to the convention.* (United Nations 1951, italics added). This violation of the most basic principle in consent-based law helped to lay the groundwork for a universal law regarding the control of extreme state violence. Similarly, the idea of a "crime against humanity"—a phrase that does not appear in any of the Geneva Conventions or similar agreements—also introduced a new universal legal norm that applied regardless of whether a particular perpetrator had adopted it.[18]

Building on these precedents—as well as a foundation of multilateral law-making treaties, resolutions passed by the General Assembly, and general peremptory legal norms—the Council has demonstrated that it regards these practices as international crimes that hold regardless of whether particular states have specifically agreed to ban them or whether they are parties to a particular treaty. Hence, when the end of the cold war enabled the Council to act as it was originally intended, it had already possessed the legal tools to act beyond the boundaries of collective security. The expansion of the Council's mandate to include the enforcement of these specific forms of state violence clearly represents an expansion of its authority inasmuch as it focuses not on violations of the territorial integrity or political independence of states, but rather the *means* through which states pursue their national interests. Although the Council has been highly inconsistent in acting in this area—often choosing to avoid becoming involved in situations where these practices occur—it has maintained its legal authority to do so when levels of state violence threatened humanitarian principles and the lives of civilian populations.

This became evident with the way in which the Council chose to address the conflicts in the former Yugoslavia during the early 1990s. In doing so, it specifically established two practices that represent a dramatic expansion in the Council's legal authority: the creation of war crimes tribunals and the designation of sovereign territory as "safe zones" designed to protect civilian populations in conflict situations, without the consent of the belligerents.

In May, 1993, the Security Council voted to establish an International Criminal Tribunal for Yugoslavia (ICTY) to try those individuals deemed to be responsible for "widespread and flagrant violations of international humanitarian law occurring within the territory of the former Yugoslavia, and especially in the Republic of Bosnia and Herzegovina (S/RES/827)." Significantly, the Statutes of this tribunal went beyond establishing procedures for prosecuting the accused. They required all states to actively cooperate with the tribunals (including arresting and extraditing suspects) even if this meant changing domestic laws to enable governments to do so.[19] Individual states were not given the option of opting out or even choosing not to adhere to this provision and were in fact legally subject to coercive sanctions if they did so.

This expansion of international law into the area of prosecuting individual leaders for crimes against humanity is well covered by Wayne Sandholtz in

Chapter 7 of this volume. Rather than delve into the details, then, I will confine my comments to several points concerning how the Council tried to provide a legal foundation for moving beyond its mandate. Although the Council mentioned Chapter VII in Resolution 827, the text of the measure clearly suggests that it was not in fact acting in response to a breach or threat of the peace or act of aggression. Rather, it claimed to be responding to violations of "international humanitarian law," a phrase that is peppered throughout the resolution but that does not in fact appear in any treaty or organizational charter. This raises two points. First, the Council is not in any way empowered to enforce the Geneva Conventions or any other treaty that was negotiated outside of the UN for that matter. Second, the term "international humanitarian law" is not a legal term drawn from any agreement, but, rather, is a description of a set of legal norms drawn from a wide range of treaties, conventions, and protocols that are designed to protect civilians and minimize human suffering by restricting the means and methods of warfare.[20] The Council did not actually claim to be enforcing any particular treaty; in fact, nowhere in the resolution authorizing the creation of the tribunals did the Council cite specific treaty violations by any party. This may be because the members of the Council did not wish to restrict themselves to the provisions of any specific document, particularly since neither Bosnia nor Croatia signed the Geneva Conventions until December of 1992 and Serbia failed to do so until 2001.

Although some might argue that as the successor state to the Socialist Federal Republic of Yugoslavia (SFRY), the newly named Federal Republic of Yugoslavia (FRY) was legally bound by the commitments made by the SFRY, both the Security Council and General Assembly specifically denied the FRY automatic membership in the UN based on the position that the FRY was not in fact a successor state (S/47/1, S/RES/757). Moreover, an arbitration commission established by the European Union similarly declared the FRY to be a new state and not successor to the Socialist Federal Republic of Yugoslavia (Murphy 2000: 677). Technically, none of the three countries were in violation of their treaty commitments (as understood under a consent-based international legal system) until that time. Yet the resolution called for prosecuting acts committed since 1991.

Neither the Secretary General's report examining the possibility of establishing a tribunal nor the text of the Council's resolutions actually accuse any particular state or military force of violating either international humanitarian law or the UN Charter. Rather, in the words of UN Secretary-General Boutros Boutros-Ghali (regarding the Balkans resolution), "the Security Council has already determined that the situation posed by *continuing reports* of widespread violations of international humanitarian law *occurring in the former Yugoslavia*, including reports of mass killings and the continuation of the practice of 'ethnic cleansing' " (S/25704. Italics added).

Boutros-Ghali clearly understood this problem when he observed in his key report to the Security Council:

The approach, which, in the normal course of events, would be followed in establishing an international tribunal, would be the conclusion of a treaty by which the States parties would establish a tribunal and approve its statute. This treaty would be drawn up and adopted by an appropriate international body (e.g., the General Assembly or a specially convened conference), following which it would be opened for signature and ratification.

(Report Of The Secretary-General (S/25704: para. 19))

The problem with this (consent-based) approach, the Secretary General acknowledged, would be (at least in part) that "there could be no guarantee that ratifications will be received from those States which should be parties to the treaty if it is to be truly effective." In other words, traditional approaches to international law could allow the perpetrators to avoid judgment by withholding their consent. Implicitly, the Secretary General was appealing to a broader understanding of international law. Thus, he continued, "in assigning to the International Tribunal the task of prosecuting persons responsible for serious violations of international humanitarian law, the Security Council would not be creating or purporting to 'legislate' that law. Rather, the International Tribunal would have the task of applying existing international humanitarian law" (S/25704: para. 19). The approach, which, in the normal course of events, would be followed in establishing an international tribunal, would be the conclusion of a treaty by which the states parties would establish a tribunal and approve its statute. This treaty would be drawn up and adopted by an appropriate international body (e.g., the General Assembly or a specially convened conference), following which it would be opened for signature and ratification.

The Security Council was in fact not creating new law, but instead was acting on the basis of legal principles that had been established over the previous few decades through a set of peremptory norms, law-making treaties, and United Nations General Assembly resolutions. While few states have considered the preservation of human rights to be a legal obligation (even though most states have signed the Covenant on Civil and Political Rights), a general consensus had been slowly developing since the end of World War II that the entire international community had an interest in developing legal restrictions on state violence when it reached the level of "a consistent pattern of gross, flagrant or mass violations" that "shock the conscience" of humankind.[21] It was on this basis that the Council created the tribunal.

The Council also expanded its authority to stop extreme state violence in the former Yugoslavia by taking the extraordinary step of imposing external restrictions on how a legally constituted government can administer its own territory, by declaring said territory to be UN protected "safe zones." In Resolution 819, which established these zones, the Council declared ethnic cleansing to be an illegal practice and justified its usurpation of sovereign territory as a way of enforcing humanitarian law and the protection of the civilian population. Even a generous interpretation of Chapter VII would be hard pressed to find a legal foundation for this type of action within a traditional consent-based international legal system. Article 15 of the Fourth Geneva Convention does provide for conflicting parties to establish "neutralized zones" to shelter civilians from the effects of the war; however, it is also very clear that these zones must be created through the mutual agreement of the parties. Nowhere does it allow an international institution to seize the territory and declare a safe zone without consent. In fact, the principle of territoriality is probably the most fundamental concept in the modern system of nation-states (Ruggie 1993). Even in cases where international law has intruded in the domestic sphere of states—for example, in the area of human rights—it has never authorized international institutions to violate the principle of territorial sovereignty in order to enforce it.

The members of the Council knew that they were entering into uncharted legal waters. Although the U.S. and Britain had unilaterally declared regions of Northern Iraq to be "safe havens" at the close of the Gulf War, they never established a legal foundation for their actions under international law, nor did they seek the support of a Council resolution.[22] Thus, when Austria proposed establishing such zones for the protection of the populations in selected areas of Bosnia and Herzegovina, it provoked considerable internal debate within both the Council and within the UN Protection Force (A/54/549). Ultimately, the Council decided to create such zones in six Bosnian towns, including its capital and largest cities.[23] Like the creation of the international tribunal, the Council did not cite specific treaties, customary practices, or violations of the UN Charter in justifying their involvement, but, rather, did so on the basis of general humanitarian law (A/54/549). In establishing these zones, Resolution 819 also declared ethnic cleansing to be unlawful, although it did not cite any particular treaties or agreements to back this up.[24] None of this is to imply that the Council did not have a legal basis for taking the actions that it did; rather, my point is that its actions were legal because it was drawing from legal norms that states accepted as universal on the basis of common consensus.

Conclusion

The expansion of the Security Council's authority is perhaps the most important development in the United Nations since its founding. It has evolved from a body charged with overseeing collective security to one that governs a wide range of practices in international relations that go well beyond the issue of international peace and security. This chapter has suggested that the explanation for this development lies with an expansion in the way international law has been practiced over the past few decades. Specifically, it reflects the growth of legal norms that are derived not from individual state consent, but, rather, from collective international consensus. I have argued that states accept the legitimacy of such a consensus because they have consented both to the process and the principles upon which said principles are articulated. In this sense, it has achieved both *purposive* and *performance* legitimacy, as we define it in the introduction. The Council's purposive legitimacy to expand its legal authority into the reduction of state violence is derived from universal legal norms that are viewed by the members as consistent with the broader norms and values of international society. Its performance legitimacy rests with its status as the body most appropriate to apply what I call consensus-based international law.

This of course suggests that there are limits to the Council's expansion of legal authority. Although the UN Charter does not stipulate *how* the Council is to determine when a particular situation is a threat or a breach of the peace, this discussion in this chapter implies that it does not have a blank check. The members expect the Council to act on the basis of either its Charter responsibilities or—as I suggest—on the basis of universal legal norms that have been accepted as such by the international community. When it fails to act—or exceeds these limits—we can expect the members to challenge its authority (as Das and Krasno discuss in Chapter 9).

Notes

1 Article 25 stipulates that the Members of the United Nations agree to "accept and carry out the decisions of the Security Council in accordance with the present Charter," while Chapters VI and VII outline the types of mandates they may issue to the membership.

2 For a complete record of Council resolutions since 1946, see www.un.org/documents/scres.htm

3 The Indian parliament, for example, refused to provide peacekeeping troops in post-war Iraq without a Security Council resolution explicitly authorizing it. See Cherian 2003.

4 For a complete listing of these agreements organized chronologically, see the Multilaterals Project at Tuft University's Fletcher School, fletcher.tufts.edu/multi/chrono.html

5 I am using the term "international community" in a legal sense; that is, as a formal association of states and other internationally recognized actors, each of whom possesses formal rights and obligations under international law.

6 Reflecting this principle, Article 34 of the Vienna Convention on the Law of Treaties explicitly states that a treaty does not create either obligations or rights for a third (non-party) state without its explicit consent.

7 In international law, the term sovereignty is defined in terms of constitutional independence; that is, the principle that states are not part of a larger constitutional structure of authority. See James 1986.

8 Schweigman (2001) cites Article 24, for example, which stipulates that the Council must act within the purposes and principles of the organization. These principles include those of "justice and international law."

9 In interviews with staff members from Council delegations, it was clear that they are acutely aware of the long-term implications of their actions. This, for example,

is one of the reasons why the Council has been extremely wary of engaging in humanitarian intervention, fearing that it would raise expectations when such situations arise in the future.

10 See, for example, the Vienna Convention on Diplomatic Relations and Protocols (1961), Vienna Convention on the Law of Treaties (1969), and the Montevideo Convention On The Rights And Duties Of States (1933).

11 See Article 53 of the Vienna Convention on the Law of Treaties.

12 Universal membership organizations are those that are open to all states so long as they accept the principles of its founding charter.

13 Von Glahn (1996: 39) refers to this as "common consent" while Oxman (1991: 143–144) calls it "diffuse consent."

14 United Nations-sponsored law-making conferences maintain very precise records detailing the substance of the discussions, including verbatim statements made by the delegates. These records, known as the *travaux préparatoires*, are available from the Dag Hammarskjöld library and its depositories.

15 This does not mean that all political leaders subscribe to this view, although outside of the United States few public officials question the legitimacy of the UN and Security Council. For an example of anti-UN views in the U.S., see Kirkpatrick 1984 and Krauthammer 1987.

16 Article 37 (2) states that, "*If* the Security Council deems that the continuance of the dispute is in fact likely to endanger the maintenance of international peace and security, *it shall decide whether to take action* under Article 36 or to recommend such terms of settlement as it may consider appropriate" (italics added).

17 For a discussion of collective security, see, *inter alia*, Wolfers 1988, Thompson 1953. For more recent treatments, see Kupchan and Kupchan 1991 and Betts 1992.

18 The Rome Statute of the International Criminal Court defines crimes against humanity as inhuman acts that are "committed as part of a widespread or systematic attack directed against any civilian population, with knowledge of the attack." Such acts include murder, extermination, enslavement, forcible transfer of population, torture, and rape.

19 See, for example, Article 29 of the Statute of the International Tribunal for the Prosecution of Persons Responsible for Serious Violations of International Humanitarian Law Committed in the Territory of the Former Yugoslavia since 1991 (UN Doc. S/25704).

20 Traditionally, international humanitarian law has referred to those provisions in the four Geneva Conventions and the two protocols that are directed toward individuals who do not take part in the hostilities (such as civilians, medics, and aid workers) and those who can no longer fight (such as the wounded and prisoners of war).

21 These phrases were taken from United Nations General Assembly Resolution 96 (I) of 11 December 1946 and Article 2(3) of the Convention against Torture and Other Cruel, Inhuman or Degrading Treatment or Punishment. They have since been used many times as the informal standard from which what I call "excess violence" has been defined.

22 Rather than seek a Council resolution to officially create "safe havens" in northern and southern Iraq, the British and American governments relied on a questionable interpretation of a previous resolution that called on the Iraqi government to stop their repression of the Kurdish population within their borders. This resolution (Security Council Resolution 688) called on the Iraqi government to end its repression of the civilian populations and allow humanitarian assistance to those regions. Nowhere did it sanction any member state to intervene in these regions nor declare any part of the territory to be "off limits" to the central government.

23 See Security Council Resolutions 819, 824, and 836.
24 Article 49 of the Fourth Geneva Convention states that an "occupying power shall not deport or transfer parts of its own civilian population into the territory it occupies"; however, the Bosnian Serb paramilitaries in question were not an occupying power.

5 The Security Council as legislature

Ian Johnstone

On September 28, 2001, the Security Council adopted resolution 1373, requiring all states to enact measures designed to suppress the financing and other forms of support for terrorist acts. On April 28, 2004, the Council adopted a similar resolution (1540) aimed at preventing weapons of mass destruction from falling into the hands of terrorists. These are unprecedented acts of law-making by the Security Council. They impose binding obligations on all states under Chapter VII of the UN Charter, and yet unlike other Chapter VII action, they are not directly related to a particular crisis or limited in time. They do not seek to enforce a decision against a particular state, but, rather, impose general obligations in a broad issue area for an indefinite period. This is qualitatively different from the Council's normal crisis management role. Some diplomats and scholars have characterized it as legislating. Others have described it as "hegemonic law" in action. Still others see it as a constructive, incremental addition to the Security Council's toolbox of devices for dealing with new security threats.

Whichever view is correct, there is little doubt that these resolutions represent an innovation in how the Council exercises its Charter-based authority to maintain international peace and security. As such, they raise important questions about the propriety of this form of Security Council (SC) action. In this chapter I explore those questions from the perspective of what I call deliberative legitimacy.[1] My central argument is that the legitimacy of Council decision-making should be judged in part by the quality of deliberations that inform its decisions. If the Council is going to act as a legislature, is the deliberative process that leads to and follows the adoption of these resolutions adequate? In seeking to answer that question, I describe the SC as a four-tier deliberative setting, composed of the five permanent members, the ten non-permanent members, the rest of the UN membership, and the constellation of experts, non-governmental actors, and organs of public opinion who keep a close watch on what the Council does. My analysis suggests that, while the Council is far from being an ideal venue for deliberation, it is less exclusive and closed than meets the eye. Moreover, it is not hard to imagine a number of politically achievable reforms (short of expanding membership) that would enhance the legitimacy of this new legislative function.

The chapter proceeds as follows. In the next, second, section, I describe the unprecedented nature of resolutions 1373 and 1540, and consider why questions have been raised about the propriety of the Security Council legislating. In the third section, I present a conception of legitimacy that draws on the theory of deliberative democracy. In the fourth section, I turn to a close examination of the negotiation and implementation of the two resolutions. In the fifth section, I assess the Council action and processes from the perspective of deliberative legitimacy, focusing mainly on the debates in and around the Security Council itself. I conclude by enumerating a number of institutional reforms that would enhance the legitimacy and therefore authority of future legislative action by the Council.

The Security Council as legislature: resolutions 1373 and 1540

The Security Council has been extraordinarily innovative in the post-cold war era, especially in the exercise of its Chapter VII powers. It imposed far-reaching obligations on Iraq in the aftermath of the 1991 Gulf War. It authorized military operations for what were essentially humanitarian purposes in Bosnia, Somalia, and elsewhere. It established peacekeeping operations in situations where there was no peace to keep and where the ultimate goal was the political transformation of a state, in Haiti, for example. It imposed sanctions on Libya to pressure it into handing over two terrorism suspects. It imposed financial sanctions on Al-Qaeda and the Taliban, and drew up lists of associated individuals who would be subject to the sanctions (see Johnstone 2006). The Council established international criminal tribunals in former Yugoslavia and Rwanda, and it adopted resolution 1422 to prevent citizens of non-parties to the International Criminal Court from being handed over to the Court. It established transitional administrations in Kosovo and East Timor, setting up the UN as the governing authority in those territories for a transitional period.

Yet all of these innovations, far-reaching as they are, are in response to discrete breaches of or threats to the peace, and as such are consistent with the Security Council's traditional role as an *executive* body charged with the maintenance of international peace and security. They are designed to resolve a dispute, to compel a state to act or refrain from acting in a certain way, or to bring about a lasting peace in the aftermath of a particular conflict. Resolutions 1373 and 1540 are different. They are acts of international legislation that establish new binding rules of international law rather than commands relating to a particular situation (Szasz 2002: 902; Alvarez 2003; Stromseth 2003: 41; Happhold 2003. Also see Alvarez 2005: 189–217). Other commentators have been careful to avoid describing the resolutions as legislation, but all acknowledge the "unprecedented" and "far-reaching" nature of this law-making act, imposing obligations of a kind usually found only in treaties (Rosand 2003: 333; Ward 2003: 298; Rostow 2002; Cortright et al. 2004: 3). They create law for all states in a general issue area, without setting any time limit or conditions for terminating the obligations. Resolution 1373 extends the application of existing terrorist conventions to all states (mainly the 1999 Convention for the Suppression of the Financing of Terrorism but also the 1998 Convention for the Suppression of Terrorist Bombings); resolution 1540 fills perceived gaps in the law relating to the proliferation of weapons of mass destruction. Both resolutions, moreover, establish monitoring committees to oversee their implementation. As Jose Alvarez (2005: 198) states: "the generalizable legal effects of the Council's work are not incidental to its efforts to enforce . . . They are express attempts to make global law."

Can the Security Council do this? When it legislates, is the Security Council acting *ultra vires*, beyond the competence granted to it by the UN Charter? In the debates on resolution 1540, a number of states expressed doubts about the power of the Security Council to legislate.[2] Matthew Happold argues that resolution 1373 is *ultra vires*, pointing to the lack of explicit authority to legislate in the UN Charter, the structure of the organization, and past practice, in which the Council has always acted in response to a particular situation rather than by laying down "abstract legal propositions" (Happold 2003: 607). Clearly, the Security Council was not set up as a legislative body and, while it has come close to acting that way in the past (for example, by creating the *ad hoc* criminal tribunals), it has never before made general law for all states with no geographic or temporal limitation. Nevertheless, a combined reading of Articles 24, 25, and Chapter VII confer broad authority on the Council to take whatever measures it deems necessary to maintain and restore international peace and security, as long as it does not run afoul of the purposes and principles of the UN. In its declarative, interpretive, promotion and enforcement functions, the Council has shaped international law. Most of these functions are not enumerated in the UN Charter and yet have come to be seen as falling within the ambit of its authority. There is no evident legal prohibition against the Council extending that authority a step further by laying down general rules in the interest of peace and security, and indeed few if any states publicly questioned the legal right of the Security Council to act in this way (Ratner 2004). Even if one considers resolutions 1373 and 1540 to be "hegemonic international law in action," the point is they are law—not manifestly beyond the competence of the Security Council (Alvarez 2005: 216).

That the Council has the legal authority to legislate, however, does not necessarily mean it should. There are at least four sets of reasons to suggest it should not. The first relates to the institutional balance between the Security Council and the General Assembly. As Marti Koskenniemi (1995: 337–9) put it in an article entitled "The Police in the Temple: Order, Justice and the UN":

> The Security Council is the Police; the General Assembly is the Temple.
> The composition and procedures of the Security Council are determined

by the single-minded purpose to establish a causally effective center of international power . . . The Security Council should establish/maintain order . . . The Assembly should deal with the acceptability of that order.

Or as the dissenting judge Sir Gerald Fitzmaurice stated in the *Namibia* case before the ICJ: "It was to keep the peace, not to change the world order, that the Security Council was set up" (International Court of Justice 1971: 294, para. 115). While the General Assembly was not given the power to legislate either, it has a quasi-legislative role in its ability to adopt multilateral treaties which, when signed and ratified by the requisite number of countries, become law. If the Security Council usurps this quasi-legislative function, the General Assembly—which Koskiennemi (1995: 344) says "faute de mieux" is the representative body best able to deal with normative controversy—could be undermined. Moreover, decisions of the Security Council are not review-able by the International Court of Justice. There is no system of "checks and balances" in the UN comparable to the executive, legislative, and judicial branches in many domestic systems (Bianchi 2007: 881, at 910–13; Happold 2003: 608).[3] In fact, some are concerned that the SC has been arrogating to itself all three functions (Bianchi 2007; Harper 1994).

A second concern is that Security Council legislation circumvents the treaty-making process—"the vehicle par excellence of community interest" (Alvarez quoting Simma, Alvarez 2003: 875). The signing and ratification of treaties is the principal mechanism by which states consent to be bound by an international legal rule. Bypassing that process usurps the power of states to legislate for themselves (Happold 2003: 609–10). This not only derogates from the principle of sovereign equality, it also encroaches on parliamentary authority within states. The concern is exacerbated by the Security Council's expanding definition of what constitutes a threat to international peace and security. In its statement at the summit meeting in January 1992, the Council referred to "economic, social and ecological sources of instability" as threats to international peace and security, and it has acted since then under Chapter VII to address human rights and humanitarian concerns. Will the SC start legislating in the field of human rights or the environment (or health or good governance) in the name of peace and security?[4]

A third, related, concern is that the Security Council lacks the requisite expertise to function as an effective legislator. Legislative drafting is a skill that ambassadors to the UN and their political masters in capitals lack. Not surprisingly, given the years of failed efforts in the General Assembly to define terrorism, resolution 1373 lacks definition, leaving considerable scope for interpretative discretion on its precise requirements and raising concerns that it would be implemented in a less than even-handed manner.[5] Moreover, legislating requires attentiveness to the range of secondary issues that may be affected by the principal subject matter of the resolution. The treaty-making process tends to balance global concerns, leading to trade-offs and bargains that account for a wider range of interests than come out of

Security Council negotiations. There were complaints, for example, that the Council was insufficiently inattentive to human rights issues in drafting resolution 1373 and to disarmament issues in drafting resolution 1540. Similar concerns have dogged the work of the Committees established to implement the resolutions (Alvarez 2005: 204, 207).

Finally, there is the obvious concern that a "non-representative" political institution like the Security Council will act in the interests of its most powerful members rather than all states. The veto-wielding members dominate, and they are immune from any action to enforce compliance with the Council's own resolutions. Beyond the P5, developed states wield disproportionate influence; if the Council begins legislating, that could exacerbate power and economic inequalities in the international system (Harper 1994: 153). Even more trenchantly, Alvarez (2003: 875; 2005: 202) claims there is little to counter the suggestion that the effect of the resolutions is to export the U.S.'s counter-terrorism laws to the world, that the U.S. is using its overwhelming influence in the Security Council to rewrite international law. He concludes that not all forms of hegemony are bad, and indeed that resolution 1373 may have been both necessary and appropriate, but "the perils of an 'imperial' Security Council are as real as the promise that it will take effective action" (Alvarez 2005: 201; 2003: 887).

Deliberative legitimacy in theory and the Security Council

The thrust of the above concerns is that legislative action by the SC, even if legal, is of dubious legitimacy and therefore lacks authority. But what is the source of the Council's legitimacy? What makes its decisions authoritative? The introductory chapter of this volume defines authority as "a relation among actors within a hierarchy in which one group is recognized as having both the right and the competence to make binding decisions for the rest of the community." Authority is a kind of power, distinguished from brute force or coercive power by its basis in legitimacy: "authority is legitimized power." Thus to grasp the scope of an institution's authority, one must determine the source and degree of its legitimacy. Legitimacy has both a substantive and procedural dimension. The substantive dimension, as explained by Ian Hurd (1999), is "the normative belief of an actor that a rule or institution ought to be obeyed." It provides an internal reason for following a rule, based on what is seen as "desirable, proper or appropriate within some socially-constructed system of norms, values, beliefs and definitions." The procedural dimension, fully developed by Thomas Franck (1990), sees legitimacy as flowing from "right process"—that is, by procedures accepted by those who are bound by the substantive decisions. Utlimately, the authority (and thus in large measure the power) of the Security Council depends on its ability to induce cooperation based on the degree of substantive and procedural legitimacy it is perceived to possess.

At the national level, legitimacy tends to be closely associated with democracy.[6] It is not my purpose to assess that claim, but it does raise an important question about the legitimacy of global governance mechanisms: What might democracy at the international level mean? A quick glance at the variety and complexity of democratic theories shows how difficult it is to answer that question: representative democracy, liberal republicanism, participatory democracy, consociational democracy, deliberative democracy (Dahl 1998; Held 1996; Cunningham 2002)?

However, this does mean talk about creating a more democratic UN—a prominent feature of the current debates about Security Council reform—should be dismissed as either cynical posturing or utopian rhetoric. The "democratic deficit" critique of international institutions does have purchase and the responses to it are increasingly sophisticated. One concept of democracy in particular is gaining a foothold at the global level: deliberative democracy.[7] A core principle of deliberative democracy is that any decision must be backed by good arguments. What constitutes a "good argument" varies from setting to setting and in accordance with the purpose of the enterprise in which the arguments are deployed. But as a general matter, good arguments in public policy-making are impartial (i.e. not purely self-serving) and are cast in terms that all who are affected understand as being relevant to the nature of the enterprise. Deliberative democrats writing about the international system find considerable evidence of that principle at work in Europe and some evidence at the global level (e.g., Habermas 2001; Zurn 2000; Eriksen and Fossum 2000; Joerges 2002; Dryzek 1999; Gutmann and Thompson 2004; Bohman 1999; Payne and Samhat 2004).

The theory of deliberative democracy holds that voting alone cannot legitimate collective decisions, that decisions must be justified through appeals to impartial and mutually acceptable principles. This does not mean that the decisions themselves must be acceptable to all (perfect consensus on every matter of public policy is not possible), but rather that decision-makers must make their case for a decision on the basis of reasons that are shared or can be shared by all who are affected. The purpose of deliberation is both to get better outcomes, and to give people the sense that their concerns have been taken into account, regardless of the outcome.

Jon Elster (1998: 6) usefully distinguishes deliberation from voting (the aggregration of fixed preferences) and bargaining. Deliberation is a third mode or element of decision-making, which entails argumentation and appeals to reasons that reach beyond narrow self-interest (Elster 1998: 12). Disagreements in a democratic society are (and should be) settled through deliberation, characterized by reciprocity: "you make your claims on terms that I can accept in principle … I make my claims on terms that you can accept in principle" (Gutmann and Thompson 2004: 55). Deliberative democrats know consensus is not always possible on matters of public policy, which is why votes are held and political bargaining occurs. But the bargains struck and outcome of votes are (and should be) shaped by engagement in public debate, argument, and reason-giving.

Deliberative democracy owes much to Jürgen Habermas' theory of communicative action, which has as its ideal discourse among equal and uncoerced participants, who seek to persuade—and are prepared to be persuaded by—each other through "the force of the better argument" (Habermas 1996). This ideal is not meant to describe an actual state of affairs, but its basic principles are presupposed in any linguistic communication (Cunningham 2003: 176). Deliberation is not a communicative free-for-all, in which any argument is as good as any other. It involves arguing in terms of "inter-subjective standards of truth, rightness and sincerity" (Eriksen 2000). If the standards are inter-subjective (*shared* meanings, rather than objective or purely subjective), then what counts as a "good argument" depends in part on the class of people to whom reasons are owed. Amy Gutmann and Dennis Thompson claim that decisions must be justified "to all who are bound by them and some who are affected by them" (Gutmann and Thompson 2004: 8 and ch. 4). In a national democratic polity, presumably this would include at least all citizens. But many non-citizens are also affected by decisions taken at the national level. Are democratic leaders expected to provide reasons affected non-citizens can accept? Put another way, does the deliberative principle extend beyond borders? To most democracy theorists, the notion of majority rule by population beyond the level of the nation-state is deeply problematic; but at least some deliberative democrats see the possibility of meaningful reason-giving across borders (Eriksen 2000; Dryzek 1999; Gutmann and Thompson 2004; Bohman 1999; Payne and Samhat 2004). Public reasoning and justification occurs in the institutions of government and intergovernmental organizations, as well as non-governmental organizations, social movements and other elements of civil society, whose activities are not confined by national borders (Benhabib 1996: 68). They see a fairly robust "public sphere" in Europe and nascent public spheres at the global level, exemplified by the growing influence of non-state actors and trans-national networks, especially in the environment field (Mitzen 2005: 401–7; Zurn 2000; Eriksen and Fossum 2000; Joerges 2002; Dryzek 1999; Bohman 1999; Payne and Samhat 2004).

The ideal of deliberation requires that participants have equal standing and equal voice in public debates (Cohen 1997: 74). Moreover, if the speakers are to speak *to* rather than *at* or past one another, they must share some experiences, assumptions and understandings of the world (Risse 2000: 10–11). At first glance, it would seem that none of these pre-conditions are close to being met in the UN Security Council: members do not share values, a history or even a language; the participants are anything but equal; and the proceedings are hardly public. Indeed, the Security Council is designed to be as heterogenous as possible, with balanced representation from each geographical region and 10 of its 15 members rotating every 2 years. Five of its members have permanent status and the veto power, which gives them disproportionate influence in the deliberations, even when they do not use the veto. The Council is composed of only a small fraction of the total UN membership and participation by non-members is restricted. The outcomes of deliberations—the resolutions and statements adopted or defeated—are public and usually accompanied by explanations of votes, but increasingly the debates themselves take place in semi-private informal consultations. The notion that only "the force of the better argument" counts seems to be so far from reality as to be all but useless in understanding how SC decisions are actually made.

A second glance, however, reveals a different picture. To begin with, perfect consensus on values and definitions of interest is not a pre-condition for meaningful discourse (if such consensus existed, there would be no need to deliberate). All that is necessary is a sense of being in a relationship of some duration, from which common meanings and expectations have emerged, and of being engaged in an enterprise the general purpose of which all understand in roughly the same way. The Security Council meets that condition. Its mission is to "maintain international peace and security" and debates are structured by a normative framework embodied in the UN Charter and Charter-based treaty law. That framework has been supplemented by the Security Council's own decisions and operational activities, opinions of the International Court of Justice and other judicial bodies, "soft law" in the form of General Assembly and ECOSOC resolutions, and decisions of other intergovernmental institutions like the human rights treaty bodies. There are standard forms of argument used to appraise and ultimately accept or reject competing claims, a legal discourse that is fundamentally about the limitations imposed by the Charter and the relative weight to be assigned to the UN's overarching purposes. These normative considerations and constraints were notoriously weak during the cold war, but there is evidence that the post-cold war era heralded some convergence of understandings about the rules of international life. The five Permanent Members of the Security Council have been dealing with each other on an almost daily basis for years, in effect debating the shape of the post-cold war world while responding (or not responding) to particular crises. Arguably, the P5 has become an exclusive club with a common history, set of experiences, and some shared understandings about the meaning of the Charter. The breakdown over Iraq in early 2003 might suggest a reversal of this post-cold war trend, but there is evidence even in those failed deliberations of a fairly robust normative framework, which structured debates and affected the course of events (Johnstone 2004; Bjola 2005).

Moreover, there are elements of Security Council practice to suggest that the notion of equal status in and access to the discourse is not entirely fanciful. The SC can be conceived as a four-tier deliberative setting. The top tier is the five permanent members of the Council, who have equal voting power and engage in deliberations on relatively free and equal terms. Differences in material power have a profound impact on the ability of each of the P5 to influence debates, but to the extent that political struggle among them takes place on the basis of deliberations, it is more evenly matched. Deliberation reduces without eliminating disparities in material power (Gutmann and Thompson 2004: 133).

The second tier is the SC as a whole. Non-permanent members are formally equal in the sense that sovereign equality is a basic principle of the Charter, each has one vote and, under Article 24, they count equally as representatives of the international community and—at least notionally—are expected to speak for all in the collective interest. Their votes count for much less than the P5, because they lack veto power, but any member of the P5 that wants to pass a resolution must solicit their support, sometimes competing with other P5 members soliciting votes for a differently worded resolution. The competition is often crass, as it is in any law-making body, but is typically characterized by appeals (both sincere and strategic) to impartial reasons, principles, and collective interests. They contribute to the deliberative process by setting the parameters of the more equal deliberations among the P5. While the debates occur against a backdrop of bargaining and with a view to voting (and in full consciousness of which SC members wield the most material and bargaining power), outcomes that cannot somehow be justified in principled terms are harder to push through.

The third tier is the rest of UN membership, who do not have votes in the Security Council. In multiparty democracies, majority party claims are "examined, challenged, tested, criticized and rearticulated" by the opposition (Benhabib 1996: 72). There is no functional equivalent of a parliamentary opposition in the Security Council, but non-members do have opportunities to wield influence. They can speak in public meetings and, although they do not participate in informal consultations (where most of the real business of the Council is now done), they are often invited to "private meetings" and so-called "Arria formula" gatherings, where the public and media are excluded. Troop contributors to peace operations meet with the Council President regularly. More often than in the recent past open debates are held before the day of a vote to give others a chance to weigh in on an issue and to gain insight into what members of the Council are thinking.

The fourth tier is the constellation of experts (lawyers, pundits, and policy wonks), engaged representatives of non-governmental organizations, organs of international public opinion, and other citizens who have a stake in and keep a close watch on what is going on in the SC. Few are heard directly by the Council as a whole (although the head of the ICRC and NGO representatives now meet regularly with the President). But many have channels for conveying their views to individual Council members, either directly or through the Secretariat. And even more important than direct participation in the debates is the audience effect of this fourth tier of actors. One need not invoke a mythical "international community" to make the case that the members of the Council feel compelled to appeal to networks of actors and citizens beyond governmental chambers. This network is part of the broader interpretive community I have described elsewhere, whose judgment—real or anticipated—matters to governmental decision-makers.[8] The Security

Council is not a sealed chamber, deaf to voices and immune to pressure from beyond its walls. If a Council member says in a closed-door meeting, "we will push this to a vote," then other members must consider whether their positions and explanations will pass muster with the outside world (and if not, whether they can bear the political, diplomatic, and economic costs of defying the weight of international opinion). Debates in private are animated by arguments that will be used later to justify positions in public.

Negotiating and implementing resolutions 1373 and 1540

Resolution 1373

Resolution 1373 was adopted seventeen days after 9/11 and close on the heels of resolution 1368, which set the stage for self-defensive military action against Al-Qaeda and the Taliban in early October 2001. A Chapter VII resolution, it obliges all states to prevent and suppress terrorist financing and to refrain from providing any other form of support to terrorist groups, including safe havens. It sets out a quite specific list of measures states must take to achieve the resolutions goals. The most important operative paragraphs come directly from the International Convention for the Suppression of the Financing of Terrorism, which had been adopted at the time but was not yet in force. The resolution creates a Counter-Terrorism Committee (CTC) as a subsidiary organ of the Security Council, composed of all its members, whose function is to oversee implementation, initially by reviewing reports submitted by states on steps they have taken to fulfill their obligations. Resolution 1373 and the CTC are primarily a capacity-building exercise, designed to raise the average level of government performance against terrorism by requiring states to upgrade their legislative and executive machinery (Rosand 2003: 334; see also Millar and Rosand 2006).

The resolution was a U.S. initiative and its unanimous passage was extraordinarily smooth. All UN ambassadors, including representatives of the P5, had received instructions from their capitals to be cooperative with the U.S. in the post-9/11 climate (Wilson 2004: interview; Mahubani 2004: interview). According to a U.S. diplomat, the prevailing mood in the UN was that the entire membership had been attacked, that "we all have been violated."[9] Moreover, while resolution 1373 was unprecedented, it did not come out of thin air. The Security Council had imposed sanctions on Libya in 1992 for its failure to hand over suspects in the Lockerbie and UTA bombings. It also imposed sanctions on Sudan in 1996, in respect of the assassination attempt on President Hosni Mubarak of Egypt (resolutions 1054 and 1070). And it imposed sanctions on the Taliban in 1999, following the bombing of U.S. embassies in Kenya and Tanzania, for which Osama Bin Laden was deemed responsible (resolution 1267). In October 1999, the Council adopted resolution 1269, characterizing terrorism as a threat to international peace and security, signaling that it would be prepared to take broader enforcement actions against terrorists (Turk 2003: 53). Meanwhile, the UN General Assembly had adopted twelve anti-terrorism treaties—including a convention on terrorist bombing initiated by the U.S. and a convention on the financing of terrorism initiated by the French—and negotiations were underway on a convention on terrorist bombing initiated by Russia.

Because counter-terrorism was a widespread cause, and because 9/11 was such a shocking event, there was very little opposition to resolution 1373. No delegation objected to the Security Council "legislating," and it is doubtful any member states even saw it in those terms (Wilson 2004: interview; Mahubani 2004: interview; Christophedes 2004: interview). There were murmurings after-the-fact, and later complaints about resolution 1540 were sometimes couched in terms of a "legislative trend" that began with 1373, but these did not surface in September 2001. And indeed opponents of this "legislative trend" could accept resolution 1373 because, while generic in its terms, it was adopted in the wake of a clear and devastatingly real manifestation of the type of threat it was aimed at preventing (Akram 2004: interview). It could be seen as a reaction to 9/11 and thus consistent with the Security Council's traditional crisis management role.

There were no explanations of votes on the day resolution 1373 was adopted, an indication of how quick and painless it was. However, there was a ministerial meeting of the SC several weeks later, on November 12, 2001. The fact that the meeting took place at all signifies an effort on the part of Council members to publicize its involvement in the war on terrorism and to give a high-profile launch to the CTC. Fifteen foreign ministers spoke, all of whom expressed support for resolution 1373 and willingness to cooperate with the CTC. Jack Straw, U.K. foreign minister, described adoption of the resolution as "an historic event"; U.S. Secretary of State Colin Powell called it "a mandate to change fundamentally how the international community responds to terrorism." No minister dissented.

The early stages of implementation of resolution 1373 also proceeded smoothly. This was due largely to the transparent approach of the CTC, and to the deft diplomacy of its first chairman, Sir Jeremy Greenstock of the United Kingdom. Ambassador Greenstock knew resolution 1373 was not likely to be enforced coercively by the Security Council. Effective implementation would require "buy-in" by the wider UN membership. To achieve that buy-in, Greenstock stressed the non-threatening character of the CTC, designed to engage states in an open-ended dialogue, not even declaring them. In its capacity-building function, the Committee acts as a "switchboard," brokering deals between states who need technical assistance and those who can provide it (S/2004/70: 8). And in an effort to reach out to the broader UN membership, Ambassador Greenstock provided briefings every other week to the non-members of the Security Council.

The approach seems to have worked, both in terms of compliance with the CTC's reporting requirement and the rate of ratification of counter-terrorism conventions.[10] In the fall of 2003, one of the CTC experts did an informal analysis of the overall picture of compliance, based on four criteria: the existence of the necessary legislation in each state, the administrative capacity to enforce counter-terrorism mandates, the presence of a policy and regulatory framework across national institutions, and participation in international counter-terrorism conventions and institutions. The expert rated the compliance of 30 countries as good, 60 more as being in transition, moving gradually into compliance, 70 as "willing but unable," and 20 as "inactive"—materially able to comply but for a variety of reasons unwilling.[11]

Despite the steady record of reporting, the dialogic approach of the CTC began to run out of steam in late 2003. The Committee and states could only go back and forth with reports and queries on those reports for so long. When Spain took over the chair of the CTC in 2003, Ambassador Arias prepared a report on the problems of implementation (S/2004/70). This prompted the Committee to propose a set of reforms to "revitalize" its work, which was approved by the Security Council in resolution 1535.[12] The thrust of the reforms was that the Committee would play a more proactive role in monitoring compliance, "enhance" dialogue with governments, facilitate technical assistance to states that needed it most, and collect information through site visits when appropriate. The most innovative structural reform was a new Counter-Terrorism Executive Directorate (CTED), created in March 2004 but not fully staffed until September 2005 and not declared operational until the end of that year. The CTED is a body of twenty experts who advise the CTC and carry out its strategic and policy decisions in a more proactive manner.

The proposal for a new CTED generated considerable controversy, reflected in a row over whether it should report directly to the CTC, or through the Secretary-General. The U.S., U.K., and Spain in particular, favored the former approach, whereas the UN Secretariat, Germany, and a number of other delegations supported the latter. The end result was a compromise in which the CTED would operate under the "policy guidance" of the CTC, but the Executive Director would be appointed by and report through the Secretary-General. Moreover, its staff members would be subject to Article 100 of the UN Charter, the cornerstone of an independent international civil service. The controversy stemmed in part from a concern that the CTED would undermine the Secretariat and authority of the Secretary-General by creating a new structure accountable only to the Security Council (and, by implication, its most powerful members).[13] That the concerns persisted until the end of 2006 is reflected in the felt need of the Security Council to clarify reporting lines between the CTED, Secretariat, and CTC (S/PV.4921: 21).

The larger issue, expressed by the representative of Switzerland in the open meeting, is "whether the fight against terrorism within the framework of the United Nations should continue to be the primary responsibility of a subsidiary body of the Security Council" (S/PV.4921: 22). Is a body of fifteen members inclusive enough to be the permanent home for the UN's counter-terrorism efforts? Does adding expert staff who would report directly (and presumably confidentially) to that body not exacerbate the problem? As the representative of India put it:

> What kind of precedent are we creating by the establishment of an enhanced mechanism such as the Executive Directorate within the Security Council? . . . How does the Council propose to ensure the accountability of the Executive Directorate and its institutionalized accessibility and appropriate consultation with Member States on their concerns and priorities?[14]

Combined with concern about the structural changes, the harmony that existed in the immediate post-9/11 period had begun to fade, and the bite of resolution 1373 was starting to be felt. Indeed, there was anxiety that the "revitalization" of the CTC might somehow modify the substance of resolution 1373 and the working methods of the committee, a perception the chairman of the committee and other supporters sought to dispel.[15] Meanwhile, the Council continued to add to the CTC's responsibilities. It was tasked with reaching out to other international and regional organizations, encouraging them to become more involved in counter-terrorism. The Council asked the CTC to develop a set of best practices in implementing resolution 1373, and in resolution 1637 "strongly urged" all states to implement forty recommendations on money-laundering and terrorist financing, including measures like requiring financial institutions to report suspicious activities.[16] In September 2005, the CTC was mandated to monitor the implementation of a Council resolution on incitement to terrorism (S/RES/1624).

Resolution 1540

Resolution 1540, also adopted under Chapter VII of the UN Charter, aims at preventing weapons of mass destruction (WMD) from falling into the hands of terrorists. It demands that all states refrain from supporting efforts by non-state actors to acquire such weapons, and to adopt appropriate legislation to prohibit that, as well as domestic enforcement measures to prevent WMD proliferation. It established for a period of two years—later extended for another two years, to April 2008—a committee to oversee implementation of the resolution. The 1540 Committee lacks a CTED-type structure, but it can call on appropriate expertise to assist in its work.

Negotiation of resolution 1540 was more contentious than 1373, for several reasons.[17] First, the political climate had changed in the years between 9/11 and early 2004, not least because of the Iraq war. Second, it came on the heels of the Proliferation Security Initiative, which generated suspicion that 1540 was designed primarily to universalize the interdiction principles a limited number of states had agreed to. Third, while resolution 1373 takes elements of international law and extends them to all UN members, 1540 "fills the gaps" in existing law. In that sense, its "legislative" character may have been more unsettling. Fourth, resolution 1540 encroaches more deeply on existing treaties (the NPT, CWC, and BWC) and the institutions established to monitor them (the IAEA and OPCW) than resolution 1373. Moreover, there was resistance to the idea of a resolution that did not also and in a balanced way address disarmament issues. Finally, many states were unhappy about adopting the resolution under Chapter VII, which they feared could trigger military enforcement action.

Pakistan, India, Brazil, Algeria, South Africa, Indonesia, Iran, Egypt, Mexico, and Cuba expressed the strongest concerns. Pakistan in particular was adamant that resolution 1540 went beyond the proper role of the Security Council.[18] The threat of terrorists acquiring WMD was real, but there had never been a concrete manifestation of that threat. Thus unlike resolution 1373, it looked like abstract legislation, which—according to Pakistan—the Council lacked the authority to enact. Moreover, the Security Council was not the best "repository of authority" on weapons of mass destruction, where disarmament by the nuclear powers was not likely to see much headway. China, Germany, Switzerland, and other European countries were less adamant, but they also took pains to stress that Security Council action should complement and strengthen rather than undermine the multilateral regimes.

Ultimately, the resolution was adopted unanimously because those who had doubts about the propriety of this kind of SC action could claim it temporarily filled a gap in the law to address an urgent threat, pending adoption of a multilateral treaty (Pakistan, New Zealand, India, Iran, Kuwait, China, and Nigeria). Many also commented on the explicit assurance in the resolution that it would "not conflict with or alter the rights and obligations" of parties to existing conventions, or with the responsibilities of the IAEA and OPCW (Ireland on behalf of EU, Australia, Jordan, Liechtenstein, Spain, and Brazil). The fact that it was explicitly connected to terrorism also made the resolution more acceptable. As an anti-terrorism rather than non-proliferation measure, it was easier to rationalize the minimal references in it to disarmament.[19]

Although many of the concerns of member states were taken into account in the final version of resolution 1540, "in the end, lots of delegations still had some misgivings about the text of the resolution," according to Germany's UN Ambassador Gunter Pleuger.[20] Pakistan worked hard to dilute the mandate of the 1540 committee, successfully stalling any substantive action until it rotated off the Security Council at the end of 2004 (Millar and Rosand 2007: 18). The Committee began to pick up steam in 2005, but by September 2006, only 132 states had submitted their first national reports—leaving 59 who had not. And of the 132 who had reported, only 84 had provided additional information as requested by the Committee.[21] The lingering misgivings may reflect dissatisfaction more with the process than the outcome of negotiations (Datan 2005). The seeds for the resolution were actually planted by the U.K., when it circulated a non-paper among EU countries in early 2003 proposing the idea of a "counter-proliferation committee," modeled on the CTC (Datan 2005). President Bush picked up the idea in his speech to the UN General Assembly on September 24, 2003, when he called for the SC to adopt a new anti-proliferation resolution, which would require "all members of the UN to criminalize the proliferation of weapons of mass destruction, to enact stringent export controls consistent with international standards and to secure any and all sensitive materials within their own borders."[22]

Consultations among the P5 began in October 2003 and proceeded exclusively among them for five months. By the end of that period, four of the five had reached agreement on a draft (China took the position that it would continue to negotiate (Mahmood: 2004 interview)). The consultations extended to other members of the Council in March 2004, and a draft was first discussed by the Council as a whole at an informal meeting on April 8. An open meeting of the Security Council followed on April 22, where the draft resolution, which had been amended twice over the previous week, was discussed at length. Meanwhile, the co-sponsors became very active in briefing regional groups (the NAM, Arab Group, Latin American group, and the African group) and "de-fanging" opponents by providing answers to questions and rumors that had been building up during the period of more closed negotiations.[23] After the open meeting, the resolution was revised once more and then adopted by unanimous vote on April 29.

A measure of the importance of process is the number of states that referred to it in the open meeting on April 22, which had been requested by Canada, Mexico, New Zealand, South Africa, Sweden, and Switzerland. Fifty-one states spoke at the meeting, totaling over one-quarter of the UN membership. More than half who spoke referred to the scope and timing of the consultations to that point, either disparagingly or in a complimentary way, and almost as many expressed appreciation for the open meeting as an opportunity to participate in the negotiations on the draft.

Assessment of resolutions 1373 and 1540 from the perspective of deliberative legitimacy

Stephen Harper suggests that a determination of whether the Security Council is acting in an executive, legislative, or judicial capacity enables a better assessment of the effect an action will have on the Council's legitimacy: if the Council has acted legislatively, then the correct inquiry is whether the Council has acted properly as a legislature (Harper 1994: 157). Most of the prudential arguments against the Council legislating relate to its unrepresentative character. The theory of deliberative democracy suggests that representativeness is too narrow an inquiry. What matters is not only who has a vote, but also the quality of deliberations: who has a say and to whom those with a say must appeal in their reasoning. The negotiation and implementation of resolutions 1373 and 1540 suggest that, while the Council is far from being an ideal deliberative setting, it has more legitimacy as a legislature than meets the eye. It also suggests that efforts to improve the manner in which the Council deliberates will render its decisions more authoritative, and thus more effective.

There was little active participation in the negotiations on resolution 1373 (indeed there was not much negotiation at all), but the sense of urgency and the post-9/11 political climate made quick adoption both possible and tolerable.[24] Participation in the debates and discussions on *implementation*, however, were quite extensive. The Ministerial meeting of November 2001, after six weeks of reflection on the implications of 1373, was an opportunity for the foreign ministers of Council members to object, yet none did. Moreover, while non-members were not invited to speak at that meeting, its high profile and highly public nature presented a perfect opportunity for states who wanted to mobilize opposition to do so. None did.

As the CTC went about its work, the Chairman made a conscious effort to operate on the basis of transparency, dialogue, and consensus.[25] Guidelines were adopted for the conduct of its work, regular briefings to member states and the media were conducted, and the CTC prepared a guide for member states to follow in submission of their reports. The burdens were quite onerous in terms of legislative drafting and the training of national personnel in the requirements of implementation of the new laws, which ranged from investigation, to border control, law enforcement, and judicial expertise. Compliance, even if the political will was there, would not be automatic. Thus unusual efforts were made to secure widespread support for the CTC's work, mainly through information exchange, persuasion, and technical assistance. In the end, according to Danilo Turk (2003: 53), Assistant Secretary-General for Political Affairs at the UN at the time, the CTC "created a tight web of communication between member states and the Security Council and provided a platform for the necessary intense cooperation among states."

As the CTC began running out of steam, proposals on how to "revitalize" it were the subject of intense and not always easy deliberations. In October 2003, the chair began consulting other members of the Committee and the UN Secretariat, following which a package of measures were agreed. Those were published as an official document in January 2004 and converted into an official proposal in February. At that point, the entire UN membership had a chance to review, consider, and comment on them informally. A formal, open meeting of the Council was held on March 4, to which all interested states were invited to offer opinions on the proposals. A total of 36 states spoke on that day. Many of the 15 Council/Committee members stressed that the Committee would continue to operate on the basis of "transparency, cooperation and even-handedness" (for example, the U.S., U.K., Germany). Many of the non-Council members expressed appreciation for the open debate, and for the transparent way in which consultations had been conducted. The statement of Ireland, speaking for the EU, is illustrative:

The European Union attaches real importance to these periodic open debates of the Security Council in which we review the work and progress of the CTC. Today's debate is of particular significance, as members' views and suggestions will provide valuable, concrete input into the revitalization process, including in the Council's ongoing deliberations on the draft resolution on this matter. Such a transparent debate will contribute to a key goal of the reform: that is, to maintain and, hopefully, to strengthen the CTC's general acceptance by—and perceived legitimacy with—all members of the United Nations family.[26]

In a similar vein, the Ambassador of South Africa stated:

We meet today at a time when the Security Council has already completed its review of the strategic direction, structure and procedures of the Counter-Terrorism Committee and has even commenced negotiations on a new resolution. We would hope that it is not too late for the views of the wider UN membership to be taken into consideration and that we can accurately express our views in the few short minutes allocated to us.[27]

It seems clear that views other than those of the most powerful Council members were taken into account, in at least two respects: (1) the CTED would be structured in a way so as not to undermine the Secretariat; and (2) it would be attentive to human rights concerns. The role of the CTC in assessing the human rights implications of counter-terrorism legislation had been a source of considerable controversy. The Committee initially took the position that it was not a human rights body and that human rights considerations should be dealt with elsewhere in the UN system. Formalizing a relationship between the CTC and the Office of the High Commissioner for Human Rights alleviated some of the concerns raised by member states, the Secretary-General, the High Commissioner for Human Rights, and human rights activists.[28] Subsequently, in May 2006, the CTC has "policy guidance" to the CTED on how to ensure human rights are respected in the implementation of resolution 1373.[29] And so while the CTC continues to be controversial, some of the sting has been taken out of the criticism. It has proven to be a well-accepted and reasonably effective instrument of counter-terrorism. The level and quality of reporting is impressive (by August 2006, the Committee had received first reports from all 191 UN member states, 4 reports from 107 states and 5 from 42 states), most countries had established legal frameworks for the expeditious freezing of assets, the administrative infrastructure (such as financial intelligence units) was being strengthened in many countries, banks and other financial institutions were aware of the new regulations, and prosecutions were starting to occur (Biersteker 2007: 29–34).

The negotiation of resolution 1540 started with consultations among the P5 only, for a period of five months. While there is general sympathy for the need of the P5 to consult first among themselves on certain issues, the far-reaching implications of a generic "non-proliferation" resolution under Chapter VII generated considerable anxiety. Would it impose non-proliferation obligations on non-parties to the key treaties? Was it an effort to generalize the Proliferation Security Initiative? Was it a backdoor way of triggering military action against "rogue states"? These not very helpful speculations prompted a uniquely open and inclusive consultation process.

A good number of statements in the public Security Council meetings invoked the language of deliberative democracy. For example, the Permanent Representative of the Philippines stated:

> My delegation appreciates the timeliness of this open debate and the value of listening to the views of the general membership, who would be implementing the resolution. *Those who are bound should be heard. This is an essential element of a transparent and democratic process*, and is the best way to proceed on a resolution that demands legislative actions and executive measures from the 191 members of the U.N. In this regard, we welcome the initiative of the sponsors to present the draft resolution to regional groups and to discuss with them and other interested parties what is in the text, and what is not in the text [emphasis added].[30]

Similarly, the Permanent Representative of Spain said: "We believe that since the Council is legislating for the entire international community, this draft resolution should preferably, although not necessarily, be adopted by consensus and after consultation with non-members of the SC. Therefore without prejudice to the—I daresay—unprecedented and intensive negotiations of the sponsors, Spain has always believed the holding of this formal open debate to be appropriate" (S/PV.4950). And New Zealand (S/PV.4950):

> The draft resolution will not succeed in its aim without the support and acceptance of Member States. Such acceptance requires the Council to dispel any impression of negotiations behind closed doors or that a small group of states is drafting laws for the broader membership without the opportunity for all Members States to express their views.

There was also "organized NGO input" into the negotiation process, especially after March 24, when a draft resolution surfaced. A group of NGOs called for an open meeting of the Council, sent a memorandum setting out its position as well as draft language for the resolution to Security Council members and other interested states, issued a media advisory, and made regular statements to the press (Datan 2005). Indeed, Merav Datan (2005) describes the entire negotiations as:

> formally closed but informally and intentionally porous. Even when the early drafts were formally circulating only among the P5, other members of the SC, states outside the SC, the press and NGO had the opportunity

to follow the deliberations and provide input. This form of practical (though relative) democracy was not the result of "security leaks," but of awareness that the political sensitivity of the issue requires as much impact by global civil society as the SC negotiating process can tolerate.

Did all of this supposed input have any impact on the draft? Changes were made: references to disarmament obligations and the integrity of existing treaty regimes were added; a reference to "interdiction" was removed; a reference to the integrity of existing treaties and regimes was added; a reference to the sovereign rights of non-parties to non-proliferation treaties was added; language on the usefulness of peaceful dialogues was strengthened; and the proposal to create a monitoring committee was introduced, with suitable reassurances about its role provided in the explanation of votes. Datan (2005) goes too far when he claims that a "counter-proliferation and PSI-type initiative . . . was transformed into a cooperative, iterative and interactive effort to address non-state access to NBC [nuclear, biological and chemical] weapons and affirm state non-proliferation and disarmament obligations." But the changes made were sufficient to induce even the staunchest critic to vote for the resolution (Pakistan), and a number of other states expressed satisfaction that their concerns had been taken into account (Brazil, Germany, Algeria, and the Philippines). Almost as significant is the effort the U.S. and its co-sponsors made to ensure a unanimous vote (the resolution could have passed with a no vote from Pakistan). Thus the Permanent Representative of Malaysia struck a chord when he said, on behalf of the Non-Aligned Movement (NAM):

> The Non-Aligned Movement sincerely hopes that the sponsors and other Council members will continue to take into consideration the views and concerns expressed by NAM member countries. We believe that it is important to ensure that the final product is realistic, generally acceptable and implementable. After all . . . governments, national legislatures and, for that matter the private sector in all Member countries are expected to cooperate and take appropriate measures, including the enactment of new legislation and the streamlining and amendment of existing legislation where applicable . . . Therefore we would counsel the need for further consultations and would request that the Security Council not rush into making a decision.
>
> (S/PV.4950: 4)

When the application of resolution 1540 was extended for two years by resolution 1673 and a new program of work was devised, similar views were expressed (Bosch and Van Ham 2007: 207–26). For legislative action by the Security Council to be effective, it requires the proactive cooperation of most if not all governments as well as a wide cross-section of non-governmental actors. The relevant constituencies—those affected by the resolution—are enormous. To make it work, they need to be consulted, heard, or at least feel their concerns have been taken into account. It is also worth noting in this connection that some of the critics and proponents of resolution 1540 stressed that it does not really legislate, because all the SC did was prescribe policy, leaving it up to member states to design and adopt laws consistent with that policy. In other words, the Council was providing "parameters for legislation," not seeking to prescribe specific legislation, which might differ from state to state (Akram 2004: interview). This point, stressed by Pakistan in the negotiations, was also made by France and Spain publicly and the U.S. privately.[31] This is a variation on the principle of subsidiarity, which holds that only what needs to be decided at the highest level should be decided at that level. Leaving the specifics of how to implement the broad (though binding) goals set by the Council creates the possibility of "democratic participation" in law-making at the national level (depending, of course, on how democratic the particular state is).

One other reason to believe that deliberative principles have informed the implementation of resolutions 1373 and 1540 concerns the dynamic between the Security Council, the CTC, the 1540 Committee, and a third committee set up to oversee the sanctions on people associated with Al-Qaeda and the Taliban imposed by resolution 1267. (The quasi-judicial function of the 1267 Committee has been the subject of commentary analogous to criticisms of the quasi-legislative action of the Security Council. See Rosand 2004; Fassbender 2000: 29–30; Watson Institute for International Studies 2006; Alvarez 2005: 176; Gutherie 2004: 503–6; de Wet and Noellkaemper 2003). The Security Council has been calling for ever-closer cooperation between the committees, including through coordinated reporting to the Council itself.[32] One of the theories circulating during the debates on the revitalization of the CTC was that the ultimate goal was the creation of a "super-committee," with its own expert staff, which would combine the functions of all three.[33] An analysis of the pros and cons of such a "super-committee" is beyond the scope of this chapter. However, it is useful to think of the Security Council and the three committees as focal points for deliberation among the broad constellation of experts, UN Secretariat officials, and international and regional organizations they consult (such as the OECD's Financial Action Task Force, the EU, OAS, CIS, APEC, ASEAN, and the Office of the High Commissioner for Human Rights).[34] While the work of the CTC is mainly operational, there is also an important deliberative dimension to it: sharing information on best practices, ensuring that national and regional standards meet the requirements of resolution 1373, and ultimately settling some of the interpretive questions left open by the resolution as to precisely what kind of action it obliges states to take. The resolution 1540 Committee has not gone as far as the CTC in specifying performance standards or coordinating its work with other international organizations, but it has the potential to play that role as well, especially in respect of its relations with the International Atomic Energy Agency, Organization for the Prohibition of Chemical

Weapons, and World Health Organization.[35] Ultimately, these committees and the networks that surround them are a place where relevant actors (government and non-government) converge to make and shape policy, or to scrutinize policy being made by others. To the extent that the often-touted spirit of openness informs those activities, the deliberative principle has purchase.

Will the SC legislate again? Probably not soon because the adoption of resolution 1540 was traumatizing for many states, and so it is unlikely that a new legislative initiative would be well received. But that could change, especially if the CTC and 1540 Committee continue to prove their worth. The U.S. might decide that it is worth taking the PSI back to the SC.[36] Or there may be another shocking event, with an impact comparable to 9/11 (like a ship carrying nuclear, chemical, or biological material blowing up in a harbor). If the SC does legislate again, the experience of resolutions 1373 and 1540 suggests a number of devices that might be introduced to enhance the legitimacy of the process.

First, state participation in the negotiations could be enhanced by engaging actively and directly with the General Assembly. More systematic engagement might entail the setting up of a joint SC–GA "consultation committee" whenever legislative action is being taken. Representatives of regional groups and specially affected or interested states could be part of this consultation committee. And even if true consultation did not come out of it, the committee could act as a sort of "shadow Council," analogous to a loyal opposition in parliamentary systems, which would keep watch on and critique Council action that seemed out of line with the interests and will of the broader membership.[37]

Second, at least one open session of the Security Council should be held before a draft resolution has been introduced, and a second once a draft is on the table but well before the vote. The meetings should be scheduled to ensure all UN members have time to examine the drafts, get instructions from capitals, and lobby for amendments. Again, this would give all interested states the opportunity to participate in the debates, and put pressure on Council members to account for their concerns in the drafting. As important, open meetings are a way of engaging civil society and the private sector, if only through the requirement of public reason giving. The more transparent and public the deliberations are, the greater the "audience effect"—the felt need of speakers to justify their actions in terms that all who have a stake in the outcome accept, even if they do not agree with the decision itself.

Third, Security Council accountability can be enhanced by submitting its decisions to General Assembly review after the fact. Again, this could be done *ad hoc* or systematically whenever the Council acts in a legislative manner.[38] After-the-fact judgment also occurs in the form of statements and resolutions of regional organizations and informal groups like the non-aligned movement, G-8 and G-20. Moreover, non-governmental groups are increasingly effective in mobilizing networks to pass cohesive judgment—either positive or negative—on Council action

Fourth, membership of the committees responsible for overseeing implementation of the resolutions could be expanded to include non-council members—with special consideration given to the selection of election of states that are most affected by the SC's counter-terrorism actions. Since compliance with these resolutions is far from automatic, implementation tends to be a process of ongoing dialogue, persuasion, and cajoling. More representative committees would not only give states whose cooperation is essential a voice, it would legitimize the process by expanding the range of views and interests that are accounted for in the deliberations.

Fifth, follow-up mechanisms should proceed on the basis of transparency. Ultimately, publicity is the main instrument for holding accountable both the subjects of Council legislation, and those who make the rules (an overlapping set). The requirement to present public reports is an accountability device, though it would be stronger if the committees were to engage in a more confrontational form of "naming and shaming." The habit of calling diplomats to explain their governments' actions to the committees enhances that sense of accountability (Biersteker 2007: 35). Chairs of monitoring committees should brief and consult non-Council members and the media regularly. Non-governmental actors, especially those whose cooperation is required for effective implementation, should be provided with channels for consultation. Non-governmental organizations should have access to some of the deliberations on implementation, not necessarily the right to participate in the discussions, but to serve as the eyes and ears of global civil society.[39]

Conclusion

This volume defines authority as a form of power distinct from coercion. From that perspective, compliance with Security Council decisions cannot be explained purely in terms of the ability of its most powerful members to enforce those decisions. While it may be possible for a few states to implement some Security Council resolutions on their own, like those that authorize small-scale peace operations, much of what the Council does requires broader cooperation. Resolutions 1373 and 1540 are cases in point. Adopted under Chapter VII and legally binding, their authoritativeness nevertheless depends on their perceived legitimacy. That legitimacy is partly a function of *substantive* content—to what extent do they reflect broadly accepted norms? It is also a function of *process*—is the procedure by which they were adopted and are being implemented generally recognized as proper? The argument of this chapter is that both substantive and procedural legitimacy—and thus the authority of the Council—are enhanced by adherence to deliberative principles. The concept of deliberative legitimacy suggests that the propriety of Security Council action depends in part on the quality of deliberations that precede and follow its decisions. When it legislates, the felt need to engage in extensive and open consultations is especially acute, ensuring widespread commitment to the substantive outcome or, at a minimum, a belief that the outcome reflects a wider range of interests and concerns than those of the most materially powerful members of the Council.

Any comparative institutional analysis would surely lead to the conclusion that the SC is far from an ideal deliberative setting. Legislating by the Council certainly has qualities of hegemonic law in action, where the materially powerful short-circuit the normal law-making process to write rules that serve their interests, while benefiting from the legitimation that working through the Council brings. But as Alvarez (2005: 215) points out, Council-generated law is not identical to old-fashioned hegemony: even the United States has to worry about the impact of its actions on the Council's legitimacy and on the risk that others will refuse to work with the U.S. through the Council in the future, when it needs their help. Beyond that strategic calculation, the informal multi-tier structure of the Security Council suggests it is a more inclusive body than it appears to be. While it may not be representative in any democratic sense, it is an imperfect but moderately accessible venue for reasoned deliberation about the rules of international life. As such, the Council should not shy away from articulating new global standards or making new law, especially when there are gaps in existing law that require urgent attention. But it will only succeed if it does so incrementally, building on prevailing norms, tested in as inclusive a deliberative process as circumstances allow. If, in seeking to legislate, the Council exceeds what the political traffic will bear, it is bound to fail and undermine its own authority in the process.

Acknowledgement

A substantially similar version of this chapter appeared as part of "Legislation and Adjudication in the UN Security Council: Bringing Down the Deliberate Deficit; American Journal of International Law (XXX).

Notes

1 I develop the concept of deliberative legitimacy more fully in Johnstone 2008. For a similar argument, applied to decisions about the use of force, see Bjola 2005.
2 United Nations Security Council S/PV.4950.
3 On nascent attempts by some judges on the ICJ to assert a power of judicial review, see Franck 1992; Alvarez 1996. Koskenniemi (1995: 346) states bluntly that the fundamental problem with the Security Council as dispenser of justice—as opposed to guardian of order—is its lack of accountability within the UN system.
4 The UN Security Council recently held its first ever debate on climate change. See United Nations Press Release SC/900, April 17, 2007.
5 Interestingly, the Security Council did adopt a definition of terrorism in resolution 1566 of October 8, 2005, following the attack on a school in Beslan, Russia.
6 Bodansky (1999: 616) argues that democracy is increasingly widely regarded as the "touchstone of legitimacy" in national governance.
7 This section of the chapter reproduces portions of I. Johnstone 2008.
8 Johnstone 2003. My argument is that in a decentralized international legal system, law operates largely through a process of justificatory discourse. The discourse is structured and constrained by an interpretive community, which can be imagined as

a series of concentric circles. In my earlier work, I described two circles: an inner circle composed of individuals directly or indirectly responsible for the formulation, negotiation, and implementation of a particular legal norm, and a more amorphous outer circle of all those regarded as possessing expertise in the relevant law or field of practice. I would now add a third circle that corresponds to the organs of what is imprecisely called international public opinion. The composition of this outer circle is not "experts," but rather interested non-governmental actors, whose values and engagement (even if only as an audience) have an impact on the terms of discourse and debate. Robert Howse (2001) prompted me to reflect on and reconsider the "technocratic" nature of the interpretive community I initially described.

9 Wilson 2004: interview. In addition to this general sense of grievance, there was also a desire on the part of some delegations—especially the French—to avoid marginalization of the UN by the U.S. (Mahubani 2004: interview).

10 Curtis Ward (2003: 299), CTC independent expert, describes the responses of states as "overwhelming and unprecedented."

11 Cortright et al. 2004: 7, based on an unpublished paper by the CTC legal expert from October 2003.

12 United Nations Security Council Resolution 1535. The Committee's proposals are contained in S/2004/124, February 19, 2004.

13 Evidence of the depth of this concern is the number of states who stressed in an open meeting several weeks prior to the adoption of resolution 1535 that the CTED should be part of the Secretariat and not in any way undermine it. S/PV.4921, March 4, 2004. Statements of Spain (as Chair of the Committee); p. 4, Benin, p. 5; U.K., p. 9; Germany (referring to the views expressed by the Secretariat in a letter of March 3, 2004), p. 15; Pakistan, p. 17; Ireland (on behalf of the EU), p. 19. S/PV.4921 (Resumption 1), March, 4 2004. Statements of Argentina (on behalf of the Rio Group), p. 4; South Africa, p. 8; and Indonesia, p. 11.

14 S/PV.4921, March 4, 2004:21.

15 S/PV.4921. See, for example, statements of Spain (as Chair); the U.S.; the U.K.; Ireland (for the EU); Mexico. For expressions of possible concern about a shift in approach, see the Philippines; India; Egypt.

16 United Nations Security Council Resolution 1617. The recommendations were prepared by the Financial Action Task Force. See Center on Global Counter-Terrorism Cooperation 2006.

17 The concerns expressed in the Security Council meetings of April 22 and April 28. S.PV.4950, April 22, 2004; S/PV.4956, April 28, 2004. They were also elaborated in my interviews with diplomats from the U.S., Spain, Brazil, India, and Pakistan, between July 19 and July 21, all of whom were involved in the negotiations.

18 The following account of Pakistan's position is from my interview with Ambassador Akram on July 20, 2004, a non-paper circulated by Pakistan to the entire UN membership in late March 2004 (on file with the author), and the statements of Pakistan in SC meetings on April 22 and 28, 2004.

19 Interviews with Davide Carrideo, Permanent Mission of Spain, July 20, 2004, and Luis Guilhermo, Permanent Mission of Brazil, July 21, 2004. Brazil in particular wanted to avoid the term "non-proliferation" in connection with 1540, as that applied to states, and instead to introduce new concepts like "non-access, non-transfer and non-availability" to non-state actors. S/PV.4950, p. 4. On the connection between 1540 and the broader counter-terrorism agenda of the Security Council, see van Ham and Bosch 2007: 7–9.

20 Lynch 2004. Similarly, Ambassador Baali of Algeria told the New York Sun, Pakistan and other members were concerned about the resolution, but "unless you are one of the five veto powers, it is very difficult to remain outside the consensus." Avni 2004: 7.

21 United Nations Security Council S/PV.5538: 7.

22 Bush's speech is reproduced in full in *New York Times*, September 24, 2003, p. A10. He repeated it again in February 2004 in a speech at the National Defense University, *New York Times*, February 12, 2004.

23 Rostow 2001 interview. One theory circulating was that resolution 1540 was a backdoor way of circumventing the IAEA process to bring states like Iran into line (Shringla 2001: interview).

24 Nicholas Rostow (2002: 482, fn. 40) states that it might not have been possible to reach agreement on the resolution even a few weeks later.

25 Ward (2003: 298) says transparency was "the hallmark of [the CTC's] operations— its modus operandi if you will." See also Rosand 2003: 335–6; Rostow 2002: 482–3.

26 United Nations Security Council S/PV.4921: 19. See also statements of India, Switzerland, South Korea, Argentina (on behalf of the Rio Group).

27 United Nations Security Council S/PV.4921: 7.

28 See statements of Brazil, p. 10; Germany, p. 15; Chile, p. 16; Ireland for the EU, p. 19; Liechtenstein, p. 3 (Resumption 1); Argentina for the Rio Group, p. 4 (Resumption 1); Mexico, p. 5 (Resumption 1); Costa Rica, p. 10 (Resumption 1); Canada, p. 12 (Resumption 1). The Secretary-General (S/PV.4435) first expressed his concern that action against terrorism should not undermine human rights to the Security Council in January 2002. On the relationship between the CTC, the High Commissioner for Human Rights and other human rights actors in the UN system, see Ward 2003: 297–8.

29 United Nations Security Council S/2006/989, S/PRST/2006/56.

30 United Nations Security Council. S/PV.4950: 2. See also statements of Brazil, China, France, Angola, U.K., Benin, Romania, U.S., Peru, South Africa, Ireland for the EU, Sweden, Switzerland, Indonesia, Egypt, Mexico, Nigeria.

31 United Nations Security Council S/PV.4950: 8. Rostow 2004.

32 S/RES/1566 (2004); S/PRST/2004/37; S/PRST/2005/16 (2005). The Mitchell– Gingrich report on UN reform suggested exploring the possibility of combining the three committees, or at least mandating closer cooperation among them. United States Institute of Peace 2005: 78.

33 The Mitchell–Gingrich report on UN reform suggested exploring the possibility of combining the three committees. United States Institute of Peace 2005: 78.

34 At a meeting sponsored by the CTC in October 2003, 110 organizations attended. Cortright et al. 2004: 20–1.

35 On the relationships between the 1540 Committee and the existing nuclear, chemical, and biological weapons regimes, see Bosch and van Ham 2007b: chs 5–7.

36 In explaining its vote for resolution 1540, the U.S. took the opportunity to appeal to all states to join the PSI.

37 A conference on creating a more democratic UN suggested the creation of a "standing committee of the General Assembly of 15 rotating, geographically representative members [who are] not at the same time members of the Security Council, to report to the Assembly on the adequacy of efforts made by the Council."

38 Informal after-the-fact review did occur with respect to resolution 1540, in the form of positive references in various General Assembly resolutions. Datan 2005: 12.

39 Much of the debate over Security Council reform in the lead-up to the 2005 summit revolved around the relative merits of expanding Council membership vs. improving its working procedures to make it more open, accountable, and transparent. Though nothing of substance came out of the summit, it is significant that much of the debate revolved around competing conceptions of "democracy"— representative and deliberative. See Johnstone 2005: 89–93.

6   The challenges and perils of normative overstretch [1]

George J. Andreopoulos

Since its creation in 1945, the United Nations has demonstrated a certain capacity of adjustment to the evolving geopolitical context and, in particular, to changes in the relations among states, as well as to the rising profile and active participation of non-state actors in the international arena. While periodic adjustments have met with varying degrees of success, they do reveal a measure of flexibility in the United Nations system, a complex assemblage of actors, processes, and programs, to respond to challenges in informal ways, as opposed to the formal and rather cumbersome amendment procedure envisaged by the Charter.

In recent years, several developments have rekindled the debate on reforming the organization to ensure effective multilateral policy-making in a whole set of key issue areas, including development, security, and human rights (United Nations General Assembly 2005). In these debates, a lot of attention has focused on the United Nations Security Council (UNSC), the key institutional authority in the areas of peace and security. In particular, UNSC is credited with having expanded the notion of "threats to the peace" in response to massive and systematic violations of human rights and humanitarian law witnessed in many post-cold war civil conflicts. In the process, the argument goes, UNSC has significantly reinterpreted and restricted the scope of the prohibition contained in Article 2(7) of the Charter, whereby the Organization is expected to refrain from intervention in matters essentially "within the domestic jurisdiction" of member states.

Yet, the "humanization" of the security discourse has come at a certain price for the integrity of the normative discourse, as well as the perceived legitimacy of the Security Council. This chapter will examine the dynamics of this trend and the impact of what I would call "normative overstretch" on the evolving role of the Security Council. By normative overstretch, I refer to collective expectations about proper conduct that create impetus for behavior in issue areas that transcend the settled cartography bounded by institutional mandates. In this context, normative overstretch refers not simply to the expansion into new areas, but to the repercussions of such an expansion on UNSC authority and legitimacy. This trend has been primarily, but not exclusively, manifested through the proliferation of human rights/humanitarian triggers for coercive action.[2] More specifically, this chapter will: (1) analyze and assess the nature and extent of this trend; (2) explore the effect of recent developments, especially those associated with the "war on terror," on the role and authority of the UNSC; and (3) offer some thoughts on their implications for the critical issue of UNSC legitimacy and the allocation of authority in the international system.

Humanizing the security discourse

Conceptually, the seeds for the humanization of the security discourse were sown during the Allied Powers' deliberations on the normative architecture of the post-World War II era. The legislative histories of the two main international instruments of that period, the Charters of the International Military Tribunal (Nuremberg) and of the United Nations, offer glimpses into the (then) tentative linkages between human rights violations and threats to/ breaches of international peace.[3] The IMT Charter linked the controversial concept of crimes against humanity to the commission of crimes against the peace. This linkage established what came to be known as the war-nexus requirement, namely that crimes against humanity could only be prosecuted in the context of an interstate breach of peace. However, the reference, in the crimes against humanity provision, to the prosecution of such crimes when "committed against any civilian population, before or during the war," created a pathway to the future internationalization of protective action irrespective of the context (war or peace).[4]

A similar type of linkage was built into the UN Charter. Although in the preamble, the reaffirmation of faith in fundamental human rights went hand in hand with the desire to save "succeeding generations from the scourge of war," operative Article 1 established a hierarchy among the organization's purposes and principles: the promotion of human rights as hierarchically inferior to the maintenance of international peace and security.[5] However, in cases where breaches of (interstate) peace did result in human rights violations, Article 1 in conjunction with Article 2(7) could likewise open pathways to the internationalization of protective action. Thus, in both instruments interstate peace trumps human rights considerations. In the absence of interstate aggression, human rights are confined to the consensual realm of "promotion," primarily in collaboration with the responsible authority structures of the states concerned (Andreopoulos 2002: 2–3). In the immediate aftermath of World War II, the message was loud and clear: the legitimacy of the human rights agenda was predicated on privileging state consent over abusive conduct, unless the said authority structures were to externalize such conduct.

The nascent human rights universe was shaped by two tracks: one track, consensual, signaled an emphasis on issues/strategies of promotion. In this context, the legitimacy of human rights initiatives hinged on state consent. The other track, coercive/non-consensual, dealt with issues/strategies of enforcement. During the cold war, enforcement-related issues took a back seat to promotion-related ones. The legitimacy of enforcement initiatives hinged on their linkages to actual or alleged threats to, or breaches of, interstate peace. Both tracks were reflective of state-centrism and converged on the formal inviolability of the sovereign prerogatives of member states; whether by consent or by coercion, state autonomy had to be invoked (consensual approach), or restored (in response to breaches of interstate peace).

However, with major advances in standard-setting, these tracks were increasingly marked by the density of points of intersection, rather than by the consensual/non-consensual divide. While there were several reasons for this emerging continuum, three are of particular relevance here. The first has to do with the long-standing porousness of sovereignty; the second relates to the unintended consequences of consensually adopted human rights obligations; and the third stems from the wide discretion provided to the organization's political organs in the determination of threats to or breaches of international peace.

Any serious examination of the troubled history of sovereignty quickly dispels certain myths about the uniqueness of the "subversive" contribution of human rights. The exponential growth of the human rights regime in the post-1945 period did not usher us into the era of erosion of conventional notions of sovereignty. As several studies have pointed out, the principles associated with sovereignty, especially in its Westphalian and international legal variants, have been persistently challenged.[6] Whether the focus is on the concern over religious toleration in the sixteenth and seventeenth centuries, on the intervention by European powers in countries viewed as "less civilized" during the last half of the nineteenth and the first quarter of the twentieth century, or on the minorities treaty regime under the League of Nations, what emerges is a picture of an ongoing erosion (Krasner 1999: 73–104; Trachtenberg 1993: 15–36; Sharp 1991; Lauren 2003). Some other analysts have gone further and argued that the challenges are embedded in the very concept, since the doctrine of sovereignty was shaped by the colonial encounter "and adopted unique forms which differed from and destabilized given notions of European sovereignty."[7] Whether one adopts the more mainstream, or the more critical perspective (i.e., the one that emphasizes the constitutive role of the colonial experience) on the origins of sovereignty, the main contribution of human rights relates to the systematization of an ongoing erosion by proliferating external sources of legitimacy (whether substantive or purely formal, via the adoption of soft as well as hard legal instruments).

The adoption of international human rights instruments points to the second reason for the growing intersections. It has been well documented that one of the main reasons for the non-binding nature of the Universal Declaration of Human Rights (UDHR) was the widespread concern among member states over the international legalization of monitoring. Yet what originally appeared as a source of weakness (i.e., non-binding nature of UDHR) proved to be, with the benefit of hindsight, a source of strength. The flexible and malleable nature of the UDHR not only made possible the progressive incorporation of key tenets of the human rights discourse in world politics, but it also paved the way for the adoption of legally binding instruments by an ever expanding number of states; in particular, it provided developing countries and their representatives with opportunities to shape the emerging legal framework, and thus with a sense of ownership of the process (drafting, debating, revising, and approving the said instruments).[8]

This process, in its turn, generated pathways for possible changes in the behavior of domestic authority structures. For example, several human rights treaties provided for monitoring and enforcement mechanisms which had an impact on the conduct of domestic authorities. The consensual nature of these initial commitments (signature and ratification) created expectations of adherence to and domestic enforcement of international rules and standards. Having said that, the record was clearly mixed. In the "high normativity" area of the Council of Europe, for example, adherence to the rulings of the European Court of Human Rights, became a key indicator of governmental legitimacy, and often resulted in changes in domestic legislation, despite the reservations expressed by affected authorities;[9] in the Inter-American system, a region marked by greater variations in normative adherence, and where the Inter-American Court of Human Rights "plays a more restricted and modest role than does its equivalent in the European system,"[10] notions of legitimacy were less influenced by failure to adhere to the findings and rulings of area organs. However, and despite variation in outcomes, this process was a contributing factor to the progressive convergence of expectations on the importance of external sources of legitimacy.[11]

The third factor relates to the provision of human rights/humanitarian issues with entry points into the high table of international security politics. The aforementioned hierarchically inferior status of human rights in the UN Charter, coupled with the emphasis on promotion, meant that, in the foreseeable future,[12] the "securitization" of the human rights agenda could constitute the only viable route towards enforcement initiatives.

To be sure, the legislative history of the Charter made it clear that the references to threats or breaches of the peace referred to potential or actual instances of direct military aggression. However, it is also true that the proposal, at the San Francisco conference, to assign the interpretation of the Charter exclusively to the International Court of Justice, was rejected. Instead, the Organization's political organs were provided with ample discretion in the delimitation of the boundaries of their respective competencies. As the subsequent record has shown, most of the interpretative work has been done by these organs (first and foremost by the UNSC), in the course of dealing with issues and responding to crises on their agenda (Franck 2002: 5).

The ample space provided to UNSC for such interpretative endeavors, clearly premised on a conception of the Charter as a "living document," proved to be a mixed blessing. On the one hand, it enabled the Council to develop a case law that slowly but steadily redefined the parameters of the domestic jurisdiction clause of Article 2(7). In this process, the promotion and protection tracks reinforced each other: standard setting opened pathways to UNSC involvement in non-traditional security issue areas, which in turn validated these pathways by strengthening, through its resolutions, the relevant norms. This interplay between the promotion and enforcement tracks was a constitutive element in shared understandings of internationally legitimate conduct.

This development is reflected in UNSC treatment of the apartheid issue and the eventual adoption of a resolution under Chapter VII, one of only two resolutions of its kind during the cold war period.[13] UNSC resolution 418 imposed a mandatory arms embargo against South Africa because its acquisition "of arms and related materiel," in light of the South African government's "policies and acts," constituted a threat to international peace and security.[14] The reference to policies and acts pointed to acts of (internal) repression and to the "defiant continuance of the system of apartheid," as well as to "attacks against neighbouring independent states."[15]

While the extent to which there was a strong relationship between South Africa's internal and external policies was and remains a matter of dispute,[16] the adoption of this resolution can only be adequately understood in the context of the spill-over effects of the momentum generated by normative and coalition building initiatives on the promotion front. In particular, activity in the United Nations General Assembly in the form of debates and resolutions,[17] earlier resolutions adopted by the Security Council which, although not under Chapter VII, called upon the government "to abandon the policies of apartheid and discrimination,"[18] the transnational mobilization of anti-apartheid activists, and a strengthening of the commitment to the norm of racial equality in regional organizations,[19] were among the key factors that contributed to the progressive delegitimation of the South African regime.[20]

To be sure, there were only two instances during the cold war in which the UNSC indicated a willingness to establish linkages between abusive internal conduct and threats to international peace.[21] Nevertheless, the reaffirmation of a commitment to the norm of racial equality (South Africa), and to majority rule (Southern Rhodesia) set important precedents for the flurry of UNSC activism in the post-cold war era. In particular, such consensus among the major powers in an often deadlocked UNSC was reflective of an incipient broadening of legitimate systemic goals, as well as means. While rationalist theories could provide some explanation as to the adoption of these resolutions in terms of converging great power interests at a particular juncture, or in terms of great power cooperation due to altered incentives, any satisfactory explanation has to take into consideration the slow but unmistakable changes in communal understandings of legitimate conduct.[22]

This is only part of the story though. As indicated earlier, there are several potential problems associated with this development. To begin with, it poses a fundamental challenge to the very essence of collective security. The designation of human rights violations as threats to the peace could exacerbate the tensions between the requisite confidence in the collective security system, in particular the system's emphasis on restraining military action, and the imperative of the system's response to a growing array of such threats/breaches.[23] The second flowed from the first: since there is no procedure for reviewing the legality of UNSC actions, and UNSC has broad discretion when determining a threat to the peace, the proliferation of possible triggers for action would deepen the accountability deficit in the organization.

More specifically, the potential increase in UN activism that such a path entailed could strengthen the hierarchical tendencies within the Council at the expense of an emerging consensus on the security implications of massive and systematic human rights violations. It could be argued that the very parsimonious nature of UNSC action during the cold war era made the emergence of such consensus possible, and enhanced the authoritative nature of UNSC statements in this issue area. The traditional emphasis on the restrictions imposed, due to U.S.–Soviet rivalry, on UNSC authority masks a more complex reality, which renders simplistic the standard portrayals of an ongoing UNSC paralysis. Any challenges to the paralysis imagery can draw sustenance from traditional international security issues as well. As the editors of this volume note, the continuing recourse, despite the looming veto, to UNSC in situations involving traditional threats/breaches reflected a shared view that "Council approval and disapproval was a consequential asset in international political competition."[24]

The end of the cold war marked a new phase for UNSC activism. On the one hand, the new geopolitical landscape offered opportunities for greater engagement. On the other hand, these opportunities were accompanied by higher communal expectations of adherence to the principles, as well as of fulfillment of the purposes of the UN Charter.

Human rights and coercive action: lowering the threshold

Arguably, one of the key characteristics of the decade following the end of the cold war was the deepening of the trend of identifying human rights and humanitarian crises as threats to international peace and security. While few would question the existence of this trend, great controversies have surrounded its nature and impact.

This trend manifested itself primarily, but not exclusively, in response to situations of massive civil strife. The legislative history of the UN Charter is of little guidance here, since it did not authorize a role for the Organization in civil wars (Franck 2002: 41). Yet not only did the UNSC address challenges posed by a growing array of situational contexts, in the process it became more sensitive to the sources of abusive conduct. What emerged was a violations-oriented approach, which focused on widespread and systematic violations of human rights and humanitarian norms irrespective of the context (inter/intra-state war, peace), or of the identity of the perpetrators (state or non-state entities).

The examples of Somalia and Angola highlight key aspects of this trend.[25] In the Somali case, it was the "very extortion, blackmail and robbery to which the international relief effort was subjected and the repeated attacks on the personnel and equipment of the United Nations" that led to the adoption of UNSC Resolution 794 authorizing the use of "all necessary means to establish as soon as possible a secure environment for humanitarian relief operations in Somalia."[26] The basis for the determination of a threat to international peace and security was "the magnitude of the human tragedy caused by the conflict . . . further exacerbated by the obstacles being created to the distribution of humanitarian assistance."[27]

In the Angolan case, the failure of a non-state armed group (UNITA) to accept the results of the 1992 elections and the continuing military activities that contributed to "the further deterioration of an already grave humanitarian situation" led to the adoption of UNSC resolution 864. The relevant determination (threat to international peace and security) was in response to UNITA's military actions. With the same resolution, UNSC imposed sanctions against the armed group.

In a similar vein, UNSC made determinations in situations involving refugee flows, genocide, mass starvation, disintegration of effective governance, and the overthrow of a democratically elected government, among others, for example, in passing resolutions 688, 929, 1101, and 940. Moreover, the security implications of non-state actor activity were reinforced during the Kosovo crisis, with resolution 1199 calling upon the KLA leadership to condemn terrorist activities. Last, but not least, with the adoption of the statute of the ad hoc International Tribunal for the Former Yugoslavia (ICTY), the UNSC engaged in legislative initiatives.[28] The ICTY Statute was included in an earlier report prepared by the Secretary-General which made determinations as to which of the relevant legal instruments constituted, beyond doubt, part of customary international law.[29]

The high point of this activist era came in 1999, in the midst of the controversy generated by Operation Allied Force, when UN Secretary-General Kofi Annan (1999) called for a more principled stance in response to massive and systematic violations of human rights. Kofi Annan's call to "humanitarian arms" generated a heated exchange in the General Assembly debate that ensued. Clearly, the precedents set during the cold war with South Africa and Southern Rhodesia had redefined a threshold which was subsequently lowered, albeit in an ad hoc rather than systematic manner. At the same time it reinforced concerns among developing countries about the direction and tenor of this interventionism.

It is this ad hocism that, among other things, played into realist/neorealist hands and made UNSC action appear as another manifestation of power policy (in normative guise). To be sure, power differentials are reflected in a more profound way in the UNSC than in any other organ of the United Nations.[30] Moreover, evolving understandings of "threats to the peace" do provide entry points for ad hoc engagements by those powers most capable and willing to act. Yet, what this picture leaves out is a realization that these decisions are not taken in a vacuum, but within an institutional context that subjects debates and resolutions to a certain process; a process whose outcomes cannot be reduced to the products of a purely instrumental rationality. In particular, these discussions unfold in a setting that "implies recognition of situatedness in a political community and openness to dialogue with other members of the community" (Koskenniemi 1996: 479–480).

In such a context, arguments to the effect that a certain situation constitutes "a threat to the peace" go beyond simplistic reiterations of a mantra reflective of "façade legitimation." On the contrary, the references to the relevant Charter articles, to precedents (whether in the form of validating or negating similarities/differences), and to the possible consequences of action/inaction, subject the participants to expectations of consistency and coherence. This web of mutual expectations presupposes the assumption of certain responsibilities vis-à-vis all those engaged in this process, and raises critical issues of accountability. In fact, it is no accident that the concern with accountability has acquired greater prominence in an era of growing sensitivity to non-traditional threats.

If these remarks are tolerably accurate, the emerging picture is one that challenges two diametrically opposed images: the first one, anchored in the long-overdue mainstreaming of human rights concerns in the security discourse, perceives developments during the 1990s as the high point in the history of the human rights movement.[31] The second one, anchored in the power asymmetries and the concomitant potential for cooptation embedded in all forays into the terrain of high politics, perceives the era of humanitarian intervention as signaling the end of human rights (Douzinas 2000). According to the latter, what we are witnessing is the emasculation of the transformational potential of human rights; from a legacy of subversion of state power to the rendering of apology for state violence (Orford 2003: 187).

In this context, challenge does not imply trivialization of the normative inroads into the security discourse, nor insensitivity to the negative effects of the uneven distribution of power. On the contrary, it views both as facets of the human rights predicament: an ongoing struggle to situate itself within the space of high politics, while maintaining a modicum of integrity and dissent. It is an effort that unfolds, as mentioned earlier, in an institutional context where open reference to rules and principles, and communal expectations of coherence and consistency, characterize the debates. No organ exemplifies better the complexities of this process than the UNSC; a place where issues of authority and legitimacy, shaped by reciprocity and related participatory precepts of international law, intersect with recurrent projections of power asymmetries. It is this very place which the ongoing "war on terror" has made the focus of institutional attention and raised questions as to its current role and future prospects.

Counter-terrorism initiatives and human rights

The attacks on September 11, 2001, and the ensuing responses have added another layer of complexity to the ongoing interplay between the participatory and hierarchical facets of the international legal process. More specifically, in the terrorism/counter-terrorism discourse, references to widely accepted standards and practices have been intermingled with "subjective assertions as to good and evil" (Duffy 2005: 2), thus raising the prospect of using the collective processes of international law, including the UNSC, to advance a particular understanding of appropriate measures/countermeasures, espoused by the international community's most powerful member (Alvarez 2003: 873).

It is beyond the scope of this chapter to address all issues relating to the use/abuse of collective processes in the "war on terror." For the purposes of our discussion, of particular concern are developments in the Security Council, especially those associated with the activities of two UNSC Committees: the Counter-Terrorism Committee (CTC) and the 1267 Sanctions Committee.

The CTC was established on the basis of UNSC resolution 1373. It "monitors the implementation of resolution 1373 by all states and tries to increase the capability of states to fight terrorism" (Andreopoulos 2005: 175–177). Resolution 1373 is a rather unusual document, since it is the first Chapter VII-based resolution that applies to all the members of the UN system (Human Rights Watch 2004: 4). It constitutes a telling example of the UNSC's legislative activism:[32] the imposition of binding orders on all states regarding counter-terrorism, unconstrained by treaty and customary law obligations (Alvarez 2003: 874), as exemplified by the à la carte treatment of the Convention for the Suppression of the Financing of Terrorism. The resolution included the treaty's enforcement provisions that suited the counter-terrorist agenda, and omitted key constraining provisions such as those relating to the rights of persons accused of terrorism-related offenses and to the requisites of international human rights law.[33]

The CTC has asked all states to report to the Committee "on steps taken or planned to implement resolution 1373." The eagerness of many countries, with well-documented records of massive and systematic violations of human rights, to submit reports cataloguing their concerted efforts to combat terrorism should be a matter of concern.[34] At this stage, it appears that the way the CTC process is structured can and does provide an opening for the international legitimation of repressive criminal laws and procedures under the banner of the anti-terrorist struggle.

There are several reasons for the well-founded skepticism that CTC's record has elicited. First, the CTC has consistently refused to address in any serious manner the human rights implications of the campaign against terrorism. The tone was set early on with Sir Jeremy Greenstock's statement that the mandate of the CTC did not include the monitoring of the human rights performance of member states.[35]

The second flows from the first: as a result of this attitude, there is a manifest lack of interest on the part of the CTC to subject to legal scrutiny member states' laws and regulations whose vague phrasing invariably violates basic criminal law principles, in particular the principle of specificity. For example, Egypt's definition of terrorism contained in Act No. 97 of 1992 includes, among other things, "any use of force or violence or any threat or intimidation to which the perpetrator resorts in order to ... *prevent* or impede the public authorities in the performance of their work." In fact, when the Human Rights Committee (HRC), the monitoring body that oversees implementation of each country's obligations under the International Covenant on Civil and Political Rights (ICCPR), examined Egypt's periodic report in November 2002, it expressed alarm at "the very broad and general definition of terrorism given in Act No. 97" (Human Rights Watch 2004: 8). No such concern was apparently raised by the CTC when it reviewed Egypt's initial report, submitted in December 2001, which contained the very same definition (Human Rights Watch 2004: 8–9).

In a similar vein, the CTC expressed no misgivings about the pending legislation related to terrorism, when it reviewed the initial report submitted by the Philippines (S/200/1290). This attitude is in sharp contrast to the reaction of the HRC when it reviewed the country's consolidated second and third periodic reports. In its concluding observations, the HRC noted, inter alia, that "While the Committee is mindful of the security requirements associated with efforts to combat terrorism, it is concerned by the exceedingly broad scope of the proposed legislation, as acknowledged by the delegation. The draft legislation includes a broad and vague definition of acts of terrorism which could have a negative impact on the rights guaranteed by the Covenant" (United Nations 2003). And it concluded: "The State party should ensure that legislation adopted and measures taken to combat terrorism are consistent with the provisions of the Covenant" (United Nations 2003).

Third, this attitude has persisted despite repeated requests by human rights officials and experts in the United Nations system for quality control mechanisms and greater collaboration between the CTC and various human rights organs. More specifically, the Office of the High Commissioner for Human Rights (OHCHR) submitted, very early on, a note to the chair of the CTC which included a set of principles that "could guide an analysis of counter-terrorism measures from a human rights perspective" (High Commissioner for Human Rights 2002). The note reaffirmed the importance of the principles of legality, non-derogability, necessity and proportionality, non-discrimination, due process, and non-refoulement (High Commissioner for Human Rights 2002).

In addressing the Commission on Human Rights on the issues of human security and terrorism, then High Commissioner Mary Robinson expressed concerns that "counter-terrorism strategies pursued after 11 September have sometimes undermined efforts to enhance respect for human rights" (High Commissioner for Human Rights on Human Security and Terrorism 2002).

In the same address, she suggested that the Commission might consider establishing "a mechanism to examine from a human rights perspective the counter-terrorism measures taken by states" (High Commissioner for Human Rights on Human Security and Terrorism 2002).

Moreover, at a HRC meeting held with the Legal Expert of the CTC, HRC members expressed concern over the post-9/11 focus in states' legislation "on counter-terrorist measures while ignoring human rights" (Human Rights Committee 2003). Some committee members pointed to instances of legislation, "which empowered the executive to accept as truth the designation made by foreign countries of organizations as terrorist organizations, without examining that designation on its merits" (Human Rights Committee 2003) while one member warned "that some policies, supposedly aimed at combating terrorism, were simply policies of repression" (Human Rights Committee 2003).

In response to these concerns and criticisms, the CTC has committed itself to ensuring a liaison between the Counter-Terrorism Committee Executive Directorate (CTED) and the OHCHR (United Nations Security Council S/2004/642). In 2006, the CTC issued a policy guidance in which it reaffirmed the need for the CTED to liaise with the OHCHR, as appropriate, when analyzing states' implementation of resolution 1373, as well as when preparing draft letters to states and organizing visits. In addition, the policy guidance stated that the CTC and the CTED, under the direction of the Committee, "should incorporate human rights into their communication strategy" (S/AC.40/2006/PG.2).

However, judging from the record so far, this "liaison" reflects a ritualistic reaffirmation of the need to take human rights seriously, with limited prospects for the adoption of concrete and substantive "next steps." Despite the fact that even certain analysts sympathetic to the work of the CTC acknowledge that the "interplay between efforts to combat terrorism and the protection of human rights" is one of the challenges confronting the CTC, the only thing that they can offer is the need for the Committee to "remain aware of the delicate relationship between counterterrorism and the protection of human rights while not losing sight of its main goal—to raise the capacity of all 191 members of the United Nations to fight terrorism" (Rosand 2003: 340).

While there are clearly no easy solutions in sight, two initial and rather modest steps in an effort to redress the human rights deficit would be (1) more regularized interaction between the CTED and the Special Rapporteur on the promotion and protection of human rights and fundamental freedoms while countering terrorism;[36] and (2) the convening of joint CTED and HRC sessions to review counter-terrorist measures for their compliance with human rights standards.

Likewise, the work of the 1267 Sanctions Committee which was established by the UNSC with the purpose of overseeing the implementation of sanctions imposed on individuals and entities belonging or related to the Taliban, Osama Bin Laden and Al-Qaeda, has generated a lot of concern.[37] The 1267

Committee was created in response to, among other things, the Taliban's continuing provision of "safe haven to Usama bin Laden;" in addition, the resolution cited the fact that the Taliban allowed Bin Laden "and others associated with him to operate a network of terrorist training camps . . . and to use Afghanistan as a base from which to sponsor international terrorist operations." In a subsequent resolution (1455), the UNSC requested the Committee "to maintain an updated list, based on information provided by States and regional organizations, of the individuals and entities designated as being associated with Usama bin Laden, including those in the Al-Qaeda organization." Finally, in resolution 1455, the UNSC emphasized the importance of the provision, by member states, of names and information to the Committee, "so that the Committee can consider adding new names and details to its list."

According to the latest information provided by the Sanctions Committee, the list includes 143 individuals and entities belonging to or associated with the Taliban, and 344 individuals and entities belonging to or associated with Al-Qaeda. Since its inception, 20 individuals and entities have been removed from the list (9 individuals and 11 entities).[38] However, the process by which individuals and institutions are listed and de-listed is not subject to any proper review or appeal process, thus raising fundamental questions concerning transparency and accountability.

One case that highlights these concerns involved three Swedish citizens of Somali origin, Abdirisak Aden, Abdi Abdulaziz Ali, and Yusaf Ahmed Ali, and one non-profit association with which these men were affiliated. Their names and that of the association appeared on the Sanctions Committee list in November 2001 (Gutherie 2004: 511). The information that led to their listing was provided by U.S. intelligence, and resulted in the freezing of these individuals' assets on the basis of a Commission of the European Communities regulation implementing UNSC sanctions.[39] In response, the three individuals brought an action, before the European Court of Justice, against the Commission and the Council of the European Union (International Court of Justice 2002). At the request of its three nationals, the Swedish government initially petitioned the Sanctions Committee to have their names removed from the list, but with no success. A subsequent joint (with the U.S. administration) petition to the Sanctions Committee proved to be more successful, and led to the de-listing of two of the three individuals in question. The third individual, Yusaf Ahmed Ali, was eventually de-listed on August 24, 2006.[40]

This incident raised troubling questions about the listing procedures followed by the Sanctions Committee. While, in response to mounting criticism, certain amendments to the existing guidelines were adopted (the most recent changes were introduced in November 2006), the end result leaves a lot to be desired.[41] In its fourth report to the UNSC, the Analytical Support and Sanctions Monitoring Team[42] noted that "Issues surrounding the fairness of the Committee's listing and de-listing process continue to occupy the attention of national and international policymakers."[43] Even in areas where the Monitoring Team felt that improvements have been made, as with the adoption of UNSC resolution 1617 which supposedly defined the term "associated with" so as to "provide enhanced clarity to States and private parties about conduct that could result in listing," problems persist.[44] In addition, until recently an individual could not directly contest his/her inclusion in the list without the support of the government of his/her country of citizenship and/or residence.[45] Last, but not least, the same body decides placing individuals/entities on the list and reviews challenges to the decisions (Gutherie 2004: 512–514).

In September 2005, the Court of First Instance of the European Communities issued decisions in two cases challenging the sanctions imposed by the UNSC and the 1267 Sanctions Committee. The applicants in these cases, Yassin Kadi from Saudi Arabia, and Ahmed Ali Yusuf and Al Barakaat International Foundation alleged that the UN-imposed assets freeze, implemented in the European Union via the aforementioned EC regulation, violated certain fundamental rights (Court of First Instance of the European Communities 2006a and 2006b). While the Court rejected all of the applicants' arguments, it did note that the Charter of the United Nations "presupposes the existence of mandatory principles of international law, in particular, the protection of the fundamental rights of the human person. . . . Those principles are binding on the Members of the United Nations as well as on its bodies." It then went on to state that "The indirect judicial review carried out by the Court . . . may therefore, in some circumstances, extend to determining whether the superior rules of international law falling within the ambit of *jus cogens* have been observed . . . in particular, the mandatory provisions concerning the universal protection of human rights, from which neither the Member States nor the bodies of the United Nations may derogate because they constitute 'intransgressible principles of international customary law' " (Court of First Instance of the European Communities 2006a and 2006b. Thus, the Court raised the possibility of judicial review of UNSC actions to ensure compliance with international human rights norms.

It is instructive to note here that the 2004 UN report produced by the High-level Panel on Threats, Challenges, and Change is unusually candid about the critical issues raised by the modus operandi of the Sanctions Committee:

> The way entities or individuals are added to the terrorist list maintained by the Council and the absence of review or appeal for those listed raise serious accountability issues and possibly violate fundamental human rights norms and conventions. The Al-Qaeda and Taliban Sanctions Committee should institute a process for reviewing the cases of individuals and institutions claiming to have been wrongly placed or retained on its watch lists.
>
> (United Nations 2004: 50)

In a similar vein, the World Summit Outcome Document (2005) called upon the UNSC "to ensure that fair and clear procedures exist for placing individuals and entities on sanctions lists and for removing them, as well as for granting humanitarian exemptions" (United Nations General Assembly A/RES/60/1: para. 109).

In response to these concerns, a series of recent studies have sought to address critical aspects relating to the fairness and transparency of listing and de-listing procedures. One of these studies was sponsored by the governments of Switzerland, Germany, and Sweden and conducted by the Watson Institute for International Studies at Brown University (2006). Among other things, the study noted that despite important improvements made over time, "criticisms persist about procedures related to the designation or listing of individuals, operations of committees, and the process for individuals and entities to be removed from the list." In addition, the study noted that "the lack of transparency of committee procedures and difficulties in obtaining information contribute to general perceptions of unfairness" (Watson Institute 2006: 3). One of the key procedural recommendations of the study was the creation of a focal point within the Secretariat to handle all de-listing requests, so that the petitioner will not have to do that through their state of citizenship or residence. With resolution 1730, the UNSC adopted a modified version of this proposal and instructed the sanctions committees, including the 1267 Committee, to revise their guidelines accordingly. The revised guidelines offer prospective petitioners a choice: to submit the request for de-listing through the focal point process, or through their state of residence or citizenship.[46] While this is a step in the right direction, other critical aspects of this problem, including the creation of independent review mechanisms, where individuals and entities may appeal decisions regarding their listing, are yet to be addressed.

What these developments indicate is that hyperactivity, a key feature of the UNSC profile during the 1990s, has by no means abated. Notwithstanding concerns about UNSC passivity, a reaction caused by its inability to reach consensus on the situation in Iraq, the main issue here is legitimacy in the context of an ongoing agenda expansion.

Legitimacy and normative overstretch: where do we go from here?

Several analysts and commentators view these developments as a reversal of the advances, albeit problematic, of the previous decade, in which human rights and humanitarian concerns acquired a more prominent place in the international community's agenda. While the relevant normative framework is under siege,[47] and, as the previous discussion has indicated, counter-terrorism policies exhibit a serious compliance deficit,[48] it would be a mistake to see the post-9/11 developments as a simple antithesis to the heady days of human rights/humanitarian activism. On the contrary, there is a considerable overlap between elements of the human rights (especially in its humanitarian intervention variant) and the "war on terror" discourses.[49]

The first facet of this overlap relates to the endorsement, albeit with reservations, of UNSC activism by organizations and groups in the human rights and humanitarian communities.[50] The opening up of the security discourse came at a price though. It provided those actors in the international system most capable and willing to project military force with an increasing array of opportunities for doing so, as well as a forum (UNSC) capable of legitimizing the relevant initiatives. In this context, the human rights discourse, by its very nature subversive of authority structures, increasingly intersected with the language of diplomacy and statecraft. In the process, it strengthened the United States' role in this activist agenda by providing the remaining superpower with continuous opportunities to "incorporate human rights concerns into its operational goals" (Farer 2003: 84).

The continuing appeal of human rights became apparent in the course of the military actions against Afghanistan and Iraq. One of the reasons cited to justify military action against the Taliban was the situation of women and girls in the country. Then Secretary of State Colin Powell argued that "the recovery of Afghanistan must entail the restoration of the rights of Afghan women" (quoted in Orford 2003: 202). In a similar vein, in the case of Iraq, the joint resolution authorizing the use of force cited both Iraq's continuing "brutal repression of its civilian population" and its "willingness to use weapons of mass destruction against . . . its own people" (United States Congress 2002). It is instructive to note here that some neoconservative analysts affirmed, in the aftermath of the weapons of mass destruction fiasco, that human rights arguments should have figured more prominently in the Administration's case for "regime change" in Iraq.

The second facet refers to the changing lens through which the terrorist threat is perceived. In the pre-9/11 period, the main focus was on places which harbored groups with an anti-Western agenda, capable of engaging in transnational acts of violence (Farer 2003: 85). The angle of vision may have now widened "to include places where prevailing conditions can foster or facilitate terrorism" (Farer 2003: 85). The transition from a focus on groups harbored by states to any disintegrating/failed or "rogue" state, a terrain potentially hospitable to all forms of abusive conduct, clearly shifts the parameters of the debate. The emerging post-9/11 consensus seems to be that these types of states constitute an inviting terrain, for the intersections between human rights protection and counter-terrorist initiatives, and, in the process, widen the menu of available discourses and policy options at the disposal of the interveners.

The above mentioned case of Afghanistan constitutes a telling example of these intersections. As the National Security Strategy document (NSS) noted, the U.S. "will continue to work . . . to provide the humanitarian, political, economic and security assistance necessary to rebuild Afghanistan so that it will never again abuse its people, threaten its neighbors, and provide a haven for terrorists." There is a seamless discursive transition from NSS to the report issued by the Secretary-General's High Level Panel on Threats, Challenges, and Change (United Nations 2004: 64) which, in addressing the preventive use of force, stated: "In the world of the twenty-first century, the international community does have to be concerned about nightmare scenarios combining terrorists, weapons of mass destruction and irresponsible states . . . which may conceivably justify the use of force, not just reactively but preventively." Thus, state irresponsibility, by raising the specter of apocalyptic consequences, renders even preventive action necessary, under certain circumstances.

The third facet relates to the emphasis on retrospective enforcement rather than proactive preventive measures. Here there are interesting parallels between the marginal place that discussions about preventing the emergence of humanitarian crises occupy within the humanitarian intervention discourse, with the marginal place that discussions about the prevention of terrorism occupy within the "war on terror" discourse. One of the most fascinating aspects of the debate concerning the most appropriate framework for fighting the "war on terror," that is, whether we should use the war, as opposed to the law enforcement framework, is the fact that very little attention is paid to strategies and tactics that do not entail at all, or not exclusively, ex post facto measures. Suppressed in both discourses are explorations of strategies for political and socioeconomic empowerment, which after all constitute part and parcel of a more holistic approach to human rights; strategies that can act as an antidote to the near exclusive preoccupation with forcible responses.[51]

In a nutshell, normative overstretch raises serious concerns due to its contribution to a troublesome interplay between the hierarchical and the participatory facets of the international legal process. In particular, by expanding the universe of potential triggers for action, it has reinforced the privileging of power asymmetries. The evolving overlap between elements of the human rights/humanitarian and counter-terrorist discourses is the latest manifestation of the former's price of entry into the realm of high politics.

In such a context, the challenge is not to disentangle the human rights perspective from the security discourse. Despite the problems that the humanization of the security discourse has entailed, such a course of action would be tantamount to "ghettoizing" human rights in the quest for an elusive purity, and, in the long run, consigning them to irrelevance. Moreover, such a course of action would accentuate the already existing accountability deficit. The main institutional pathway to continuing relevance (i.e., adherence to international human rights norms and standards) is also the sine qua non of institutional legitimacy.[52] What is needed at this juncture is accountable UNSC activism, activism which perceives conformity to these norms and standards as the chief source of its legitimacy. It is the type of activism that can narrow the growing gap between the UNSC's role in international affairs (expanding) and its authority (diminishing). This, however, is a formidable task.

Recent initiatives, undertaken in response to the new security challenges, have compounded the elusiveness of the quest for accountability. The UNSC is not only expected to address an ever growing array of threats and challenges, but it is expected to do so with a wider range of means, including the preventive use of force.

The Report of the High Level Panel on Threats, Challenges, and Change (United Nations 2004: 88) is instructive here. It confirms the drastic changes that the landscape of security has undergone since the founding of the UN. While originally the UN was concerned primarily with interstate aggression, now the organization must be prepared to address "any event or process that leads to large-scale death or lessening of life chances and undermines States as the basic unit of the international system" (United Nations 2004: 2) which is the report's understanding of what constitutes a threat to international security. The report identifies six clusters of threats: economic and social threats, interstate conflict, internal conflict, nuclear, radiological, chemical and biological weapons, terrorism, and transnational organized crime (United Nations 2004). When it comes to the discussion of the means and methods of addressing these threats, the report endorses the preventive use of force, but only in the context of UNSC action; in other words, "collective action authorized under Chapter VII" (United Nations 2004: 64). Going a step further, the report urges the UNSC "to be more proactive on these issues, taking more decisive action earlier, than it has been in the past" (United Nations 2004).

What is most striking about this report is the lack of any substantive discussion on UNSC accountability commensurate with its expanding agenda. This is indeed remarkable, given the UNSC's own track record, and the concerns about legality and legitimacy that are raised in the report. On the issue of legality, the report simply asserts that the preventive use of force is not an issue in the context of UNSC authorized action, since such action can be taken by the UNSC "at any time that it deems that there is a threat to international peace and security" (United Nations 2004). On the issue of legitimacy, the report almost verbatim adopts the threshold/precautionary criteria associated with the collective international responsibility to protect norm, which is characterized as an emerging norm.[53] The reaffirmation of UNSC's wide discretion in the determination of threats to the peace coupled with the adoption of the said criteria raises critical questions concerning the legitimacy/legality nexus in the quest for a "new security consensus." In particular, wide discretion exercised in the context of self-policed normative boundaries increases its receptivity to the siren calls of enlightened despotism, rather than to communal expectations of responsible conduct.

In a similar vein, there is very little of substance on accountability in the "war on terror," despite the acknowledgment of the problems that this ongoing situation poses for the rule of law and human rights. While the report makes reference to the concerns expressed by governments and civil society organizations as to the corrosive impact of the "war" in question on human rights and the rule of law (United Nations 2004: 48), as well as to the questionable listing and de-listing practices of the Al-Qaeda and Taliban Sanctions Committee (United Nations 2004), it does not offer any specific recommendations for making this "war" conform to the said standards.

Given the critical role of the UNSC in fashioning what the report calls "a new and broader understanding . . . of what collective security means," the failure to address, in any substantive way, UNSC accountability in the context of an ever expanding agenda is indeed troubling. This silence undermines any serious effort to articulate this new and broader understanding, and erodes the limited advances in the humanization of the security discourse. It is a posture (silence) that has been replicated, rather than challenged, in subsequent UN documents.[54]

To be sure, accountability at the international level is a highly complex issue with no easy solutions in sight. The main concern here is not the lack of answers; rather, it is the fact that, in a milieu characterized by growing power asymmetries and by an expanding universe of non-traditional threats, policy-makers have yet to acknowledge, beyond the occasional routine references, accountable activism as a major world order issue.

There are several possible ways to explore accountability enhancing mechanisms for the UNSC (as well as the other main organs of international governance). Any such effort must be based on three important premises: first, while standards of legitimacy are important in all mechanisms, not all standards have to be formally encoded in law (Grant and Keohane 2005: 35–36); second, and related to the previous one, the importance of human rights norms as standards of legitimacy strengthens the argument for both hard and soft law accountability options; and third, accountability does not entail the elimination of power asymmetries, but rather a greater convergence on understandings of legitimacy in a setting that, as noted earlier, implies recognition of situatedness in a political community. Accountability options can strengthen, as well as be sustained by, such recognition.

More specifically, there are a couple of mechanisms that deserve further exploration at this juncture (the list is by no means exhaustive). On the legal front, the time has come to place the issue of judicial review of UNSC decisions, preferably by the International Court of Justice (ICJ), on the global agenda. Broad discretionary powers are/should not be equated with lack of accountability. To bring just one example: while the UNSC, as mentioned earlier, has broad discretion in the determination of threats to the peace, this, as the ICTY noted in the Tadic case, "is not a totally unfettered discretion" (*Prosecutor v. Dusko Tadic* 1995). While the ICTY characterized "threats to the peace" as "more of a political concept," it duly noted that the determination "has to remain, at the very least, within the limits of the Purposes and Principles of the Charter" (*Prosecutor v. Dusko Tadic* 1995). Needless to say, this conclusion is consistent with a standard interpretation of the provisions of Article 24 of the UN Charter, in accordance with Article 31 of the Vienna Convention on the Law of Treaties.[55]

Another possibility is to consider ways of strengthening the relation between the UNSC and the International Criminal Court (ICC). As is well known, according to Article 13(b) of its Statute, the UNSC, acting under Chapter VII, can refer a situation to the Prosecutor. In fact, the UNSC has already done so in the case of Darfur. Following this path, one can consider a reciprocal relation whereby an indictment issued by the Prosecutor would place a particular situation on the UNSC agenda for a determination as to whether it constitutes a threat to international peace and security. Such a move, while not problem-free, could potentially contribute to more principled deliberations on such determinations.

On the non-legal front, a possible mechanism relates to what Grant and Keohane have identified as peer accountability (Grant and Keohane 2005: 37). In the context of our discussion, it relates to the exploration of mechanisms that would strengthen expectations among member states as to the voting behavior of those states which serve on the UNSC; expectations that the said behavior would meet the requirements of transparency, as well as those mandated by widely accepted standards of legitimacy. One possible way to operationalize peer accountability would be via the introduction of ex ante and ex post review mechanisms along the lines suggested in the context of military interventions (Buchanan and Keohane 2004: 1–22).

This is clearly very preliminary. The main point, however, is to go beyond a posture of silence and commit to a deliberative process that views transparency and standards of legitimacy as key pathways to accountable activism. The commitment undertaken at the 2005 World Summit "to continue consideration of the responsibility to protect" within the framework of the General Assembly provides an opportunity that should not be squandered.

Conclusion

The conceptual lenses through which the intersections between human rights and collective security are perceived have clearly evolved. From a hierarchically inferior position in the normative architecture of the UN Charter, the human rights discourse has been engaged in an ongoing struggle to situate itself within the space of high politics. In its efforts to meet the main challenge, the transformation of human rights/humanitarian issues from peripheral into more high-profile items on the security agenda, the discourse has exposed itself to the perils of cooptation. After all, this effort has centered on the UNSC, the main locus for the privileging of power asymmetries in the United Nations system.

These intersections have also posed a challenge for the UNSC: how to balance the interplay between the hierarchical and participatory facets of the international legal process. In particular, the key task is to ensure legitimacy in a milieu marked by competing pressures from above (the widening of power asymmetries), and from below (shared expectations of adherence to communal values and standards).

The ever expanding universe of non-traditional threats (the "war on terror" being the most recent and troubling addition) has added another layer of complexity to these intersections. The opening up of the security discourse has provided those most capable and willing to project force with more opportunities for doing so. Thus, human rights considerations could be viewed as facilitators to the legitimation of a growing array of coercive practices. There is another side to this coin though: the need to fashion, in light of proliferating non-traditional threats, a new and broader understanding of collective security, has exposed the UNSC to growing questions of authority and legitimacy. Herein lie the related perils: for human rights it is either retrenchment, in the quest for an elusive purity and hence irrelevance, or cooptation; for the UNSC (as the main organ for collective security) it is the image of enlightened despotism at best and sheer puppetry at worst.

While human rights are still the hierarchically inferior partner, it is now clear that they are needed more than ever before. If the fashioning of a new and broader understanding of collective security is to have any chance of success, it needs the legitimating input of that discourse. Accountable UNSC activism, premised on widely shared human rights norms and standards, may not constitute the magic bullet; however, it offers a credible way to narrow the gap between the UNSC's expanding role in international affairs and its diminishing authority.

Acknowledgment

The author, editors, and publisher are grateful for permission to use material from *The Law of Armed Conflict*, by Howard M. Hensel (September 2005), Aldershot: Ashgate (ISBN 0 7546 4543 6).

Notes

1 Parts of this chapter are based on a paper presented at the Columbia University Seminar on Human Rights in May 2006, and on a paper presented at the American Political Science Association Convention, Philadelphia, August 30–September 3, 2006. I would like to thank the participants in these sessions for their useful comments.

2 Although very often in the literature the terms human rights and humanitarian are used interchangeably, there are important differences between the relevant normative frameworks (international human rights law and international humanitarian law), as well as among the organizations (human rights/humanitarian) that operate on the basis of their respective principles. Some of these differences persist despite the growing convergence between these two bodies of law. I have addressed some of the key similarities and differences in "On the accountability of non-state armed groups" in Andreopoulos, Zehra, Arat, and Juviler 2006: 239–278; Meron 2000.

3 To be sure, there have been earlier, but less successful attempts, at establishing such linkages. For example, in the aftermath of World War I, the Treaty of Sevres stipulated in Article 230 that "The Turkish Government undertakes to hand over to the Allied Powers the persons whose surrender may be required by the latter as being responsible for the massacres committed during the continuance of the state of war on territory which formed part of the Turkish Empire on August 1 1914." This provision referred to the massacres of the Armenian population. The Treaty of Sevres was never ratified; see Biddiss 2004: 45; and Bass 2000: 135–136.

4 As is well known, the Nuremberg Tribunal did not condemn as criminal the perse-

cutions that the Nazi regime "had inflicted on its own citizens or ex-citizens during the peacetime years of the 1930s"; see Biddiss 2004: 48.

5 The inclusion of references to human rights in the Charter was made possible primarily due the mobilization of small countries participating in the San Francisco Conference, as well as to the activities of sympathetic NGOs; see Gordon Lauren 2003: ch. 6; William Korey 1998: 29–42.

6 For the use of these terms, see Krasner 1999: 14–25. As Krasner (1999: 25) has noted, "Understood more generally as a problem of the relations between rulers and ruled, human rights are but one more incarnation of a long-standing concern in the international system."

7 Anghie 2005: 6. According to Anghie, the agenda of the "civilizing mission," the project of governing non-European peoples, is constitutively significant for the discipline of international law, and not a peripheral issue. For similar views, see Orford 2003: 25–26.

8 Johannes Morsink (1999: 20) has argued that "The fact that the Declaration itself is not intertwined with any piece of this machinery of implementation gave it from the start an independent moral status in world affairs and law." For similar remarks, see Falk 2002: 24. For the contribution of the global south, see Waltz 2002: 51–71; Waltz 2004: 799–844.

9 See, for example, *Dudgeon v. United Kingdom*, Ser. A, No. 45, 4 EHRR 149 (1981).

10 Steiner and Alston 2000: 881. While acknowledging the limitations confronting the Court, a more positive assessment of its effectiveness can be found in Pasqualucci 2003: 326–350.

11 Arguably, some of the most notable successes did not even involve legally binding arrangements. For example, a lot has been written on the impact of the Helsinki Final Act (1975), whose "human rights basket" was originally thought of as a sideshow, a compromise struck by the Soviet Union, so as to ensure the recognition by Western powers of the boundaries established in Eastern Europe in the aftermath of World War II. Yet, in a short period of time, this "basket" energized civil society actors in the Soviet Union and in several Central and Eastern European countries to challenge the human rights policies of their respective regimes during periodic follow-up conferences. The human rights provisions of the Helsinki Accords acted as a catalyst for the transnational mobilization of human rights activists, an outcome that no one would have predicted back in 1975, let alone the Communist regimes themselves, which initially viewed the Helsinki Final Act (HFA) as a victory for their cause. On the HFA and its impact, see Thomas 2001: 159–288.

12 Despite the post-1960s explosion in international human rights law-making, the weak enforcement mechanisms would ensure the relevance of securitization, albeit as a last resort.

13 The other resolution related to Southern Rhodesia's Unilateral Declaration of Independence. In this resolution, the UNSC condemned "the usurpation of power by a racist settler minority" and declared that the continuance of the situation "resulting from the proclamation of independence" constituted a threat to international peace and security; United Nations Security Council resolution 217, November 20, 1965. The resolution was adopted with one abstention (France).

14 United Nations Security Council resolution 418, November 4, 1977. The resolution was adopted unanimously.

15 Ibid. The wording is from the resolution's preamble.

16 The Western Powers rejected the existence of such a relationship, and cited South Africa's confrontational foreign policy as the reason for the adoption of the mandatory arms embargo, thus delinking internal abusive conduct from external aggression; see Klotz 1995: 50–51. In support of this argument, Klotz (1995: 51) refers, among other things, to an earlier and unsuccessful draft resolution, which

declared internal repression as constituting a threat to international peace and security.

17 See, for example, United Nations General Assembly resolution 1663 on the question of race conflict in South Africa resulting from the policies of apartheid of the Government of the Republic of South Africa, November 28, 1961; and United Nations General Assembly resolution 1881 on the policies of apartheid of the Government of the Republic of South Africa, October 11, 1963.

18 United Nations Security Council resolution 181, August 7, 1963. This resolution reaffirmed the language of an earlier resolution (134, April 1, 1960) which recognized that the situation in South Africa (the discriminatory policies of the regime) "has led to international friction and if continued might endanger international peace and security." Both resolutions were adopted with two abstentions (France, U.K.).

19 Here it is important to stress the role of the Organization of African Unity as well as that of the Commonwealth; see Klotz 1995.

20 Another important factor had to do with South Africa's continuing occupation of South West Africa (Namibia); see Crawford 2002: 329–340. In 1970, the United Nations General Assembly and the UNSC sought an advisory opinion from the International Court of Justice on the consequences for Namibia of South Africa's presence. The Court concluded that "the continued presence of South Africa in Namibia being illegal, South Africa is under obligation to withdraw its administration from Namibia immediately"; International Court of Justice 1971.

21 For a differing view on resolution 418, see Klotz 1995. However, and in addition to the arguments about the previous UNSC resolutions on apartheid, one cannot ignore the impact of the 1976 Soweto riots, which took place less than a year before the resolution's adoption. Klotz (1995: 51) acknowledges the possible influence of these events when she writes that "The 1976 Soweto riots may have been partly responsible for provoking the UN arms embargo," but she goes on to say that "domestic unrest does not convincingly explain the permanent members' decisions."

22 In the context of South Africa, this will necessitate explaining the country's transformation, in less than twenty years, from the status of an important international actor and founding member of the United Nations, to that of a pariah state, or to use more current terminology, to that of a "rogue" state.

23 As Claude (1984: 258) has noted, "it [collective security] can expect to retain their [participating states'] loyal support only if it succeeds in reducing, rather than increasing, their exposure to the perils of military involvement."

24 See the Introduction to this volume.

25 In the discussion of Somalia and Angola, I follow my piece on "Violations of human rights and humanitarian law and threats to international peace and security," in Biddiss 2004: 84–86.

26 United Nations Security Council resolution 794, December 3, 1992.

27 Ibid.

28 United Nations Security Council resolution 827, May 25, 1993.

29 According to the Report, these were, the 1907 Hague Convention IV Respecting the Laws and Customs of War on Land and the Regulations annexed thereto, the Charter of the International Military Tribunal, the Convention on the Prevention and Punishment of the Crime of Genocide, and the 1949 Geneva Conventions. In resolution 827, the UNSC, acting under Chapter VII, approved the S-G's report.

30 This argument is separate and distinct from the argument that challenges the extent to which the composition of the UNSC accurately reflects current geopolitical realities. It may be true that there are other countries which are more deserving of permanent membership than some of the current ones, but this does not negate

the fact that no other institution reflects power differentials as profoundly as the UNSC, even in its present form.

31 See, for example, Michael Ignatieff (2002: A25) who has characterized the 1990s as the decade in which "human rights has become the dominant moral vocabulary in foreign affairs."

32 There is no consensus in the literature as to the features that UNSC resolutions must have to qualify as legislative acts. For some scholars, resolutions that have determined the applicability of certain international legal instruments in particular situations, or have imposed economic sanctions, qualify as legislative acts, while for others it is the general and abstract character of the obligations imposed that characterizes international legislation. For a general discussion, see Koskenniemi 1995; Talmon 2005.

33 Alvarez 2003: 875. Article 17 of the Convention includes a specific reference to international human rights law; untreaty.un.org/English/Terrorism/Conv12.pdf

34 Uzbekistan, for example, is highlighting, among other things, provisions of its criminal legislation relating to crimes against public security which include "the creation or direction of or participation in religious extremist, separatist, fundamentalist or other banned organizations" (Art. 244–2). In the 2006 U.S. Department of State Country Reports on Human Rights Practices, Uzbekistan is characterized as "an authoritarian state" whose "security forces routinely tortured, beat, and otherwise mistreated detainees under interrogation to obtain confessions or incriminating information";www.state.gov/g/drl/rls/hrrpt/2006/78848.htm

35 Sir Jeremy Greenstock stated that "Monitoring performance against other international conventions, including human rights law, is outside the scope of the Counter-Terrorism Committee's mandate." He then went on to note, "But we will remain aware of the interaction with human rights concerns, and we will keep ourselves briefed as appropriate." United Nations Security Council 2002/S/PV.4453 5. See also Human Rights Watch 2004: 6. Sir Jeremy Greenstock was the first chairman of the CTC.

36 For the Special Rapporteur's most recent report, see Human Rights Council 2007.

37 Andreopoulos 2007.

38 United Nations Security Council *The Consolidated List of Individuals and Entities Belonging to or Associated with the Taliban and Al-Qaida Organization as Established and Maintained by the 1267 Committee*, www.un.org/sc/committees/1267/consolist.shtml. Accessed April 15, 2007.

39 Ibid. The regulation in question is Commission Regulation (EC) No. 2 199/2001 of November 12, 2001 amending, for the fourth time, Council Regulation (EC) No. 467/2001 prohibiting the export of certain goods and services to Afghanistan, strengthening the flight ban and extending the freeze of funds and other financial resources in respect of the Taliban of Afghanistan and repealing Regulation (EC) No. 337/2000; *Official Journal of the European Communities*, L295/16–18.

40 Gutherie 2004: 512; see the *Consolidated List of Individuals and Entities*, supra, note 38.

41 United Nations Security Council *Security Council Committee Established Pursuant to Resolution 1267 Concerning Al-Qaida and the Taliban and Associated Individuals and Entities. Guidelines of the Committee for the Conduct of its Work*, www.un.org/Docs/sc/committees/1267/1267_guidelines.pdf. Accessed February 22, 2007.

42 This is known as the Monitoring Team and is composed of independent experts appointed by the UN Secretary-General. While the Team operates under the direction of the 1267 Sanctions Committee, "the views and recommendations expressed in its reports do not necessarily reflect the views of the Committee or of the United Nations."

43 United Nations Security Council 2006 S/2006/154: 13.

44 Ibid. While UNSC 1617 is an improvement over the previous situation, it still leaves room for arbitrary conduct. According to the resolution, the list of activities indicating that an individual, group, etc., is associated with Al-Qaeda, Osama Bin Laden or the Taliban include "otherwise supporting acts or activities of."

45 See below for recent developments with UNSC resolution 1730.

46 United Nations Security Council Sanctions Committee "Guidelines of the Committee for the Conduct of its Work," (www.un.org/sc/committees/1267/pdf/1267_guidelines.pdf) Accessed April 15, 2007. In a letter dated March 30, 2007, the Secretary-General notified the President of the UNSC about the establishment of the focal point for de-listing.

47 For a good discussion of the issues relating to the application of international humanitarian law and international human rights law in the "war on terror," see Duffy 2005: 217–378.

48 The compliance deficit refers to human rights and humanitarian law standards.

49 Parts of this section follows Andreopoulos forthcoming.

50 Andreopoulos n.d. The use of force for human rights protection purposes has often generated heated debates both within, as well as among organizations in these two communities. For a good overview of the relevant issues, see International Council on Human Rights Policy 2002.

51 Here it is important to stress that the quest for political and socioeconomic empowerment should not be confused with the current neoconservative mantra about spreading freedom and democracy all over the globe as a way to address many of these problems. Leaving aside the fact that this language is yet to be tested, a human rights-based understanding of empowerment does not look merely at possible gains for all involved, but at "whether the distribution of gains is *fair or acceptable*"; as Amartya Sen (2004), echoing John Nash, noted, "The criticism that a distributional arrangement from cooperation is unfair cannot be rebutted by just noting that all the parties are better off than would be the case in the absence of cooperation; there can be many—indeed infinitely many—such arrangements and the real exercise is the choice among these various alternatives."

52 On human rights norms as standards of legitimacy in world politics, see Grant and Keohane 2005: 35.

53 United Nations 2004: 66–67. For the responsibility to protect, see International Commission on Intervention and State Sovereignty 2001. For the concept as an emerging norm, see Knight 2003.

54 Most notably in the Secretary-General's own *In Larger Freedom* report and in the *2005 World Summit Outcome* document. In the latter, there are mainly two very general references to UNSC legitimacy and accountability. The first correlates enhanced legitimacy with expansion (references to reform that will make the UNSC "more broadly representative") and the second advocates adaptation of UNSC working methods, so as to increase non-UNSC member states' involvement, "enhance its accountability to the membership and increase the transparency of its work". (United Nations General Assembly 2005).

55 See Article 31 (General rule of interpretation) of the Vienna Convention on the Law of Treaties.

Part III

The exercise of Council authority

7 Creating authority by the Council

The international criminal tribunals

Wayne Sandholtz

International prosecution of the perpetrators of war crimes and other gross human rights violations has emerged as one of the most significant expansions of international authority since the founding of the United Nations system. Beginning in 1993 with the International Criminal Tribunal for the former Yugoslavia (ICTY), the Security Council has had a hand in establishing a number of special purpose courts, some purely international (like the ICTY and its counterpart for Rwanda, the ICTR) and some "mixed" (with both international and national elements, as in East Timor, Sierra Leone, and Cambodia). The new international and mixed tribunals represent a dramatic expansion of international authority into the judicial domain. In these courts, individuals are held accountable for violations of international humanitarian law. When these tribunals hand down punishments, they act on behalf of international society.

The growth of international tribunals opens a second layer of conceptual and empirical questions regarding international authority, legitimacy, and the Security Council. As the Security Council has played a central role in establishing these new kinds of courts, it has not only been exercising authority, it has been creating authority. When we think of Security Council authority, we tend to invoke its capacity to act, by imposing sanctions, for instance, or sending peacekeepers. We could label these direct interventions in international affairs "first order authority." "Second order authority" is the competence to create new institutions that, in turn, exercise first order authority (the capacity to act in international affairs).[1]

Authority and legitimacy, as Cronin and Hurd argue in the introduction, are inextricably intertwined, and the creation of the tribunals inevitably raises questions regarding both. The punishment of crime has historically fallen within the core competences of states. How can international bodies legitimately take custody of, prosecute, and punish individual citizens of sovereign states?[2] On what basis can the Security Council expand international authority into the judicial domain? The Security Council does not have the authority to prosecute individual crimes; how can it create judicial authority that it does not itself possess?

The questions just posed are of more than theoretical interest, for at least two reasons. First, the creation of the Yugoslav and Rwandan tribunals provided a crucial impetus to the establishment of a permanent International Criminal Court (ICC). That impulse was a dual one. The ICTY and the ICTR demonstrated that the international community could create functioning criminal tribunals; they showed that it could be done. Second, the Yugoslav and Rwandan tribunals, plus the subsequent special courts, raised the issue of the proliferation of international criminal jurisdictions (Shany 2003). With a growing number of war crimes prosecutions underway or potentially on the horizon, the natural question was whether it would not be more efficient to try such cases in a permanent criminal court rather than create a new *ad hoc* tribunal for each humanitarian crisis. Such considerations strengthened the case for a standing International Criminal Court. Indeed, there is a plausible argument that without the ICTY and ICTR, the International Criminal Court would not have come into being, at least not when it did (Lee and Price 2004).

This chapter seeks to answer some of the questions of authority and legitimacy posed by the international and mixed tribunals.[3] It focuses on the necessary transition from purposive and procedural legitimacy to performance legitimacy. In general, though the international tribunals generally began with considerable purposive and procedural legitimacy, their record in achieving performance legitimacy has been decidedly uneven. The special courts for East Timor and Cambodia, in particular, have failed to establish performance legitimacy. The high cost and seemingly slow pace of the Yugoslav and Rwandan tribunals have, despite important judicial outcomes, raised questions about the value and legitimacy of such courts (Cobban 2006).

The failure to achieve performance legitimacy would normally have serious consequences for an institution, placing in question its continuing viability. An institution lacking performance legitimacy would find it difficult to attract resources, and compliant behavior, from other actors. Though the *ad hoc* tribunals are all temporary and will close their doors in the near future, a failure on their part to earn performance legitimacy could undermine the international prosecution of major atrocities in general, and the International Criminal Court in particular. The ICC begins with a substantial reservoir of legitimacy. Its purpose—to prosecute individuals for serious war crimes and crimes against humanity—is clearly consistent with and supportive of widely shared international human rights norms and values, and its creation accorded with the norms of multilateral treaty-making. The conclusion briefly addresses the legitimacy challenge facing the ICC in light of the experience of the international tribunals. To preview, though the ICC begins as an "institution for the common good" (Cronin 2003), it, like the tribunals before it, will have to earn ongoing performance legitimacy.

Purposive legitimacy and the tribunals

Opposition to the tribunals' existence has been minimal (criticism of their operation is another issue, to be discussed below). In this section, I contend that the tribunals have been widely accepted because their purpose—the prosecution of persons accused of major war crimes and crimes against humanity—is consistent with, and supportive of, well-established international human rights norms. The special courts therefore enjoy a high degree of what we have labeled "purposive legitimacy."

The story of the emergence of international human rights norms since World War II is well known; I will recapitulate pieces of that account in order to support my point that the international criminal tribunals fit firmly within a well-established constellation of values and norms. The UN Charter repeatedly affirms that one of the organization's principal purposes is to promote respect for universal human rights, beginning with the preamble: "We the peoples of the United Nations determined . . . to reaffirm faith in fundamental human rights, in the dignity and worth of the human person, in the equal rights of men and women." Among the "Purposes and Principles" delineated in Chapter I of the Charter are "promoting and encouraging respect for human rights and for fundamental freedoms for all without distinction as to race, sex, language, or religion" (Art. 1(3)). Article 55 repeats the language in Article 1(3) and Article 56 pledges all members to take separate and joint action in cooperation with the United Nations to achieve the Article 55 purposes.

Among the first major acts of the General Assembly was the unanimous (with eight abstentions) passage of the Universal Declaration of Human Rights (1948). The International Covenant on Civil and Political Rights and the International Covenant on Economic, Social, and Cultural Rights both entered into force in 1976; 154 states are parties to the first and 151 are parties to the second (United Nations 2005). Together with the Universal Declaration, the two Covenants form what is sometimes referred to as the "International Bill of Rights." Additional treaties proscribe specific categories of abuses. Most relevant to the international tribunals are the Genocide Convention—signed in 1948, currently 136 parties—and the Convention Against Torture and Other Cruel, Inhuman, or Degrading Treatment—signed in 1984, currently 139 parties (United Nations 2005). The large numbers of states parties to these conventions is an indicator of the broad consensus underlying the norms expressed in the treaties.

A parallel body of rules has developed under the rubric of the laws of war. The Hague Conventions (1907) and the Geneva Conventions (1949, plus the two Additional Protocols of 1977) contain rules on permissible means of combat; the treatment of the sick, wounded, and prisoners; and protections for non-combatants, detainees, and civilian property. Together these conventions are also referred to as "international humanitarian law" (International Court of Justice 1996). The Hague Conventions have long since acquired the status of customary international law, meaning that all states—not just the parties—are obligated to abide by their provisions. The Judgment of the International Military Tribunal at Nuremberg declared that "by 1939 these rules laid down in the [1907 Hague] convention were recognized by all civilized nations, and were regarded as being declaratory of the laws and customs of war" (Roberts and Guelff 1989). By unanimous vote, the UN General Assembly on December 11, 1946 passed Resolution 95(I), which affirmed "the principles of international law recognized by the Charter of the Nuremberg Tribunal and the judgment of the Tribunal," thus confirming the customary law status of the Hague Conventions (United Nations General Assembly A/236). More recently, the International Court of Justice affirmed that "the provisions of the Hague Regulations have become part of customary law, as is in fact recognized by all the participants in the proceedings before the Court" (International Court of Justice 2004).

The 1949 Geneva Conventions may also be regarded as having attained customary international law status (Meron 1998). In fact, the International Court of Justice has declared that the Hague and the Geneva rules must "be observed by all States whether or not they have ratified the conventions that contain them, because they constitute intransgressible principles of international customary law" (International Court of Justice 1996). The Court furthermore quoted approvingly from the Secretary-General's Report on the Statute of the ICTY, which was unanimously endorsed by the Security Council. That Report declared, "The part of international humanitarian law which has beyond doubt become part of international customary law is the law applicable in armed conflict as embodied in" the Geneva Conventions, the Hague Convention (IV) and Regulations, the Genocide Convention, and the Charter of the Nuremberg Tribunal (International Court of Justice 1996). In short, the key rules defining war crimes, in both international and internal conflicts, are by now seen as applying universally, as customary international law.

Finally, the Security Council during the 1990s dramatically expanded the range of actions that it, on behalf of the international community, was willing to take in response to large-scale war crimes and crimes against humanity. In several instances, the Security Council authorized the use of force in response to gross violations of international human rights norms (see Sandholtz 2002; Tesón 1997; Murphy 1996; Ramsbotham and Woodhouse 1996; Holzgrefe and Keohane 2003). The number of such missions generated a label for them: "humanitarian intervention." The Security Council authorized the use of force in the former Yugoslavia in 1992 and 1993, in response to widely publicized evidence of concentration camps, systematic rapes, mass killings, and forced dislocations ("ethnic cleansing"). Additional interventions mandated by the Council included Somalia (1992), Rwanda (1994), and Haiti (1994). In other instances, the Security Council welcomed (though it did not authorize in advance) the intervention of troops from the Economic Community of West African States (ECOWAS) in the brutal civil war in Liberia (1990) and in that in Sierra Leone (1997). Britain, France, and the United States claimed to be acting under Security Council resolutions when they intervened to protect the Kurds in northern Iraq in 1991; that intervention was generally condoned if not explicitly authorized. Similarly, the

Security Council did not approve in advance the NATO intervention in Kosovo (1999), but it also declined the opportunity to condemn it. The Australian-led military mission to East Timor (1999), authorized by Security Council resolution, was not a humanitarian intervention in the same sense as, say, Somalia or Haiti because Indonesia consented, but it was a close cognate. The willingness to approve armed humanitarian interventions is evidence of the solidity of the underlying international human rights norms. The enforcement of international human rights norms was thus widely seen as a legitimate purpose for international action. The criminal tribunals enjoyed the same purposive legitimacy.

The Security Council and procedural legitimacy

With respect to procedural legitimacy, the question is the following: Was the creation of the international criminal tribunals (ICTs) consistent with the rules governing the exercise of authority by the Security Council? The brief answer is "yes," if only because the rules establishing Security Council authority are exceptionally permissive. In essence, the UN Charter allows the Security Council to do whatever it can agree upon. The proper boundaries of Security Council authority are certainly subject to contestation, but there is little question that the current rules permit the Council to create institutions like the ICTY and the ICTR.

Article 24 of the Charter confers on the Security Council "primary responsibility for the maintenance of international peace and security." In fact, this is the only duty of the Security Council explicitly mentioned in the Charter. In carrying out this mandate, the Security Council "shall determine the existence of any threat to the peace, breach of the peace, or act of aggression," and shall "decide what measures shall be taken" (Art. 39). Thus the Security Council itself determines, in any specific instance, whether there is a breach of or threat to the peace and, if so, what action the United Nations should take. The relevant Charter provisions place no limits on the measures that may be ordered, including the use of force (Art. 42). With respect to actions not involving the use of force, Article 41 offers examples of what measures the Security Council *may* authorize (economic sanctions, curtailing diplomatic relations), but sets no bounds.

The Charter also grants to the Security Council wide scope for creating additional institutions. Article 29 declares, "The Security Council may establish such subsidiary organs as it deems necessary for the performance of its functions." Thus, if the Security Council determines that international tribunals are necessary for the performance of its mandate to maintain the peace, then it is fully entitled to create such tribunals. The only Charter limitation on Security Council prerogatives is similarly broad: "In discharging these duties the Security Council shall act in accordance with the Purposes and Principles of the United Nations" (Art. 24(2)). Finally, there is no formal institutional mechanism for any outside body to review or check actions taken by the Council.[4] In short, the rules and procedures governing Security Council action impose virtually no limits. The only real check on Security Council prerogatives is a practical or political one: it can act only if nine members agree and none of the permanent members (the P5) votes against.[5]

But the absence of meaningful formal limits on Security Council authority does not make assessments of the procedural legitimacy of its actions impossible. As in all social settings, legitimacy exists in the eyes of the relevant communities, which constantly evaluate the procedural legitimacy of an institution. Even when formal rules and procedures may be quite expansive, the actors involved in the institution necessarily develop informal understandings of the institution's authority. An institution enjoys procedural legitimacy when its actions stay within the bounds established by the consensus of the relevant actors. Those actors may be constantly negotiating or contesting the boundaries of legitimate institutional action, but their evaluation at any given moment reveals the location of informal social norms regarding legitimate process. With respect to the Security Council, the relevant actors include Council members and other actors affected by the Council's actions. We therefore look to the assessments of Security Council members and other affected states in order to draw conclusions about the procedural legitimacy of the creation of the tribunals.

Because the first two tribunals, the ICTY and the ICTR, were essentially decreed into existence by Security Council resolutions, an assessment of the procedural legitimacy of those actions is crucial. The Yugoslavia and Rwanda tribunals also formed points of reference, to which the discussions in subsequent cases (East Timor, Sierra Leone, and Cambodia) constantly referred. The Special Panels in East Timor were not created directly by the Security Council, but rather by the UN governing authority established by the Security Council. The two last tribunals emerged out of various kinds of agreements between the United Nations and national governments.

The Yugoslav Tribunal illustrates how the Security Council utilized the latitude created by the Charter's expansive grants of authority. In the ex-Yugoslavia, the intensifying wars of the early 1990s transmitted to the rest of the world reports and images of gross violations of international humanitarian law, including mass killings, ethnic cleansing, prison camps, torture, and systematic rape. Several actors, including the Council on Security and Cooperation in Europe, the UN Human Rights Commission rapporteur, the co-chairs of the International Conference on the former Yugoslavia (Cyrus Vance and Sir David Owen), and a Commission of Experts appointed by Secretary-General Boutros-Ghali in October 1992, had recommended the creation of an international criminal tribunal to try those responsible for large-scale violations of international humanitarian law. The Secretary-General submitted a further report and attached to it a draft statute for an international tribunal. The ensuing Security Council Resolution 827 (May 25,

1993) cited "reports of widespread and flagrant violations of international humanitarian law" in the former Yugoslavia, including "reports of mass killings, massive, organized and systematic detention and rape of women, and the continuance of the practice of 'ethnic cleansing'." In the following paragraph, the resolution expressed the Council's determination "that this situation continues to constitute a threat to international peace and security." The resolution ordered the creation of the international tribunal, acting under Chapter VII of the Charter, and required all states to cooperate with the tribunal. The vote was unanimous.

The only objection to the procedure establishing the ICTY came from China. The Chinese representative argued that the tribunal should have been established by an international treaty, and ratified by the concerned governments. To create the tribunal by Security Council resolution was "not in compliance with the principle of State judicial sovereignty." Nevertheless, China voted in favor of the resolution in view of the "special circumstances" in the former Yugoslavia, and insisted that the tribunal would "not constitute any precedent" (United Nations Security Council S/PV.3217). Of course, the ICTY constituted a powerful precedent.

The following spring, for about 100 days between April and July, the Rwandan government incited members of the Hutu community to carry out the slaughter of Tutsis and moderate Hutus. Eight hundred thousand, and possibly a million, Rwandans were killed. Though the United Nations refused to intervene to halt the genocide, the Security Council did decide to seek punishment for those responsible. Security Council Resolution 955 (November 1994) followed the pattern established by the Yugoslav tribunal resolution: it found that the situation in Rwanda continued "to constitute a threat to international peace and security," invoked Chapter VII authority, established the ICTR, and ordered all states to cooperate with the tribunal. The ICTY prosecutor would be responsible for the same duties as the ICTR, which would also share the appeals chamber at the Hague.

When resolution 955 came to a vote in the Security Council, thirteen countries voted in favor, with China abstaining and Rwanda, ironically, voting against. China affirmed that it did not favor reliance on Chapter VII to create an international tribunal. The Rwandan representative explained that his government objected to the short temporal jurisdiction of the ICTR (January–December 1994), given that the planning of the genocide (and other acts of mass killing) had taken place in previous years (United Nations Security Council S/PV.3453). Rwanda had also asked for more judges than the statute provided for, requested that the ICTR have its own prosecutor and its own appeals chamber, and suggested that the court sit in Rwanda. Rwanda also regretted that the ICTR statute ruled out the death penalty, which was permitted under Rwandan law (S/PV.3453). Despite the Rwandan objections, the international community broadly accepted the legitimacy of the process that led to the ICTR, as evidenced by the vote of the General Assembly endorsing the Security Council's decision.[6]

The procedure that produced the Special Panels in East Timor was similar to the ICTY–ICTR process, but with an added layer of delegation. During the period leading up to and following the September 1999 referendum on independence in East Timor, anti-independence militias, supported by the Indonesian military, inflicted widespread killing and destruction throughout East Timor. The Security Council authorized a military intervention led by Australia (and agreed to by Indonesia as it withdrew its forces from the territory) to establish order. The United Nations assumed responsibility for government functions in East Timor. The vehicle for that mission was the United Nations Transitional Administration in East Timor (UNTAET), created by Security Council Resolution 1272 in October 1999 under Chapter VII authority. Using the familiar formula, the Security Council determined that "the continuing situation in East Timor constitutes a threat to peace and security." Resolution 1272 conferred upon UNTAET "all legislative and executive authority, including the administration of justice".

Special investigations sponsored by the United Nations led to proposals for an international tribunal, modeled after the ICTY and the ICTR. Secretary-General Kofi Annan declined that proposal, apparently preferring to accept the pledge of the Indonesian government to investigate the human rights abuses and try any Indonesian perpetrators, and to cooperate with parallel processes in East Timor (Bowman 2004). Meanwhile, UNTAET, in turn, in its Regulation 2000/15 ("On the Establishment of Panels with Exclusive Jurisdiction over Serious Criminal Offenses"), created special panels of judges within the District Court and the Court of Appeals in Dili. The special panels would include two international judges and one local judge, and would have sole jurisdiction over the crime of genocide, war crimes, and crimes against humanity committed between January and October 1999 (Shraga 2004). Though there was nothing technically improper in the establishment of the East Timor Special Panels, they came into existence with a lower level of procedural legitimacy than they might have done. It is not a question of the presence or absence of such legitimacy, but rather one of degrees. UNTAET was essentially an administrative agency, whereas the Security Council is the top decision-making body in the United Nations. The imprimatur of the Security Council would have conveyed a greater degree of procedural legitimacy on the East Timor courts.

In contrast, the Special Court for Sierra Leone and the Cambodian tribunal ("Extraordinary Chambers") were established via treaties signed by the United Nations and the respective governments. In the case of Sierra Leone, the request came in the form of a June 12, 2000 letter from President Alhaji Ahmad Tejan Kabbah to Secretary-General Kofi Annan. The Security Council was not willing to establish an international court under Chapter VII, but it did authorize the Secretary-General to negotiate an agreement to establish a mixed (national and international) court in Sierra Leone. The result was an Agreement between the United Nations and the Government of Sierra

Leone on the Establishment of a Special Court for Sierra Leone (Agreement Between the United Nations and the Government of Sierra Leone 2002) signed on January 16, 2002 and ratified by the parliament of Sierra Leone in March 2002 (Shraga 2004). The Special Court has jurisdiction to prosecute "persons who bear the greatest responsibility for serious violations of international humanitarian law and Sierra Leonean law" committed since November 1996 (Statute of the Special Court for Sierra Leone 2002). As in East Timor, international judges form the majority in the Special Court's chambers. Unlike East Timor, the Special Court is not part of the national judiciary. The treaty mechanism used to establish the Special Court for Sierra Leone is well established in international law and politics, and thus raises few issues of procedural legitimacy. The same procedure applied to Cambodia, however, did raise legitimacy issues.

For Cambodia, the crimes referred to the mass killings perpetrated by Pol Pot and the Khmer Rouge between 1975 and 1979. Approximately 2 to 2.2 million people died, amounting to one-quarter to one-third of Cambodia's population (Etcheson 2004). The process in Cambodia began in 1997 and remains unfinished. Though a UN Group of Experts recommended an international tribunal modeled after the ICTY, the government of Cambodia rejected that approach. China had also promised to veto such a tribunal (Etcheson 2004; Shraga 2004). Cambodia then, in 1999, requested UN assistance in preparing a statute for a special domestic court, with international involvement, to try Khmer Rouge leaders. Secretary General Kofi Annan's legal advisors concluded that the Cambodian statute would not meet international standards and urged that the UN drop out of the discussions (Etcheson 2004). Annan persisted, but finally in February 2002 withdrew from the process, declaring that the court being discussed would not meet UN standards of independence and objectivity (Shraga 2004). The Cambodian government then passed a tribunal law of its own. The General Assembly in December 2002 asked the Secretary General to restart the negotiations; several countries (including the United States, France, Japan, and India) instructed the Secretariat to reach an agreement quickly. Thus the UN and Cambodia signed an agreement in March 2003 outlining the structure and operation of the tribunal, which would conform to Cambodia's preferences. After approval by the General Assembly (May 2003), the UN signed the formal treaty with Cambodia (June 2003) (Etcheson 2004; Shraga 2004). The evident differences between the Secretariat and the General Assembly diminished the procedural legitimacy of the creation of the Cambodian tribunal. The Secretariat was charged with negotiating with Cambodia a tribunal that would meet UN standards. The General Assembly's intervention, mandating an agreement that fell short of those standards, raised questions about procedural legitimacy. Again, the General Assembly's action was not technically improper, but it did raise questions about the integrity of the process and, therefore, about the legitimacy of the Cambodian tribunal.

To summarize, in the case of the two tribunals directly established by the Security Council—the ICTY and the ICTR—there was minimal criticism of the procedures followed. China was the only state to object explicitly to the creation of international tribunals by Security Council resolution, preferring international treaties. Still, China voted in favor of the ICTY resolution and abstained on the ICTR resolution. Rwanda's negative vote on the ICTR was based on substantive, not procedural, criticisms. The other Security Council members supported the creation of the tribunals, and the General Assembly specifically endorsed the ICTR. The international community, then, broadly accepted the procedural legitimacy of the creation of the ICTY and the ICTR. The same is true for the Special Court for Sierra Leone, which came into existence via treaty.

The tribunals for East Timor and Cambodia, however, were created by processes that, though not on their face improper, did raise questions of procedural legitimacy. For East Timor, the Secretary General turned aside the proposal for an international tribunal similar to the ICTY, and accepted instead an arrangement that relied on the willingness of Indonesia to prosecute its own officers. An international tribunal created by the Security Council would have enjoyed fuller procedural legitimacy than did the Special Panels established by UNTAET. The mixed tribunal in Cambodia likewise came into existence under a procedural cloud. Though the agreement between the United Nations and Cambodia was not formally improper, the General Assembly had instructed the Secretariat to agree to a tribunal that the Secretariat had concluded would be unacceptably subject to political influences and would fall short of international standards. Table 7.1 summarizes key features of the five tribunals.

Performance legitimacy: the tribunals in action

Though the creation of a new international body may be widely accepted as legitimate, in both purposive and procedural terms, new institutions do not enjoy automatic legitimacy forever after. Actors shift their attention from the founding to the functioning. An institution must then be able to reaffirm its legitimacy by satisfactorily achieving the community's purposes. Procedural and purposive legitimacy may be necessary, at least initially, but that legitimacy can diminish if the new institution is seen as ineffective, incompetent, or unfair. The international and mixed tribunals vary substantially in the effectiveness with which they are achieving their mandated purposes.

The ICTY

Because the ICTY is the first and longest running of the courts, assessments of its performance are bound to play a critical role in the overall judgment of the international tribunals. Though the ICTY has been criticized for being

Table 7.1 Comparison of the international and mixed tribunals

Tribunal	Legal basis	Year created	Subject matter jurisdiction	Rules of criminal procedure	Judges total (international)	Prosecutors and registrars
International Criminal Tribunal for the former Yugoslavia (ICTY)	Security Council resolution	1993	Grave breaches of the 1949 Geneva Conventions; violations of the laws of war; genocide; crimes against humanity	ICTY rules	16 permanent, pool of 27 *ad litem*, all international	International
International Criminal Tribunal for Rwanda (ICTR)	Security Council resolution	1994	Genocide; crimes against humanity; violations of Article 3 common to the Geneva Conventions	ICTR rules	16 permanent, pool of 18 *ad litem*, all international	International
Special Panels, East Timor	UNTAET regulation	2000	Genocide, war crimes, crimes against humanity based on Rome Statute; some common crimes		Trial panel: 3 (2) Appeals panel: 5 (3)	Prosecutor: International, with mixed staff Registrar: E. Timorese courts administration
Special Court for Sierra Leone	Agreement between the UN and Sierra Leone	2002	Crimes against humanity, war crimes, based on ICTR and Rome Statute	Based on ICTR Rules of Procedure and Evidence	Trial chamber: 3 (2) Appeals chamber: 5 (3)	International
Extraordinary Chambers for Cambodia	Agreement between the UN and Cambodia	2003	Genocide; crimes against humanity as in Rome Statute; grave breaches of Geneva	Cambodian law, with reference to international law if necessary	Pre-trial chamber: 5 (2) Trial chamber: 5 (2) Appeals chamber: 7 (3)	Investigating judges: 2 local, 1 international Prosecutors: 2 local, 1 international Registrar: Cambodian, w/international deputy

slow and expensive, it has developed into a functioning judicial institution, whose jurisprudence is gaining respect.

The beginning, however, was rocky. After its creation in 1993, the ICTY faced an array of difficulties that did not bode well for its credibility. The search for the first chief prosecutor dragged on. The judges were left to compile their own rules of procedure. The tribunal was slow to issue indictments, and even when it did, it confronted huge obstacles in obtaining evidence and in gaining custody of the accused. Severe financial and personnel constraints added to these challenges. However, once the key personnel and procedures were in place, the tribunal gradually gathered momentum, and credibility.

Despite its successes, the ICTY raises ongoing doubts about specific aspects of the international prosecution of individual defendants. One of these concerns time: the process works slowly. Given the scale of the crimes, the evidentiary demands are complex (prosecutors must prove multiple elements of various crimes) (Jorda 2004). The witnesses and evidence are located thousands of miles away, in countries where a great deal of physical infrastructure was destroyed in the wars and where many people (understandably) retain feelings of deep distrust and resentment. The long preparation periods for each case mean that defendants can spend years in custody awaiting trial, and then face lengthy trials. On the one hand, the right of the accused to a speedy trial is compromised; on the other hand, observers might doubt whether perpetrators will ever be convicted of their crimes. Those doubts were renewed when in March 2006 Slobodan Milosevic died in his cell at the Hague, where he had been on trial since 2001.

A second area of concern is the question of which perpetrators are prosecuted. The number of participants in war crimes and crimes against humanity in the former Yugoslavia is certainly in the thousands or tens of thousands. Given such numbers, the ICTY cannot possibly bring to justice every person involved in serious violations of international law. Can a tribunal that is able to prosecute only a small fraction of the thousands who committed serious war crimes and crimes against humanity in the former Yugoslavia be seen as fairly and effectively fulfilling its purpose? That question also arises with respect to high-profile indictees—namely Radovan Karadžić and Ratko Mladić—who remain at large.[7]

The concern with time led to a series of reports by ICTY presidents (chief judges) to the Security Council, which in turn produced a "completion strategy" in resolution 1503 (August 2003). The completion strategy called on the ICTY to complete all investigations by 2004, all first-instance trials by 2008, and all appeals by 2010. The ICTY subsequently took various steps to increase speed and efficiency. Even so, the caseload expanded, with 21 indictees arrested and handed over to the tribunal in 2005. The current president of the tribunal acknowledges that proceedings will continue into 2009 (Ahmedani et al. 2006b).

Under the terms of its "completion strategy," the tribunal will focus on prosecuting the "highest-ranking" leaders. Where does that leave the prosecution of middle- and low-ranking perpetrators? The ICTY has worked out a solution that maintains its legitimacy while dealing pragmatically with the problem of thousands of potential defendants at varying levels of responsibility. Middle-level defendants will be indicted by the ICTY, then handed over to a specialized court in Bosnia-Herzegovina (Jorda 2004). Pursuant to a plan agreed by the ICTY and the Office of the High Representative for Bosnia and Herzegovina, and approved by the Security Council, the creation of a specialized war crimes chamber within the State Court of BiH is underway. International judges and prosecutors will be appointed to the special war crimes chamber during a transition period (Mundis 2005). An interesting feature of this arrangement is that it represents a delegation of criminal justice authority from the international to the national level (albeit with important international participation).

Despite the problems, the ICTY's performance has earned it considerable respect and widespread international legitimacy. The tribunal has carried out its mission while adhering to high standards of due process and protections for the rights of the accused. The ICTY has indicted 161 persons. Of those, 48 have been convicted and sentenced and five have been acquitted. Eleven cases have been referred to national courts, while 36 accused have either died or had their indictments withdrawn. Sixty-one cases are currently in process at either the trial or the appeals stage. Six accused remain at large, but the ICTY has no police arm and must rely on national governments to apprehend and hand over indictees (International Criminal Tribunal for the former Yugoslavia 2007a). The failure to arrest high-profile accused is therefore generally blamed on certain states (like Serbia) and not on the tribunal itself. ICTY cases are now regularly cited by legal scholars and by other courts. Frustration with drawn-out trials and mounting costs is real, but there have been no serious calls to close the tribunal, and the Security Council continues to allocate the funds needed for the ICTY to complete its tasks.[8]

The ICTR

The beginnings of the ICTR were less auspicious than those of the Yugoslav Tribunal. Created by Security Council resolution 955 in December 1994, the tribunal opened its offices in Arusha (Tanzania) after a one-year delay. Though officially open, the ICTR lacked staff, including key prosecutorial and administrative personnel, and basic communications infrastructure. For its first several years, the tribunal's budget was inadequate, though the financial constraints eased after 1998 and by 2001 its annual budget amounted to over $90 million (International Crisis Group 2001). Organizational features may also have contributed to the slow development of the tribunal: for instance, the chief prosecutor for the ICTY was also the chief prosecutor for the ICTR. The two tribunals also shared the same appeals chambers, which were located in The Hague.

Serious concerns quickly emerged regarding the management of the court and the fairness of its proceedings. A 1996 UN audit found serious mis-management at the tribunal, and over the next several years key personnel—including lead prosecutors, investigators, defense attorneys, and court administrators—were found to be incompetent and dismissed (Amnesty International 2002; International Crisis Group 2001). The first trials began in 1997, but ongoing mismanagement and incompetence, combined with a lack of cooperation on the part of the Rwandan government, brought the tribunal's work to a near standstill. The inability of the prosecuting staff to present well-prepared, effective cases, and the failure of the judges to manage trials efficiently (or even to do their work at all), drew intense criticism. A 1998 Amnesty International report lamented the extensive delays that seemed to plague every stage of the tribunal's work, from indictments to motions to trials (Amnesty International 1998). For a 15-month period in 1999 and 2000, the tribunal held only one trial, with one defendant (International Crisis Group 2001). By 2001 the ICTR had rendered only nine verdicts; that same year, two defendants had been in prison for five years and two for nearly six, without coming to trial (International Crisis Group 2001), calling into question the right to be tried within a reasonable time. Even when the trial chambers managed to complete trials, the rendering of verdicts often entailed further delays. For example, a judgment handed down in February 2003 came nine months after the conclusion of the trial; another verdict emerged eleven months after the trial (International Crisis Group 2003b). On top of that, several defense investigators were on the Rwandan government's list of genocide suspects, and another was arrested by the prosecutor in 2001, accused of participating in the genocide (International Crisis Group 2001). The ICTR faced a crisis of legitimacy.

A series of reforms has helped the tribunal to begin to establish credibility and build a degree of performance legitimacy. In 2002, the Security Council created a pool of 18 *ad litem* judges; a resolution the following year increased the number of *ad litem* judges who could be assigned to the Trial Chambers at any one time from four to nine. These temporary judges are not permanent members of the tribunal, but they greatly increase its capacity to try cases. In addition, the Security Council in August 2003 gave the ICTR its own chief prosecutor. In addition, the General Assembly has dramatically increased the budget of the ICTR, which reached about $250 million for 2006–2007 (International Criminal Tribunal for Rwanda 2007), up from $57 million in 1998 (International Criminal Tribunal for Rwanda 1998). The Security Council also required the ICTR, like the ICTY, to submit a "completion strategy," a plan for finishing all trials by the end of 2008 and all appeals by the end of 2010.

The plan submitted by the ICTR president in May 2004 informed the Security Council that the tribunal would concentrate on fewer defendants, focusing "on the accused bearing the heaviest responsibility for the crimes" (United Nations Security Council S/2004/341). The plan also reported that among those tried or awaiting trial were many of the top leadership responsible for the genocide, including the former prime minister, 11 ministers, the president of the National Assembly, 4 prefects, and 4 military officers (S/2004/341). The December 2006 report on the completion strategy noted further progress: a total of 31 judgments rendered, 2 trials completed with judgment pending, trials involving 25 persons in progress, and 11 detainees awaiting trial. Eighteen indictees remain at large. The report forecasts that the ICTR will complete all trial-stage work by the end of 2008; however, that target will be reached by transferring up to 17 prosecutions to national jurisdictions (International Criminal Tribunal for Rwanda 2006). On the basis of its progress in recent years, the ICTR has built a moderate degree of performance legitimacy.

East Timor Special Panels for Serious Crimes

The Special Panels for Serious Crimes and the Special Crimes Unit (SCU, the investigation and prosecution office) came into being in East Timor via regulations issued by the UN administration (UNTAET) in March 2000. By June 2000, the UNTAET held in custody 50 members of the militias that had carried out large-scale atrocities during the period surrounding East Timor's referendum on independence (September 1999). In December 2000, the SCU issued its first indictments for crimes against humanity. But the Special Panels and the SCU were meagerly funded and suffered from a lack of trained, experienced personnel (judges, prosecutors, defenders, court administrators, interpreters). As a result, the work of the court proceeded slowly, and criticism mounted. For example, a 2001 report by Amnesty International concluded that the SCU "has suffered from a combination of inadequate resources, a shortage of experienced staff, poor management and a lack of political support. The slow pace and questionable quality of its work has resulted in a loss of confidence among the East Timorese in UNTAET's ability or will to bring perpetrators to justice" (Amnesty International 2001).

In response to concerns, including those of representatives of the Security Council who visited Dili in November 2000, UNTAET sought to improve the capacity of the SCU, but the defender's unit and the courts themselves continued to be grossly ill-equipped for major international human rights trials. The judges, even the international ones, lacked experience in international humanitarian law. They had no clerks, researchers, or secretaries; they had to take their own notes. There was no law library and, until late 2001, no Internet access. With frequent vacancies on the bench, there were long stretches during which the trial panels could not sit; the resulting backlog meant that defendants could be in custody for over three years with no trial date set. Of the public defenders (including the internationals), none were experienced criminal defense lawyers and only one had a background in international humanitarian law. The defenders had no investigators and interpreters, and no budget for field work or bringing witnesses to the court. In the first 14 trials, not one witness appeared for the defense (Bertodano 2004; Cohen

2002). Genuine reforms were virtually impossible given the meager financial resources allocated to the Serious Crimes process. The budget for the East Timor Serious Crimes apparatus ranged from $6.1 million in 2002 to $7–8 million in 2004–2005 (Cohen 2006a). (Compare those sums to the $276 million allocated to the ICTY for the two-year period 2006–2007; see International Criminal Tribunal for the former Yugoslavia 2007b.)

After East Timor (officially, Timor-Leste) gained independence in March 2002, the Special Panels established under UNTAET continued to function, albeit in a growing crisis of legitimacy. In May 2002, the Security Council responded to the serious challenges facing the new country by creating a UN Mission of Support in East Timor (UNMISET); UNMISET took over UNTAET's role in supporting the Serious Crimes process. Two years later, responding to a request from the Secretary General, the Security Council reduced the size of UNMISET and extended its mission for one year (through May 2005), requesting that East Timor and Indonesia cooperate with UNMISET in prosecuting the 1999 perpetrators of serious crimes. The resolution was, in effect, a recognition that the prosecution of the 1999 atrocities was not progressing well.

In addition to the internal, structural problems, the Special Panels had only limited reach. The political and military leadership behind the 1999 crimes was almost entirely Indonesian. After Indonesia withdrew from East Timor, Indonesian officials suspected of responsibility for atrocities returned to Indonesia. In response to UN and international pressure, Indonesia created in Jakarta an Ad Hoc Human Rights Court for East Timor, which would have jurisdiction over Indonesian perpetrators (Khumprakob et al. 2004). Indonesia's previous conduct with regard to prosecutions invited skepticism: though Indonesia had pledged to cooperate with the East Timor Special Panels, none had occurred (Linton 2001). As of December 2004, out of 392 persons indicted, 303 remained at large in Indonesia (Amnesty International 2005a). Indonesia had not handed over a single suspect, nor had it responded to any Timorese requests for witnesses then residing in Indonesia (Bertodano 2004; Khumprakob et al. 2004). As a result, the East Timor Special Panels could prosecute and punish only the lower-level militia leaders, who were East Timorese. This inequity has undermined the credibility of the Panels as a mechanism of justice (Human Rights Watch 2005c). Only 6 of the 18 persons indicted by the Jakarta court had been convicted by 2004, and all of those convicted were East Timorese (Khumprakob et al. 2004). Five of those convictions were overturned on appeal (Rouleau et al. 2005).

In short, the Special Panels in East Timor faced a sizeable legitimacy deficit. As the East Timorese judge who sat on the panel that handed down the first conviction remarked, "Speaking as a Timorese and not as a judge, I think this system is not fair. Is it fair to prosecute the small Timorese and not the big ones who gave them orders?" (Cohen 2002). A September 2004 conference of East Timorese victims, government officials, jurists, diplomats, and activists in Dili expressed a complete lack of confidence in the Special

Panels and "overwhelmingly advocated for an international criminal court akin to" the ICTR and the ICTY (Khumprakob et al. 2004).

In response to the criticisms, Indonesia and Timor-Leste in December 2004 agreed to a bilateral Truth and Friendship Commission, which would investigate the 1999 human rights abuses and crimes. At about the same time, the United Nations formed a Commission of Experts to evaluate the independence and objectivity of the Human Rights Court in Jakarta and the Special Panels in Dili (Rouleau et al. 2005). However, the governments of both East Timor and Indonesia expressed the view that the Truth and Friendship Commission was the means for addressing the 1999 atrocities, and that the UN Commission was redundant. Human rights activists feared that the bilateral commission would do nothing to promote legal accountability for the perpetrators, and that the legal mechanisms would wither under official indifference (Rouleau et al. 2005).

The UN Commission of Experts evaluated the Special Panels in Timor-Leste and the Ad Hoc Court in Indonesia and submitted its report in May 2005. The report highlighted serious deficiencies in the East Timor court, including inadequate funding, a lack of independence of the prosecutor from the East Timorese government, and a lack of access to suspects and evidence in Indonesia. The report concluded that the Special Panels had "not yet achieved full accountability of those who bear the greatest responsibility" for the 1999 atrocities. With respect to the Indonesian Ad Hoc Human Rights Court, the Commission found that the prosecutions conducted there were "manifestly inadequate," and that the court itself "did not provide for a credible judicial forum that would inspire confidence in the public mind"; rather, the Jakarta process revealed "scant respect for or conformity to relevant international standards." The Commission recommended that the United Nations support the Special Panels until it completed its task of investigating and prosecuting serious human rights abuses. Failing that the Commission urged the creation of an international criminal tribunal under Chapter VII of the UN Charter (United Nations S/2005/458). The Security Council declined to take either of these steps, and when the UNMISET mandate expired in May 2005, the Special Panels in East Timor shut their doors.

Since then, independent evaluations of the Special Panels have been even more critical than the UN Commission of Experts report. Cohen concludes, on the basis of extensive interviews and examination of the documents, that the Serious Crimes process in East Timor "was so deeply flawed from the beginning that, despite the important and successful efforts of key individuals to make structural improvements, egregious problems remained until the very end." His analysis of the proceedings and the Panels' judgments cast doubt on "the basic fairness of a significant number of the Serious Crimes trials" and on "the legitimacy of some of the ensuing convictions."[9] Much of the blame for the courts' failure fell on the United Nations, which "failed so utterly to provide the resources (human, technical, and financial), cooperation, oversight, and political backing necessary to meet the standards" that had been set by the ICTY, the ICTR, and the Sierra Leone Special Court (Cohen 2006b). Indeed, the East Timor Special Panels failed to achieve any degree of performance legitimacy.

Sierra Leone's Special Court

The Special Court for Sierra Leone took shape quite quickly. In January 2002 the United Nations and Sierra Leone signed the agreement creating the court; by July 2002 it had opened its offices in Freetown. The Chief Prosecutor issued the first indictments in March 2003. From the outset, the court's officers, and its supporters in the international community, emphasized that the tribunal should accomplish its tasks efficiently. It would try only the leaders bearing "the greatest responsibility" for the worst atrocities committed during Sierra Leone's civil war; the number of defendants would be limited to fewer than 30 and their trials would be completed in three years (International Crisis Group 2003a). Funding for the Special Court comes from voluntary contributions by states, which has proven to be a somewhat erratic source. In each year of its operations, donations have fallen short of pledges and thus expenditures have exceeded income (Special Court for Sierra Leone 2004, 2005b, 2006). The Special Court has filled the funding gap with special allocations from the United Nations General Assembly (Special Court for Sierra Leone 2005a), and its financial situation has not been nearly as dire as that of the Special Panels in East Timor.

The Special Court has faced some challenges with respect to its international legitimacy. One early difficulty was the perception of excessive U.S. political influence. The United States was the first and largest donor to the Court's funding, and Americans dominated the prosecution staff (including the post of chief prosecutor). The concern was that the United States was using the Special Court to demonstrate the viability of alternatives to the recently created International Criminal Court, which the Bush Administration strongly opposed (International Crisis Group 2003a). Second, though the Court has adhered to its plan of prosecuting the top leaders, that emphasis has given rise to some fairness concerns, as a number of notorious mid-level commanders, not to mention the direct perpetrators, have not been brought to justice (Human Rights Watch 2005b; Kendall and Staggs 2005; Sriram 2006).

Still, the Court has been able to build considerable legitimacy by its performance. First, the perception of U.S. dominance of the staff dissipated with the hiring of internationals from other countries (notably Britain and Canada) and with the recruitment and training of Sierra Leonean personnel (International Crisis Group 2003a). Indeed, in the most recent year, the Court employed 187 Sierra Leoneans out of a total staffing of 315 (Special Court for Sierra Leone 2006). Second, the Court has been seen to carry out its mandate by indicting and prosecuting those responsible for major crimes.

As of mid-2006, the Special Court had indicted 11 suspects, of which one remained at large. Among the indictees were leaders of all of the factions that participated in Sierra Leone's civil war. The Court achieved its greatest coup when it gained custody of former Liberian president Charles Taylor in March 2006.[10] The first trials began in June 2004, and the process accelerated with the opening of a second trial chamber in March 2005. Court proceedings have finished for one set of cases, and the first judgments should appear in 2007. Though concerns remain, the Special Panel for Sierra Leone is widely seen (internationally) as, to a reasonable degree, effectively and fairly fulfilling its mandate. In that sense, it has acquired considerable performance legitimacy.

Cambodia's Extraordinary Chambers

Grave doubts regarding the Extraordinary Chambers of the Courts of Cambodia (ECCC) undermined their legitimacy from the beginning. The General Assembly approved the agreement between Cambodia and the United Nations despite the objections of Secretary-General Kofi Annan and the Secretariat's experts. That June 2003 agreement conformed largely to Cambodia's preferences rather than international standards (Meijer 2004). Just as Cambodia was content to stretch out the negotiations leading up to the agreement, it has consistently acted to slow its implementation. For instance, the Cambodian government did not fill key positions (court administrator, chief prosecutor, judges) until 2005 and 2006, and only designated a site for the Extraordinary Chambers in early 2006 (Ahmedani et al. 2006a, 2006b). The government does not necessarily want to reopen the conflicts surrounding the Pol Pot era, especially since prominent members of the Khmer Rouge joined the government in 1998 (Shraga 2004). Indeed, Prime Minister Hun Sen was himself a member of the Khmer Rouge. In a few more years, the Khmer Rouge leadership will have passed away, and the issue of trials will die with them. Cambodia may well be playing a complex political game. On the one hand it gives the appearance of cooperating with international actors that favor trials, in order to continue receiving substantial aid from Europe, Japan, and the U.S. On the other hand, Cambodia seeks to please China by ensuring that progress is slow enough that there is no prospect of trials. China, which is adamantly opposed to prosecutions, will then keep its substantial aid payments flowing (Etcheson 2004).

The structure of the ECCC guarantees that the Cambodian government will have a hand in virtually every part of its operation, further eroding the Chambers' legitimacy. The Chambers are part of a national judicial system that is viewed as corrupt and closely controlled by the government (Human Rights Watch 2006). The government appoints the director of administration, the chief prosecutor, and a majority of the judges in both the trial and appeals chambers. The United Nations designates the deputy director and nominates candidates for international co-prosecutors and judges. The judges met in November 2006 to decide on rules of evidence and procedure, but the Cambodian participants, led by chief prosecutor Kong Srim (closely tied to the deputy prime minister), insisted that the Extraordinary Chambers' rules must be consistent with those of Cambodia's domestic courts. That demand was unacceptable to the international judges, as some of Cambodia's internal rules fall short of basic international standards (Human Rights Watch 2006). In addition, the government-controlled Cambodian Bar Association (CBA) instructed Cambodian attorneys not to attend a training program on international standards being organized in Singapore by the International Bar Association (IBA). The IBA canceled the conference and strongly criticized the Cambodian Bar Association's actions.[11] Finally, Cambodia has failed to provide its $13 million share of the ECCC's funding (the United Nations is contributing $43 million). The ECCC is therefore seeking additional donations (Ahmedani et al. 2006b).

In short, though the idea of the ECCC enjoys widespread purposive legitimacy—there is broad international agreement that the perpetrators of the killing fields should be held accountable—the Extraordinary Chambers themselves will almost certainly fail to earn performance legitimacy. The Chambers are widely seen as deeply flawed with respect to their independence and adherence to international standards (Williams 2004). As the Human Rights Watch, *World Report 2005*, declares, "The Cambodian government's record of interfering with courts and intimidating judges, as well as the grossly inadequate training of many judicial officials, gives reason for concern that prosecutions could be politically influenced" (Human Rights Watch 2005a). Amnesty International reached a similar conclusion (Amnesty International 2005b). The Secretary General at the outset expressed (diplomatically phrased) doubts regarding the ability of the Chambers to meet international standards (United Nations General Assembly A157/769).

In sum, the performance legitimacy of the international and mixed tribunals is decidedly uneven. The most international of the courts—the ICTY and the ICTR—seem, despite their difficulties, to have achieved a substantial degree of international performance legitimacy. The Special Court for Sierra Leone is gaining credibility. But the East Timor Special Panels were unable to earn performance legitimacy, and the Cambodian Extraordinary Chambers seem to be sliding toward failure as well.

Conclusion

The Security Council, by establishing the international and mixed tribunals, launched a process that has expanded international authority in criminal justice. Prosecution of serious crimes—including international crimes—had previously fallen under national jurisdiction. The ICTY and the ICTR, both created by Security Council resolution, opened the door to this new form of international authority. Their perceived legitimacy was an indispensable foundation for the subsequent mixed tribunals and, more importantly, the

International Criminal Court. Because the Security Council initiated this chain of events, it is fair to conclude that the United Nations was indispensable in "legitimizing judicial intervention" (Scheffer 1996: 38).

Still, as I have argued, though the tribunals generally began with procedural legitimacy (regarding the means by which they were created) and substantial purposive legitimacy (regarding their purposes and objectives), they must earn performance legitimacy if they are to remain viable and functioning. Because legitimacy is the flip-side of authority, declining legitimacy implies diminishing authority. Put differently, to the extent that actors perceive that an institution is losing legitimacy, they will be less likely to accept its authority claims, and will be less likely to comply with its rules and requests. Table 7.2 summarizes the five tribunals with respect to the three types of legitimacy.

Though the procedural legitimacy of the tribunals may be mixed, their purposive legitimacy is substantial. These new international institutions are consistent with, and supportive of, fundamental international human rights norms and values, as these have evolved over recent decades. However, the tribunals cannot live on purposive legitimacy alone. Once functioning, assessments of legitimacy shift to performance. Tribunals that are seen as unfair or ineffective may dissipate some of their initial legitimacy.

In that regard, the mixed tribunals for East Timor and Cambodia seem already to have squandered much of their beginning fund of legitimacy. The Special Panels in East Timor have not been able to prosecute those most responsible for atrocities. The Extraordinary Chambers in Cambodia are still not functioning and are so institutionally vulnerable to government manipulation that there is little hope that they will ever produce justice. The Special Court in Sierra Leone is widely deemed reasonably effective, and the Yugoslav and Rwandan tribunals are handing down credible sentences to major perpetrators and generating a serious jurisprudence.

The legitimacy of the international and mixed tribunals may seem of secondary importance because each has a fixed lifespan. Within a matter of years, all five of these courts will have shut their doors. But the perceived legitimacy of their work could be of significant consequence, for two reasons. First, the experience of the international and mixed tribunals matters for the

Table 7.2 Legitimacy of the international and mixed tribunals

	Purposive legitimacy	*Procedural legitimacy*	*Performance legitimacy*
ICTY	H	H	H
ICTR	H	H	M
East Timor	H	M	L
Sierra Leone	H	H	M/H
Cambodia	H	M	L

Notes: L = low; M = medium; H = high

International Criminal Court (ICC). The ICC began its existence with substantial procedural and purposive legitimacy. But, like its predecessor tribunals, the ICC must be seen to function fairly and effectively, if it is to maintain its authority and gain cooperation and compliance from national governments. The ICC has now received its first referred cases.[12] The stakes are high, not just for the concerned parties but for the ICC itself, whose legitimacy will inevitably be judged by its performance in its initial cases. In addition, to the extent that the international and mixed tribunals lose legitimacy, they may undermine support for international criminal prosecutions in general and for the ICC in particular. Second, the legitimacy of the international and mixed tribunals matters because, despite the existence of the ICC, they may not be the last *ad hoc* tribunals. In some future humanitarian crisis, a special purpose tribunal may be seen as preferable to, or more feasible than, prosecutions at the ICC. At present, 104 states are parties to the International Criminal Court, meaning that some 90 states are not. If, in a future conflict involving genocide, war crimes, or crimes against humanity, some of the states involved are not ICC members, a new *ad hoc* tribunal may well be the best, or the only, mechanism for prosecuting perpetrators. The likelihood of future prosecutions therefore depends in part on the legitimacy of the current set of tribunals.

Notes

1 The distinction parallels the one drawn by H. L. A. Hart between primary rules and secondary rules. Primary rules regulate actions, whereas secondary rules confer the power to make, modify, and interpret primary rules (Hart 1994).
2 Gary Bass assesses the periodic recurrence, and limited role, of international war crimes trials; see Bass 2000.
3 The International Criminal Court was established not by the Security Council but by international treaty. It is therefore outside the scope of this chapter, though the analysis does refer to it periodically.
4 Though no organ has yet formally ruled on the legality of a Security Council action, the International Court of Justice has, in recent cases involving Bosnia and Libya, indicated that there are, in principle, legal limits to the Security Council's powers and that those limits are, in principle, judicially reviewable. See Alvarez 2001; Martenczuk 1999.
5 There is ongoing discussion of whether the composition and procedures of the Security Council need to be modified to reflect changes in international society, but those debates do not bear directly on the procedural legitimacy of the creation of the tribunals. See Hurd 2002; Farley 2005: A4.
6 United Nations General Assembly 1994. Other actors have challenged the procedural legitimacy of the ICTY and the ICTR, arguing that the Security Council exceeded its authority in creating the tribunals. The challenges have come from defendants challenging the authority of the tribunals to prosecute them. The ICTY's Appeals Chamber, in the *Tadic* case, ruled that the Security Council had acted within its legal powers, and that therefore the tribunal was legally established (*Prosecutor v. Dusko Tadic* 1995). The ICTR Trial Chamber reached the same conclusion on a similar jurisdictional motion (*Prosecutor v. Joseph Kanyabashi* 1997). The Special Panel for Sierra Leone similarly ruled that the agreement

establishing the court was valid and that the Security Council had not excessively delegated its own powers (Sriram 2006). Of course, though legality can be an important element of legitimacy, it is not equivalent. It is certainly possible for formally legal conduct to be widely considered illegitimate (Jim Crow laws came to be seen as illegitimate in much of America before they were found to be unconstitutional). Similarly, formally illegal acts may sometimes be seen as legitimate. One assessment of the ICTY views its creation as illegal but legitimate; see Davis 2002.

7 A third area of concern has been the cost of the tribunal, which has totaled more than $1.2 billion from 1993 through 2007; see International Criminal Tribunal for the former Yugoslavia (2007b). Normally, the issue of cost is separate from that of legitimacy. One may acknowledge the legitimacy of an institution yet question the costs incurred. Of course, if high costs were traceable to gross waste, financial mismanagement, or personal corruption, then the performance legitimacy of the institution could also come into question because its capacity to fairly and effectively carry out its mission could be compromised.

8 The ICTY probably enjoys greater legitimacy in the international community (which is the subject of this chapter) than it does in Serbia, where it is frequently regarded with distrust and disdain.

9 Assessments of specific parts of the Special Panels' operations are even more damning, including the conclusion that "legally incoherent decisions . . . call into question the basic competence of some of the international judges of the Court of Appeal" (Cohen 2006b). Indeed, all of the Special Panel judges failed a competency examination in early 2005, a result that may have indicated both inadequate judicial training and incompetence in the preparation of the examination (Cohen 2006b).

10 As leader of a guerrilla army in Liberia, and later as president of Liberia, Taylor was accused of providing advice and material support to the Revolutionary United Front, perhaps the most brutal of the factions in Sierra Leone's civil war. Besieged politically and militarily, Taylor resigned as Liberian president in August 2003; Nigeria granted him asylum. International pressure induced Nigeria in March 2006 to agree to extradite Taylor to Liberia, which would then turn him over to the Special Court for Sierra Leone, which had indicted him in March 2003. Taylor then disappeared, only to be captured while trying to cross into Cameroon. United Nations troops transported Taylor to Liberia and then on to Sierra Leone, where he was placed in the custody of the Special Panel. Taylor's trial will be conducted by the Special Panel in the Hague, where Taylor was transferred in June 2006.

11 Human Rights Watch 2006. The president of the CBA was Ky Tech, who had assumed that position in 2005. With the help of Kong Srim and the Cambodian courts, Ky Tech engineered the nullification of the CBA election that had produced a victory for the independent candidate. Ky Tech, the government candidate, won the new election; see Human Rights Watch 2006; Zagaris 2007.

12 The ICC's first cases include the situation in the Democratic Republic of the Congo, the situation in Uganda, the situation in the Central African Republic, and the situation in Darfur. The situations in Uganda and Darfur in particular appear to pose significant legal and practical challenges.

8   NGOs and the Security Council

Authority all around but for whose benefit?

Jonathan Graubart

In this chapter, I fully subscribe to the core premises of the editors of this volume regarding the significance of the Security Council. It is a body with extraordinary power because it enjoys the authority to govern on behalf of the entire global community. Moreover, since the end of the cold war, the Council has much more frequently exercised its authority and, more significantly, extended its scope of authority into the domestic governance of states. Yet while interjecting a valuable new analytical perspective on a global body only thinly examined theoretically in the international relations scholarship, the editors and the bulk of the contributors to this volume give scant attention to two important characteristics of Council authority. First, Council authority is far from neutral or benign. Rather, it is primarily shaped by policy-makers of the most powerful states, especially the United States, known informally as the "Permanent One" (P1) in UN circles (Malone 2004: 8). To be sure, as Johnstone notes (Chapter 5), deliberation occurs among the "Permanent Five" (P5), the "Elected 10" (E10) and even outside actors, but at the end of the day, the most influential actors in setting the Council's agenda are policy-makers from the United States and its allies. Similarly, the nature of Council authority is largely one-directional, whereby the Council is mostly shaped by the United States and other powerful Western states to exercise authority primarily over weaker states in the Southern hemisphere. Indeed, for much of the Southern population, the authority of the Council to engage in extensive intervention appears to be based substantially on coercive pressure from powerful Western states rather than acceptance of the Council's legitimacy. By mentioning this hierarchical aspect, I do not deny the Council's considerable authority. I do want to emphasize, however, that the Council's authority is politically contentious and skewed.

Second, Council authority does not simply rest on the behavior and attitudes of states. In fact, a set of prominent transnational NGOs in recent years, especially those that provide humanitarian relief to distressed parts of the world, have played a crucial role in expanding the Council's scope of authority to encompass fundamental reconstructions of a state's political, economic, and social infrastructure (so-called "peacebuilding"). Without the involvement of NGOs in these peacebuilding activities, the Council's authority to authorize a type of domestic governance that goes well beyond the original scope of governance allotted to it would not be sustainable. What humanitarian NGOs, like Oxfam, CARE, and World Vision, offer the Council are practical expertise and a globally recognized commitment to humanitarian values. They enable societal reconstruction to proceed with a modicum of competency and to gain wider global acceptability as a sincere humanitarian effort rather than a quasi-imperialistic intervention by great powers to reshape a Southern state.

These two characteristics—authority exercised by and on behalf of the most powerful global actors and the role of nonstate humanitarian actors—are not unrelated. After all, Council-ordered peacebuilding activities occur not simply in response to the degree of humanitarian crisis at stake but due to broader political calculations on the part of the dominant actors that set the Council's agenda and invest the most resources into the peacebuilding. Specifically, the Council orders peacebuilding when policy-makers for the United States and other powerful states have concluded that the operation will likely be compatible with their own political interests in the target state and surrounding region. Hence, these agenda-setting actors welcome the enlistment of humanitarian NGOs as the latter offer practical expertise and moral bona fides to the peacebuilding operation. One can also expect the powerful backers of the operation to cajole participating NGOs to cooperate with their broader political reconstruction plans for the target state.

The remainder of this chapter reviews Council authority, especially its recently acquired peacebuilding authority, with respect to the two commonly neglected characteristics introduced above. In the first part of the chapter, I show how the evolution of Council authority corresponds with broad changes in power politics and in prevailing global norms on the relationship between global security, sovereignty, and appropriate forms of domestic governance. I then situate the growth in influence of transnational, humanitarian NGOs within these broader trends. In so doing, I challenge a common claim in studies of transnational activists (of which humanitarian NGOs represent an important subset) and argue that certain characteristics of influential transnational activists cause them to advance the political agenda of dominant global actors rather than resist it. Finally, I turn to the politics of Council peacebuilding activities and the involvement of humanitarian NGOs to demonstrate how these are primarily designed and implemented to promote the political interests of the powerful sponsors rather than the subject population. Through this review, I hope to provide a wider and more critical lens on the nature of Council authority and on the increased involvement of humanitarian NGOs in Council activities.

Situating the evolution of Council authority in broader global trends

The Security Council has been an important global actor since its inception at the end of World War II. Naturally, it does not operate in a political vacuum. Its influence and scope of activity has been influenced by broader global trends. Most notably, changes in the global political order since the end of the cold war have led to considerable growth in the Council's prominence. This section reviews important changes in the global political order from the cold war era to the present and connects them to evolution in the role played by the Council in global governance. I will show that the Council has shifted from a pluralist cold war approach to one that is aggressively interventionist and partial to the preferences of policy-makers from the United States and allied states.

The post-World War II order featured a predominant United States, a cold war between the United States and the Soviet Union, and the emergence of a Third World, consisting of Latin America and the newly decolonized states of Asia and Africa. Much of the global security tensions centered on the Third World. Both the United States and Soviet Union sought to expand their spheres of influence although the U.S. reach was far greater. At the same time, North–West tension developed over Western military and covert interventions into Southern states and over Southern efforts for a more egalitarian global order (Krasner 1985; McCormick 1989).

Perhaps because of the political impasse between the United States and the Soviet Union and collective demands from the recently decolonized states of the South to reduce great power dominance, the cold war era was marked by a great deal of pluralism. Helping this pluralism was the UN Charter's codification of norms prohibiting the use of force and prioritizing sovereign equality and non-intervention. Although the United States, the Soviet Union, and other states violated these norms in practice, they never denied the norms' applicability and always justified their interventions as either extended self-defense or the product of an invitation from a local government (Gray 2004; Byers 2005). Overall, the global community was pluralist in that it, including the superpowers, accepted the legitimacy of a number of political and economic systems. Even with respect to the noncommunist developing world, it was generally accepted by policy-makers in the United States, other Western states, and in international economic organizations like the World Bank and IMF, that developing states could engage in extensive and varied forms of government intervention into the market (Biersteker 1992; Yergin and Stanislaw 2002).

The Security Council's activities during the cold war followed this pluralist attitude. The framers of the UN Charter envisioned an important but focused role for the Security Council in the post-World War II era. The Council was tasked with assisting in the peaceful settlement of international disputes (under Chapter VI), determining acts of international aggression and

breaches of peace, and enforcing the restoration and maintenance of international peace and security (under Chapter VII). Conceptually, this collective
security function rested on a conventional notion of security from interstate
military aggression. Politically, it was understood that the collective security
role would depend on the support of the great powers. The P5, accordingly,
was given permanent membership and veto power to block Council actions
with the understanding that each would commit itself to the principle of
collective security (United Nations 2004: 64).

During the cold war, the Council rarely exercised its Chapter VII authority
to implement coercive peace enforcement. With the exception of Southern
Rhodesia's extreme racial discrimination, the Council made no sanctionable
judgments on any state's political, economic, or social system (Murphy
1996: 117; Chandler 2006). Instead, the Council adopted a category of
consent-based peacekeeping, whereby the Council authorized neutral outside
forces to serve as a buffer between two belligerent states (Gray 2004: 201–2).
It also passed a number of declaratory resolutions that proclaimed bench-
marks for resolving disputes, such as Council resolutions 242 and 338 on the
Israeli–Arab–Palestinian conflict, and labeled certain behaviors unacceptable,
such as resolution 276 on South Africa's occupation of Namibia (Ratner
2004: 593–600). The Council's behavior reflected the U.S.–USSR divide and
broad support for sovereign equality. The Council exercised considerable
authority but did so in a way that rested on a very broad consensus and that
respected the principle of non-intervention.

With the end of the cold war, the global parameters that guide Council
behavior have shifted considerably. Most notably, the Soviet Union has been
dissolved. Although the Soviet Union was dwarfed in overall power and
influence by the United States, it partially checked U.S. interventionism.
While Russia is a powerful state that is not a U.S. ally, it is far less influential
than the Soviet Union and less of an obstacle to the global ambitions of U.S.
policy-makers. As a result, the United States has become more aggressive in
promoting its global agenda. Another notable change in the global order that
predates the end of the cold war is a shift in the prevailing global economic
order. Up to the 1980s, the international community was both pluralist in
general with respect to a state's choice of economic systems and tolerated
considerable variation even within the part of the world that roughly sub-
scribed to capitalist economics. Prior to the 1980s, it was accepted that liberal
economics are embedded in social concerns whereby it is appropriate for
states to exercise considerable state intervention and selective protectionism
(Ruggie 1983). Since the 1980s, the prevailing liberal framework has become
less socially embedded. This "neoliberalism" emphasizes greater conform-
ance with market economics, a reduced public sector, and liberalization of
trade and investment (Williamson 1990).

Collectively, the demise of the Soviet Union and the global transformation
in favor of neoliberalism has resulted in the shift, albeit tentative, from a
pluralistic vision of sovereignty to a more assertive liberal global order. Under

the emerging new order, the United States, Western Europe, and regional and global bodies are increasing pressure on states, especially in Central and Eastern Europe and the South, to adopt liberal democratic systems that feature contested elections, a strong private sector, individual rights, and a rule of law.

Such changes in the global order have dramatically altered the role of the Council. To begin with, the end of the U.S.–USSR divide has enabled it to exercise its Chapter VII coercive authority, in a manner largely conducive to the goals of U.S. policy-makers. Thus, in 1990, the Council passed a Chapter VII resolution to enable a U.S.-led coalition to remove Iraqi troops from Kuwait. Subsequently, it has approved more than twice the number of military interventions (be it peace enforcement or peacekeeping) than those approved during the entire cold war span (Paris 2004: 17). More fundamentally, the Council has successively reinterpreted its mandate in favor of aggressive intervention into the domestic governing and societal practices of certain states. This change originated in 1991, after Saddam Hussein repressed an insurrection in the Shiite-dominated south (Murphy 1996). The U.S.-led coalition took no action against Hussein's response because it was an internal Iraqi matter. The coalition, however, changed course by the subsequent crackdown in the north and prohibited Iraqi forces from entering the Kurdish-dominated areas (Murphy 1996). In acquiescing to this action done under the implied mandate of a Council resolution, the Council extended its authority to internal matters (Weiss 1999b: 22). Thus, the most influential states and global policy-makers agreed that human rights atrocities and mass instability implicate international security and merit outside intervention (Murphy 1996: 284). The Council has since authorized interventions in other areas facing internal violence and instability, such as Somalia, Bosnia, and Haiti.

These authorized interventions go further than simply halting the immediate domestic crisis. In fact, the Council authorizes interventions that are empowered to engage in extensive reconstruction of the crisis state's political, economic, and social institutions. Consistent with the emergence of an assertive global liberal order, the intervention aims to insert a liberal democratic model that features contested elections, limited government, a strong private sector, and globally open markets (Duffield 1997: 530; Paris 2004). The Council has, hence, redefined global security so that it is linked to the domestic adoption of liberal democratic political, economic, and social systems. This agenda corresponds with the liberal assertiveness promoted in general by policy-makers in the United States and Western Europe.

Overall, the Council's exercise of authority in the post-cold war era primarily benefits a particular set of powerful global actors rather than the global community at large. This one-sided nature is reflected in the way the Council delegates its authority. Since its inception, the Council has delegated authority because of limited operational capacity. During the cold war, member states contributed troops voluntarily to Council peacekeeping operations, who were under Council control (Chesterman 2001). What is new in the post-cold war era is that the Council has largely surrendered supervisory authority for peace enforcement operations to "coalitions of the willing," meaning the state or states authorized to carry out the military intervention (Chesterman 2001). The United States initiated this practice in the first Persian Gulf War. After the death of eighteen U.S. soldiers in Somalia in 1993, President Clinton made this arrangement permanent by resolving that the United States would only participate militarily in UN operations where it retained complete control over its soldiers and where a clear U.S. national interest is at stake.[1] Other states, like Australia in East Timor, have followed suit. These interveners often resume a predominant role in subsequent peacebuilding.

A common view expressed by global diplomats and academics is that the expanded scope of Council authority reflects and furthers a collective shift from conventional state sovereignty to a global community ethos (see, for example, United Nations 2004). This characterization is substantially misleading. Rather than reflect global community values, the Council's post-cold war interventionist norm reflects the interests and values of the United States and other powerful Western states. After all, the United States and its allies play the main role in attaining a Council resolution authorizing intervention and in shaping the intervention to follow liberal norms.[2] Moreover, Council-authorized interventions are not applied universally but limited to relatively weak, conflict-ridden states that are mostly located in the South. Accordingly, the Council's new interventionist agenda does not reflect a wholesale undermining of sovereignty but, rather, an attack on sovereign equality, whereby only weak states without influence lose their sovereign protections from coercive intervention. It is this disjuncture that triggers discontent in much of the South at the new norm of intervention.

Why transnational humanitarian NGOs have become important players in the Council's agenda

The other major innovation in Council authority in recent years, along with its intervention into the domestic affairs of selected Southern states, has been the substantial incorporation of prominent humanitarian, human rights, and development NGOs into Council activities. These groups lobby the Council to take actions, meet regularly with Council members, shape various Council initiatives, and most significantly, play a lead role in implementing the state reconstruction tasks called for in peacebuilding. Just as Council authority cannot profitably be viewed in a vacuum, neither can the extensive recent involvement of transnational NGOs in Council-mandated operations. This section provides a context for understanding why humanitarian NGOs, in particular, have become important actors in Council-ordered peacekeeping and how such involvement comports with dominant global trends. I focus on two important global developments over the past several decades: the rapid growth in influence of transnational activists and the coming to prominence of a market-friendly, neoliberal view of political economy among elite global policy-makers. These two trends have converged to make transnational humanitarian NGOs the agents of choice in Council-authorized interventions for providing emergency relief and economic and political reconstruction.

The growth in influence of transnational activists

As transnational humanitarian NGOs are a subset of transnational activists, it is useful to first understand the major characteristics of transnational activists and how they attain influence. Activists are actors that derive their identity primarily from a commitment to principled norms of right and wrong rather than conventional material interests (Keck and Sikkink 1998: 1–9; Abbott and Snidal 2002). Transnational activists operate beyond state borders by working on global causes, networking with activists in other states, utilizing international institutions, and invoking international norms. Transnational activists seek to interject principled norms onto the global agenda, mobilize popular support, and pressure states to comply with such norms. They focus on human rights, environment, peace, and global economic governance (Smith 1997; O'Brien et al. 2000; Graubart 2004).

Although transnational activism has a long history, it has rapidly expanded in the past several decades due to advances in communication and travel, increased global interdependency, and a transformed understanding of social values, like human rights, poverty reduction, and environmental sustainability, as global concerns (Smith et al. 1997; Keck and Sikkink 1998). Perhaps the most important stimulus is the proliferation of global institutions and meetings at the UN and elsewhere. These enable activists to boost the status of their cause and gain new allies (Smith 1997; Keck and Sikkink 1998).

To attain influence, transnational activists rely foremost upon their reputation as committed upholders of principled norms of right and wrong. In addition, activists gain influence through their expertise, their connections to a network of actors, including local activists and influential policy-makers, and their public support. In short, activists count on their legitimacy as appropriate, competent, and untainted actors for promoting and implementing well-regarded norms of behavior, such as human rights. They employ a mix of tactics. One valuable tactic is dissemination of information to the media, the broader public, allies, and officials of governments and global bodies (Keck and Sikkink 1998: 16–22). Activists report on the factual situation (e.g., the level of human rights violations) and on the legal-normative standards (Smith et al. 1997: 69–73). Other important tactics include recruiting and mobilizing supporters, protesting, and lobbying (Smith 1997: 42; Keck and Sikkink 1998: 16–26).

The extent of influence is open for debate but transnational activists have undoubtedly become significant global actors. They have strengthened local movements, pressured changes in states' foreign policies, influenced the policies of global bodies, like the World Bank, and helped draft multilateral treaties, like the Rome Treaty that established the International Criminal Court (Brett 1995; Willets 1996; Welch 2001). The most sustained success is gaining access, which includes consultative status at the UN's Economic and Social Commission and regular audiences with officials at states and at major global bodies, like the World Bank, the World Trade Organization, and the Security Council (O'Brien et al. 2000; Paul 2004).

De-romanticizing transnational activists

The scholarship on transnational activism imparts valuable insights on such aspects as the creative strategies applied by activists, the means by which they take advantage of political platforms to advance their agenda, their networking abilities, and the optimum conditions and issues for success. It suffers, however, from a romanticized view of transnational activists. Such scholarship assumes that because transnational activists are driven by principled norms, they exert a meritorious and antisystemic influence that impels global bodies and governments to elevate grassroots-driven moral principles over *realpolitik* interests of the powerful (e.g., Keck and Sikkink 1998; O'Brien et al. 2000). As a result, the literature fails to appreciate certain salient dynamics of transnational activists that legitimate and reinforce existing inequalities in the global order, rather than challenge them.

One such dynamic is Western-centricism. The leadership of the prominent, transnational NGOs is predominantly Western. As a result, the groups privilege a set of Western liberal norms based on equality, individual rights, and contested elections. Similarly, Western-centricism leads transnational NGOs to be less attentive to issues of particular concern to populations in the South, such as local political, social, and economic practices, deep West–South inequalities, and the role of Western elite actors in maintaining a stratified global order (Duffield 1997; Mutua 2001; Mazurana et al. 2005).

A second common dynamic of transnational activism is an elite Western-based incentive structure. For example, many prominent humanitarian and development NGOs rely on Western governments and Western-dominated global bodies for the bulk of their funding (Duffield 1997; Mutua 2001). Hence, they face strong incentives to justify their activities not to the populations they purportedly serve but to Western benefactors (Schloms 2003). Success, then, is measured according to values and interests of Western states and global bodies. In addition to funding, transnational activists depend primarily on Western populations for membership and support. To gain Western interest, such groups often employ what some critics refer to as a "fairy story" of Southerners as victims and Westerners as rescuers (De Waal 1997; Chandler 2001). Under this narrative, the emphasis is on blameless victims and murderous villains (both in the target state) and the appeal is for an outside "savior" from the West. Success is bringing Western liberal values to troubled Southern states. Deeper historical and structural patterns that complicate the picture are slighted.

Given the Western-centric and opportunistic tendencies of transnational NGOs, their insistence that principled norms, like human rights, trump the principle of state sovereignty presents troubling implications for West–South relations (Chandler 2006). In the abstract, this priority is sensible with respect to the prevention of massive human rights atrocities. Yet when seen in the context of great global power imbalances, the disregard for sovereignty is far less benign. Even putting aside the Western-centricism of the benchmark norms used to justify intervention, the implementation of this post-sovereignty principle will be decidedly one-sided. Specifically, the states that will experience intrusions upon their sovereignty will not all be states that fail to uphold the benchmark norms but only those that lack power and prestige to resist outside intervention. Such states are mostly in the South. Similarly, given the costs of such intervention, the parties called upon to engage in the intervention will often be powerful Western states. Accordingly, the effect of weakening sovereign protections will be a selected, rather than generalized, eroding of sovereignty, to the detriment of Southern states.

Of course, transnational activists encompass a broad variety of actors. Some, like solidarity social justice groups, may not exhibit these more problematic, status-quo enforcing characteristics. Such is not the case, however, for the bulk of transnational humanitarian NGOs, to be discussed below.

The growth in prominence of humanitarian NGOs

Humanitarian NGOs have become one of the most influential groups of transnational activists. Originally, such groups were not activists in the sense of advocating for specific causes. Rather, like the standard bearer, the International Committee for the Red Cross (ICRC), humanitarian groups existed to provide relief to all victims of conflict and other calamities (Weiss 1999a). In more recent decades, a number of activist transnational humanitarian groups have emerged, such as Medecins Sans Frontieres (MSF), Oxfam, and CARE, that provide relief services and advocate (Weiss 1999b; Chandler 2001). Such advocacy has until recently meant insisting that all parties provide civilian access to relief services and comply in general with international humanitarian standards set forth in the Geneva Conventions and customary international law (Torrente 2004: 32).

Humanitarian NGOs have employed common transnational activist tactics to attain influence and gain access to governments and influential global bodies. What has really helped them, however, is the global predominance of neoliberal economic governance. Neoliberalism features market-oriented, deregulatory economic policies. These policies feature a restricted state role in the economy and reduced state spending on infrastructure and social welfare (Eichengreen and Kenen 1994: 32; Kitson and Mitchie 1995). The leading advocates of neoliberalism since the 1980s have been the U.S. and

U.K. governments and officials from the leading global economic governing bodies, such as the World Bank and IMF (Haggard 1995). Neoliberalism's prominence became manifest in the South, especially in Latin America and Africa, in the wake of severe debt crises in the 1980s. Prodded by internal changes among leading political and economic figures and pressure from the U.S. government, private banks, the World Bank, and IMF, many of these states fundamentally restructured their economies away from populism and heavy state intervention into the economy (Biersteker 1992; Haggard 1995). Taking their place was a set of policies known as the "Washington Consensus," which includes reductions in state spending, liberalization of markets, and privatization (Williamson 1990).

This new paradigm has changed the nature of foreign aid. Consistent with the Washington Consensus, assistance from the United States, global bodies, and other wealthy Western states has been made conditional on the recipient state restructuring its economy along neoliberal lines. Particularly important for donors is a reduction of the state's involvement in the economy. One major means applied by governments and global bodies to express their wishes is channeling their assistance through NGOs rather than directly to the governments of the recipient states (Duffield 1997: 532; Chandler 2001: 686). Since the 1990s, NGOs have served as the vehicle for well over 10 percent of total public development assistance and more than that distributed by all UN agencies (Weiss 1999b: 20). Some of this aid is distributed to local NGOs in the recipient states (Weiss 1999b: 29). The primary NGO beneficiaries, however, have been a small subset of well-endowed transnational NGOs involved in humanitarian relief and, sometimes, development, such as Oxfam, CARE, World Vision, and MSF (Weiss 1999b: 11; Stoddard 2003). Such large and federated NGOs are considered more convenient partners for UN agencies and other donors (Smith and Weiss 1997: 606).

It bears remarking that some of these NGOs are quite critical of neoliberalism and genuinely supportive of local, sustainable development. Nevertheless, their substantial role in allowing governments and global bodies to bypass local governments in giving aid to Southern states has facilitated a neoliberal paradigm. In fact, the prominent transnational humanitarian NGOs have proved remarkably cooperative in the recent effort of policymakers in the United States and other Western states to use Council-authorized peacebuilding as a new means to advance a neoliberal agenda.

The Council–NGO partnership in peacebuilding

Having situated the recent activities of the Security Council and prominent humanitarian NGOs in a set of global dynamics that advance the agenda of the most powerful global actors and effectively undermine North–South sovereign equality, I turn to the most intrusive Council activity of recent years, peacebuilding. This is the area of Council activity in which NGOs, especially humanitarian ones, have been most influential. Global policy-makers and academic commentary have been largely favorable toward peacebuilding and of NGO partnership in this enterprise. At face value, peacebuilding is indeed quite appealing. It is prescribed by the Council as a necessary response to a "complex emergency," which is defined by the UN's Inter-Agency Standing Committee as "a humanitarian crisis in a country, region, or society where there is a total or considerable breakdown of authority resulting from internal or external conflict" (cited in Weiss 2005: 12). Rather than just halt the immediate conflict, peacebuilding aims to address the root socioeconomic and political causes and reconstruct the society (Camilleri, 2002: 247; Keating and Knight 2004: xxxii–xxxiv). A close probing, however, reveals that peace-building is initiated by elite global policy actors, supported by transnational NGOs, with the aim of imposing Western friendly, liberal institutions upon mostly Southern states.

Peacebuilding involves extensive "social engineering," whereby outside par-ties reconstruct a state's security, political, economic, and social institutions (Paris 2004; Weiss 2005). The Council has authorized numerous peacebuild-ing missions in the post-cold war era, which extend to Central America, Africa, Asia, the Balkan states, and the Middle East (Paris 2004). The degree of reconstruction has ranged from modest police reforms to the comprehen-sive nation building in East Timor, Kosovo, Afghanistan, and Iraq. The manner of delegation has also varied with UN agencies in charge in some areas, such as Kosovo and East Timor, and coalitions of the willing assuming command elsewhere, as in Bosnia and Iraq (Matheson 2001; Chandler 2006). What unites all peacebuilding operations is a liberal democratic orientation based on a market economy and global openness, contested elections, indi-vidual rights, a strong private sector, a modest public sector, and a rule of law (Chinkin 2003: 868; Paris 2004).

For much of the reconstruction, the authorities directing the peacebuilding have contracted with transnational humanitarian NGOs, such as CARE, World Vision, and Oxfam, and with human rights and democracy NGOs to perform relief and reconstruction tasks, like humanitarian services, nurturing of private businesses, development of public infrastructure, creation of legal and political institutions, and human rights monitoring (Smith and Weiss 1997: 614; Mazurana et al. 2005: 20). This extensive delegation reflects a wide appreciation of NGOs' expertise, resources, contacts, and status (Weiss 1999b). Many NGOs have welcomed the delegated tasks and supported a partnership with the intervening parties (O'Brien 2004). They view Council endorsement of the peacebuilding mission as an opportunity to enhance their primary mission of aiding communities in crisis.[3]

Not only participating humanitarian NGOs but also a broader liberal internationalist community of high-level global diplomats and academics are strong proponents of peacebuilding. Starting with Boutros-Ghali's call for an Agenda For Peace (1992), UN Secretary Generals have commissioned several multinational task forces to, in part, rally increased global resources and support for peacebuilding.[4] Policy-makers of Western states are especially supportive (International Peace Academy 2001). Even the present Bush Administration, which is at odds with the UN over the unauthorized U.S. invasion of Iraq, has embraced peacebuilding. In both Afghanistan and Iraq, it has embarked on extensive state reconstruction along liberal norms and received the authorization of the Council (Berger 2006). By contrast, there is much resistance in Asia and Africa to the Council authorizing such activities (International Peace Academy 2001).

Genuine supporters among global policy actors and NGOs laud peace-building as a means of moving beyond a global order based on self-interest and *realpolitik*. They assume that peacebuilding is based on a commitment to a set of norms that are neutral and universal and, thus, in the public interest of the target society. This assumption does not hold up to close scrutiny. After all, the consistent liberal democratic emphasis on peacebuilding belies the claims from intervening parties that peacebuilding is only concerned with restoring sustainable self-government. The benchmark liberal democratic norms are not the ideas of local populations but, rather, those of a network of elite global actors, like the United States, other Western states, the Council, and other global bodies (Paris 2004). These norms are not unique to peace-building but parallel the Washington Consensus framework advanced by the United States, other Western states, and global economic bodies for reconstructing political and economic institutions in developing states.[5]

Supporters of peacebuilding defend liberal democratic values and point to peacebuilding missions that have improved humanitarian and human rights conditions. Yet the liberal democratic bias of peacebuilding is far more prob-lematic than the picture presented in UN-sponsored task forces or scholarly analysis. For one thing, its narrow prism excludes from diagnosis of root causes important structural global factors, such as West–South inequalities, weak Southern representation in global governance, damages inflicted by historic and, often persisting, direct and indirect great power interventions, and the ways neoliberal-led economic globalization has generated economic dislocation, greater inequality, and social unrest in many developing states. Hence, the prescription to reduce the role of the state, adopt market econom-ics, and freely open one's economies to international trade and investment can readily exacerbate societal instabilities (Paris 2004). For another thing, the insistence upon a standard liberal democratic framework hinders incom-patible indigenous forms of reconstruction. Interveners have dismissed as spoilers factions in target states that reject the liberal democratic framework (Richmond 2004: 94).

One may hope, along with supporters of peacebuilding, that the involve-ment of humanitarian NGOs would check the tendencies of policy-makers from the United States and allied states to use Council-authorized peace-building for their own agenda. To be sure, transnational NGOs have con-tributed a few positive features to peacebuilding. The most notable are facilitating delivery of humanitarian assistance, enabling local groups with pre-existing relationships to transnational NGOs to take part in the peacebuilding, and persuading the administrators of the peacebuilding to promote protection of fundamental human rights (Weiss 1999b). Overall, however, transnational humanitarian NGOs have supported rather than challenged the elite domination of peacebuilding.

Contrary to common scholarly expectations of transnational activists playing an antisystemic role, it is actually not surprising that the involvement of humanitarian NGOs in peacebuilding has exacerbated an elite-friendly vision of reconstruction. As discussed above, humanitarian NGOs in the age of neoliberalism have adopted, at least to some degree, a subservient relationship with policy-makers in the United States, other wealthy industrialized states, and global governing bodies, like the World Bank. Specifically, they have willingly been used as a prime vehicle for funnelling aid from the United States, Western Europe, and U.S.-dominated global bodies in a way that bypasses government agencies of the recipient states and thus encourages a weak state apparatus.

The dynamics pushing humanitarian NGOs to adopt a subservient attitude are magnified in the peacebuilding setting. After all, they are dependent on the parties in charge of the peacebuilding for the contracts to provide services and for access to the target populations (Gordenker and Weiss 1997). Generally, the administering party expects participating NGOs to cooperate with the security and broader political objectives of the intervention (Torrente 2004; Rieff 2004). The United States has been especially demanding, as in Afghanistan, where Secretary of State, Colin Powell, implored U.S.-based NGOs to promote American values and be a "force multiplier for us."[6] Although NGOs considered Powell's comments to be inappropriate (Scott 2004: interview), they have generally been cooperative in peacebuilding. As the advocacy director for CARE in Afghanistan remarks, a number of humanitarian NGOs have shifted their understanding of humanitarianism to consider the underlying political factors that enable the humanitarian crises (Weiss 1999b: 214–219; O'Brien 2004). In so doing, they have shed their traditional neutrality and linked their mission to political-security objectives of the interveners (Weiss 1999b: 215). Such linkages typically include targeted withholdings of relief until the region's dominant faction agrees to disarm or to some other major concession (Weissman 2004b; Rieff 2004).

Reflections on Council authority, peacebuilding, and the role of NGOs

There are a number of lessons to be drawn from the partnership between humanitarian NGOs and the Council in peacebuilding, some of which directly relate to the principal concerns of this volume on the nature and significance of Council authority. Other lessons concern far-reaching normative implications on Council authority in the contemporary era.

Lessons on Council authority and on how it interacts with the authority of NGOs

One very useful lesson to be drawn from Council-authorized peacebuilding is the pivotal role humanitarian NGOs play in enabling the Council's extraordinary extension of its authority into nation-building. Both the Council, collectively, and its most influential members, realized in the aftermath of the first Persian Gulf War that neither the Council, the coalition of willing states, nor the UN's humanitarian and development agencies were capable of administering the massive reconstruction efforts called for in the expanded Council mandate (Weiss 1999b). Given its limited capacity and heretofore limited association with humanitarian causes, the Council would have likely seen its legitimacy to order such extensive interventions quickly dissipate. What saved the Council's authority was its delegation of many reconstruction tasks to transnational humanitarian NGOs. The latter provided a much needed boost in the legitimacy and capability of such extensive operations.

A related lesson is the generating effect of Council authority on the authority of NGOs. As the editors note in the introduction, the enhanced Council authority does not necessarily detract from state authority. In fact, as discussed in this chapter, policy-makers of the United States and other influential states are well aware that Council authority can boost the authority of their own states to engage in extensive intervention. Thus, they have welcomed the extension of Council authority into peacebuilding because it legitimates interventions by coalition of the willing states as interventions done on behalf of the global community. In turn, the actions of the coalition of the willing give teeth to the Council's authorization power, even if they are implemented with minimal Council supervision. A similarly complementary relationship exists between the authority of the Council and the authority of a group of transnational humanitarian NGOs. Such NGOs are looking to elevate humanitarian concerns over sovereignty norms and to promote their own competency and commitment to providing for humanitarian needs. By authorizing peacebuilding operations and contracting directly with the NGOs to provide substantial relief and reconstruction tasks, the Council lends a powerful imprimatur to the NGOs. Indeed, the Council often justifies its authorization of peace enforcement operations as needed to secure access to humanitarian relief (Duffield 1997: 530; Reindorp 2002: 31). As such, the Council is validating the authority of transnational NGOs to bypass state sovereignty with respect to states undergoing internal crises.

There is one significant distinction, however, between the complementary relationship of Council and NGO authority and that of the Council and intervening states. While the latter enjoys virtually plenary control, NGOs' authority is decidedly subordinate to that of the intervening parties. Although the supervision can be limited at times (Gordenker and Weiss 1997: 451–2), the dependence of NGOs on the funding and military access of the intervening troops means they will be pressured to conduct their activities in a manner consistent with the political-security objectives of the intervening parties (Torrente 2004). As a result, there has been considerable tension, with some NGOs, like MSF, harshly critical of this constraint on their autonomy and neutrality (Torrente 2004; Bradol 2004). Accordingly, the Council–NGO relationship has not been completely synergistic. Rather, it has negatively affected the autonomy and, by extension, authority of NGOs. This dynamic invites profound normative concerns to be addressed below.

Authority all around but for whose benefit?

Security Council authority and the involvement of humanitarian NGOs with respect to peace enforcement and peacebuilding raises momentous normative questions. After all, the global community is bestowing upon the Council the authority to enable powerful coalitions of the willing to embark upon vast military, political, economic, and social interventions into the domestic affairs of mostly Southern states. To be sure, there is some seductive appeal to granting the Council this extensive authority. Sadly, there is no shortage of areas facing deadly conflict and humanitarian calamities. Moreover, the Council is the only external actor with widespread authority to intervene and attempt to redress the situation. Council-authorized interventions are the only external, armed interventions that do not radically disrupt an acceptable international legal process (see Cronin's chapter (4) in this volume).[7] A further appeal of directing these domestic interventions (sometimes referred to as "humanitarian interventions") through the Council is that it ensures some form of multilateral process, even if far from universal. All Council coercive actions require affirmative votes of nine member states and the acquiescence (either by affirmative vote or abstention) of all P5 states. As the High Level Panel on Threats, Challenges, and Change and other supporters maintain, such a multilateral process backed by legal authority is preferable to unilateral interventions, such as has substantially been the case with the U.S. invasion and reconstruction of Iraq.

One can also see the appeal of significantly incorporating prominent transnational humanitarian NGOs into the peacebuilding. They, collectively, possess extensive networks in place throughout the globe, experience and commitment, and expertise in providing humanitarian relief. Such qualities enable Council-authorized interventions to be more effective and connected to local organizations.

What is disturbing about most of the supportive commentary from a community of global diplomats, academics, and prominent NGOs is their inattention to the most worrisome aspects of Council authority to order wholesale interventions. Such interventions go well beyond halting the armed conflict or alleviating the immediate humanitarian crisis. In addition, they are typically delegated to a powerful state or coalition of states who enjoy virtually plenary control (Chesterman 2001). Given the considerable resources the intervening states are expending, they are likely to privilege a restructuring that furthers their own political-security-economic interests over that of the affected population. As a result, expanded Council authority is legitimating interventions of regional or global powers into the affairs of weaker, mostly Southern states.

Even the multilateral Council decision-making requirement is not an effective impediment where one or more of the P5 states is able to secure the consent of the others for a self-interested intervention. Such a scenario is readily plausible in light of the unprecedented power and influence of the United States (see Ferguson 2004). The United States has even been able, repeatedly, to cajole the consent (via abstentions) of China and Russia to accommodate U.S. interests. True, the United States was unsuccessful in securing Council approval for the invasion of Iraq in 2003. Yet it secured a number of favorable preliminary and post-invasion resolutions to, at least, partially facilitate extensive U.S. restructuring of Iraq.

In fairness, the level of delegation to a single state or a coalition of the willing varies across the Council-authorized peacebuilding operations. But even the interventions that are not directly controlled by a powerful state are still shaped by a skewed collective norm of liberalism (Paris 2004). Under all such interventions, the normative framework of a limited state sector, a strong private sector, a market-based and globally open economy, and contested elections is imposed by a great power-dominated body upon a vulnerable state. By contrast, there is little consideration for alternative visions more rooted in the values and experiences of the affected population. It is this one-sidedness in intervention that undermines sovereign equality to the detriment of less influential Southern states.

The involvement of transnational humanitarian NGOs does not mitigate this biased form of intervention. In fact, as argued above, they generally advocate for intervention from powerful Western states and, at least to some degree, the adoption of Western-style political, economic, and social institutions. As a result, they have been readily enticed to cooperate with the policies followed by the intervening parties, who offer access, resources, and official prestige. Moreover, the involvement of humanitarian NGOs legitimates the intervention as a humanitarian one. Active cooperation by the NGOs in the determination of where and how to provide humanitarian relief supports the intervener's story of which belligerent party is at fault and what the political resolution should entail. Furthermore, NGOs' cooperation in the political and socioeconomic reconstruction advances the development agenda of the interveners, who seek to impose a neoliberal model.

Finally, NGO co-optation to the political-security interests of the intervening states undermines the neutrality of humanitarianism. Such neutrality involves a separation of humanitarian activity from political goals and a decision-making process based exclusively on meeting the needs of the besieged population (Stoddard 2003; Torrente 2004). By politicization, I do not mean the practice made famous by MSF of openly denouncing states and nonstate belligerent parties who violate humanitarian principles. Rather, I mean linking relief to broader political-security goals, often formulated by the intervening states, such as disarmament and agreement to a particular political settlement (Weissman 2004b). Besides undermining a fundamental global norm institutionalized in international humanitarian law (Benvenisti 2004) with an ad-hoc, easily abused political calculation, such politicization fundamentally hinders the capacity of humanitarian NGOs to provide relief. Having become viewed as tools of the outside intervening parties, relief workers have been banned from territory controlled by belligerent forces and targetted for kidnapping and murder (Gidley 2004; Logan 2004).

One may still wish to argue on behalf of Council-authorized peacebuilding and peace enforcement on the basis that, however problematic, it can still be better than no outside intervention. Perhaps the levels of suffering under certain regimes can justify this revived license to undermine the sovereignty of states in the Southern hemisphere. Yet it is imperative to confront the troubling costs of such interventions to North–South equality as well as the possibilities for abuses.

Conclusion

By highlighting the politically biased nature of Council authority in the present era, I do not deny that the global body enjoys authority, as defined by the editors of this volume. The Council is indeed recognized by a wide group of policy-makers to have the right to engage in a vast sweep of global governance, including fundamental intervention into the domestic affairs of crisis states. But, like Robert Cox (e.g., 1986) and other critical theorists of international relations, I wish to emphasize that authority is not neutral. Rather, it is the product of historical developments and political contestation and is disproportionately shaped by the values and interests of the most powerful actors. It is therefore essential to situate Council authority in the historical context of the major developments and pivotal struggles of the post-World War II era concerning political, economic, and social orders. In so doing, one readily appreciates that Council authority is not universal nor static. In the post-cold war era, where Council authority has dramatically expanded, it is not surprising to find considerable discontent. Not surprisingly, the frustrations and challenges are most pronounced in the parts of the world that have little influence but are most pressured to submit to the Council's invigorated authority. There may very well be emerging a bifurcated dimension to Council authority, whereby its authority is well established among prosperous, influential Western states but is tenuous among the poorest and politically weakest states. Such a state of affairs could impact upon the long-term sustainability of the Council's post-cold war leap in authority.

Finally, it is worth stepping back and reflecting whether the extraordinary growth in Council authority is actually desirable for global order and justice. To date, much of the policy and academic discussions on the Council have concerned reforming the institution in order to make it a more effective and representative body to carry out the vast global governance expected of it (e.g., United Nations 2004). Such a reformation, however, would have to be quite deep to justify allotting to the Council the right to, in effect, impose political, economic, and social orders upon a subcategory of states in the global order. Assuming even that such issues are an appropriate global agenda, they should under any defensible principle of global justice be deliberated upon by the broader global community, with an especially prominent voice given to Southern states. To put it mildly, it is quite difficult to imagine that the United States or other P5 states would agree to such a transformation.

The original Charter mandate, by contrast, has the virtue of accepting that while the Council would be a great-power-dominated body with considerable coercive authority, its scope is restricted to keeping the peace between states. As a dissenting International Court of Justice judge commented, "It was to keep the peace, not to change the world order, that the Security Council was set up" (cited in Koskenniemi 1995: 17). Even assuming good faith on those shaping Council-mandated peace enforcement–peacebuilding operations, its underlying premises rest on a fundamentally flawed assumption, as articulated by Martti Koskenniemi (1995: 19):

> The theoretical objections to the comprehensive concept of security relate to the extent that it seems to assume both that we know (or can reasonably ascertain) those social conditions in which security flourishes and that everybody would, of necessity, have good reason to agree on their enforcement through the Security Council.

In fact, as Koskenniemi continues, the last attempt to impose European political systems on newly decolonized states in Africa turned out quite badly.

Let us hope this is not the case of history repeating itself, the first time as tragedy, the second as farce (Marx 1970: 72). I have no doubt that the motivations of academics and of some global diplomats to keep expanding the reach of the Council are well meaning (as, no doubt, were their counterparts in prior historical eras). They could stand, however, a great deal more of attention to historical context and the unsettling implications of granting virtually boundless authority to a great-power-dominated body.

Notes

1 Chesterman 2001: 181; Barnett 2002: 43. In fact, the U.S. troops in Somalia were under U.S., not UN, command. See Byers 2005.
2 To be sure, the United States and its allies often face resistance from China and Russia. Yet the level of resistance is far less than it was during the cold war.
3 Other humanitarian NGOs, like MSF, have rejected the partnership concept and warned of the negative consequences of losing neutrality. See Stoddard 2003; Weissman 2004a.
4 Other commissions are the Panel on UN Peace Operations, which released the Brahimi Report in 2000, the Secretary General's Commission on the Prevention of

Armed Conflict of 2002, and the High-Level Panel on Threats, Challenges, and Change of 2004.

5 Richmond 2004; Soederberg 2006. Peacebuilding includes policing and human rights norms not included in the standard neoliberal agenda of global economic bodies like the World Bank and IMF.

6 Calas and Salignon 2004: 82. U.S. government pressure on NGOs has been even more intense in Iraq. In an address to U.S. NGOs, USAID director Andrew Natsios informed NGOs under U.S. contract that they are "an arm of the U.S. government" and need to better emphasize their ties to the U.S. government (Brauman and Salignon 2004: 284).

7 Although a strict reading of the UN Charter does not allow the Council to intervene in internal conflicts (Glennon 2001), there has emerged a consensus that internal conflicts involving great casualties can be deemed threats to peace (see United Nations 2004).

9 The Uniting for Peace resolution and other ways of circumventing the authority of the Security Council

Jean Krasno and Mitushi Das

One way to test if a governance body has legitimate authority is to see what attempts have been made to circumvent that authority. If the Council had no legitimate authority, there would be no need to find a legal means of getting around its normative power. As stated in the opening chapter, authority is legitimized power, not based on the threat of coercion but based on rules. In that sense, if the Council is an authority based on rules, then there must be rules set in place to circumvent that authority and transfer the authority temporarily to another body when needed. The Uniting for Peace resolution passed in the General Assembly in 1950 is just that instrument. By setting rules for how to transfer authority, the members of the UN, in so doing, acknowledged the legitimate authority of the Council. This chapter tells the story of how the Uniting for Peace resolution came into being, why it was necessary, and how it has been used over time.

The big question?

With the increased activity of the Security Council and the expansion of its authority into spheres well beyond the visions of the founders of the UN, is there still a need to find a legitimate means to circumvent the Council when it fails to act? This chapter hopes to fully address that question. The Uniting for Peace resolution was written in 1950 in order to pass authority from the normally privileged Security Council to the General Assembly. The purpose initially was to wrestle the use of the veto away from the Soviet Union at the time when the United States and the West wanted the United Nations to legitimize action taken to defend South Korea from encroachment from the north. It actually was not the first time that the Western powers had maneuvered an issue into the General Assembly to avoid Soviet blockage and it happened several times again after 1950. The question today is: When the Security Council is unable to act for reasons of the veto or any other obstacle, can "Uniting for Peace" action be utilized as an effective and legitimate strategy? Or not? This chapter will examine the history of this strategic tool, and other similar maneuvers, and make an attempt to analyze the potential for its future use.

A look at the language

Disgruntlement over inaction and lack of cooperation among Security Council members emerged soon after the United Nations met for the first time in London in January 1946. If the Council were unable to act, its legitimate authority would wither away. General Assembly resolution 290 passed on December 1, 1949, clearly demonstrates this frustration:

290 (IV). Essentials of Peace

The General Assembly

Calls upon the five permanent members of the Security Council.

10. *To broaden* progressively their cooperation and to exercise restraint in the use of the veto in order to make the Security Council a more effective instrument for maintaining peace.

Only a few months later in November 1950, the General Assembly was ready to take up the responsibilities of peace and security and make use of its relative advantage of being free of the constraints of the veto. The passage of the Uniting for Peace resolution was initially orchestrated to enabled the Assembly to address the conflict in Korea, despite Soviet objections. In addition, the resolution was intended to establish for the record a mechanism for taking action if and when the Security Council was unable to agree. If legitimate authority is based on rules, then rules had to be made to shift authority when needed. The resolution reads:

377 (V). Uniting for Peace

The General Assembly

Recalling its resolution 290 (IV) entitled "Essentials of Peace," which states that disregard of the Principles of the Charter of the United Nations is primarily responsible for the continuance of international tension, and desiring to contribute further to the objectives of that resolution,

A1. *Resolves* that if the Security Council, because of lack of unanimity of the permanent members, fails to exercise its primary responsibility for the maintenance of international peace and security in any case where there appears to be a threat to the peace, breach of the peace, or act of aggression, the General Assembly shall consider the matter immediately with a view to making appropriate recommendations to Members for collective measures, including in the case of a breach of the peace or act of aggression the use of armed force when necessary, to maintain or restore international peace and security. If not in session at the time, the General Assembly may meet in emergency special session within twenty-four hours of the request thereof. Such emergency special session shall be called if requested by the Security Council on the vote of any of its seven members, or by a majority of the Members of the United Nations.

The resolution clearly states that if the Security Council is unable to act when there is an imminent threat to international peace and security, the General Assembly may take up the issue under two conditions: (1) that the Security Council votes to do so, today with any nine votes in favor among the current fifteen member Council; or (2) that a majority of UN member states votes to do so. The vote count in the Security Council would not be subject to the veto as it would be considered a procedural matter, as stated in the resolution "any of its seven members." Maneuvering around the veto was a clever and useful strategy for a period of time but could this be repeated effectively today and why was the veto created in the first place if it seems to only throw roadblocks in the way of progress?

How the veto emerged: the debate at San Francisco

The principle that there should be a veto was settled among the major powers prior to the 1945 San Francisco conference that finalized the UN Charter, but the issue was again raised in San Francisco. The word veto does not appear in the Charter and the San Francisco participants often referred to it as the "unanimity clause." The Charter states:

Voting: Article 27:

1. Each member of the Security Council shall have one vote.

2. Decisions of the Security Council on procedural matters shall be made by an affirmative vote of nine members [in 1950, seven members of the then eleven-member Council].

3. Decisions of the Security Council on all other matters shall be made by an affirmative vote of nine members including the concurring votes of the permanent members.

This explains the careful wording in the Uniting for Peace resolution, using the phrase "lack of unanimity" instead of the word veto in reference to "the concurring votes of the permanent members." The establishment of the veto, or unanimity of the five permanent members was meant to protect the interests of the great powers (Krasno 2004a: 19–46). It was believed that the major powers (the United States, the Soviet Union, China, the United Kingdom, and France) that fought together as allies to defeat the axis powers would need to remain united in a common cause to deter any aggression that might lead to a third world war. Any serious disagreement among the powers could in essence lead to a clash and perhaps war. That was to be avoided and in fact, the U.S. would not have become a member of the UN without it. At San Francisco: "Smaller countries were generally opposed to the veto, the Latin Americans in particular, but eventually they, along with Philippines and Australia had to retreat, because there would have been no charter without it [the veto] and they couldn't afford not to have a charter" (Finkelstein 1990: interview). The final vote in San Francisco on the "unanimity clause" was 33 in favor, 2 against, and 15 abstentions. The small powers had agreed to accept the veto on the condition that the General Assembly should be granted under Charter Article 11, paragraph 2, the right to discuss any question and to make recommendations unless the Security Council is seized of the matter.

> Article 11: paragraph 2:
>
> The General Assembly may discuss any question relating to the mainten-ance of international peace and security brought before it by any Member of the United Nations, or by the Security Council, or by a state which is not a Member of the United Nations . . . and . . . may make recom-mendations with regard to any such questions to the state or states con-cerned or to the Security Council or both.

At San Francisco, the Soviet Union had objected to the General Assembly's right to take up any issue including security, even if its resolutions were only recommendations and not binding. However, under pressure by the U.S. and the smaller states, particularly from Latin America, the Soviets eventually had to back down. To protect the prerogatives of the Council, the Charter states that as long as the Security Council is seized of a matter, the General Assembly is not allowed to intervene. Article 12 of the Charter states:

1. While the Security Council is exercising in respect of any dispute or situation the functions assigned to it in the present Charter, the General Assembly shall not make any recommendation with regard to that dispute or situation unless the Security Council so requests.

2. The Secretary-General, with the consent of the Security Council, shall notify the General Assembly at each session of any matters relative to the maintenance of international peace and security which are being dealt with by the Security Council and shall similarly notify the General Assembly, or the Members of the United Nations if the General Assembly is not in session, immediately [when] the Security Council ceases to deal with such matters.

The Soviets must have felt a sense of security with that interpretation, not anticipating what would occur only a few years later.

The United Nations Special Commission on the Balkans (UNSCOB)

It is generally perceived that there was no precedent to the 1950 Uniting for Peace resolution which allows the General Assembly to make recommendations in lieu of the Security Council on a matter of peace and security. However, UNSCOB (the UN Special Commission on the Balkans) was deployed in 1947 under the authority of the General Assembly, not the Security Council. This observer mission was sent to monitor complaints that outside support by communist guerrillas from Albania, Bulgaria, and Yugoslavia for the communist movement in northern Greece was destabilizing the Western-backed Greek government. When the Soviets used their veto to block the mission, the U.S. maneuvered the issue onto the agenda of the General Assembly. UNSCOB was the first UN-sponsored fact-finding mission and was also the first attempt by the UN to deploy a peace observation mission in the midst of armed conflict (Durch 1993: ch. 5). The creation of UNSCOB by the General Assembly instead of the Security Council demonstrated the first attempt to consider a procedural vote by the Council as a means to circumvent Soviet objections and have the veto-free Assembly address the issue.

The history leading up to UNSCOB demonstrates the frustration members had with the Security Council and its inability to act. The failures of the League of Nations were still fresh in the minds of diplomats who did not want the newly created UN to be paralyzed in the same way as the League had been. The issue of violent incidents on the border between Greece and Albania was initially raised by the Ukrainian representative on August 24, 1946. The United States suggested the establishment of an investigative commission to look into the matter. However, the proposal was vetoed by the Soviet Union. On December 3, 1946, the Greek government brought complaints before the Security Council against Albania, Bulgaria, and Yugoslavia for supporting communist guerrillas in northern Greece. This time the Soviet Union went along with the proposal made by the U.S. However, this support was short-lived as the Commission found evidence of support for the insurgency affirming the Greek claim. The Soviet Union disagreed with the results and repeatedly used the veto against Security Council resolutions that were based on the recommendations of the report with regard to the insurgency. The Security Council then removed the item from its agenda to allow the General Assembly to deal with the matter.

The General Assembly called on all parties for restraint and established the UN Special Commission on the Balkans (UNSCOB) on October 21, 1947, to be composed of the then-eleven members of the Security Council. However, the Soviet Union and Poland refused to serve on the Commission bringing the number down to nine. A unique trait of the mission was that its members represented and received instructions from their respective states and not the UN. In addition, the military observers reported their findings to their national governments.[1] The Commission reports were issued to the General

Assembly and not the Security Council. UNSCOB remained in existence until 1951, submitting regular reports on the growing refugee problems, arms trafficking, and the abduction of children across international frontiers. On December 7, 1951, the General Assembly decided to discontinue the Special Commission but due to the situation in the Balkans decided to request the Peace Observer Commission to establish a Balkan Sub-Commission (contemplated in resolution 377 (V), section B).

The Korean question

In 1950, the Soviet Union had boycotted the Security Council on grounds that the UN had failed to grant the People's Republic of China (Communist China), which had achieved control of the mainland after 1949, the seat of China in the UN and on the Council. Instead the UN continued to recognize the Chiang Kai-shek regime in Taiwan as the legitimate member. When war broke out between North and South Korea, with the Soviets absent from the Council, the West was free to authorize the use of force under UN auspices without the threat of a Soviet veto. During this period the Council passed three resolutions on Korea: the first on June 25, 1950; the second on June 27, 1950; and the third on July 7, 1950. The three gave authority to the member states led by the U.S. to take action against the North Korean attack. In August 1950, realizing its blunder, the Soviet Union returned and Soviet Ambassador Malik took up the Council presidency for the month of August. With the Soviet Union back on the Security Council, it was no longer possible to take action with regard to Korea because of Soviet opposition. They were supporting North Korea. Previous discussions about the role of the General Assembly in the area of peace and security and the experience of UNSCOB encouraged Washington to seek a way to involve the Assembly in finding a solution to the Korean conflict. A careful study of the Charter by legal analysts revealed the right of the General Assembly to discuss questions of peace and security and make recommendations as long as the Security Council was not considering the matter. The U.S. sought support from other nations and drafted what was referred to as the "multi-power" resolution. The proposal was cleverly named the "Uniting for Peace" resolution, to cast it in a more positive light and obfuscate the fact that it was actually a political/legal maneuver to sideline the Soviets. Leonard Meeker (1990: interview), who was working in the U.S. State Department at the time on UN affairs, recounts:

> During the summer when August 1 came and Malik went back to the Security Council to take up the role of President (since it was his turn to be President in August) it was recognized that the Security Council, with the Soviet Union present, would no longer be able to function in regard to Korea. The Soviet veto would prevent any action. There had been earlier discussion about the role of the General Assembly in the field of

peace and security and, in fact, a sub-organ called the Interim Committee had been set up a couple of years earlier. As I recall it now, during August of 1950 there were meetings in Washington which included Dean Rusk, Harding Bancroft, John Foster Dulles (who came down from his retreat in northern New York State) and myself to discuss what might be done to put the General Assembly in a position to act in some way in the Korean War. It was recognized that the Security Council at the most had made recommendations. And it was believed by all of us that if you looked carefully at the different articles of the Charter dealing with the powers of the General Assembly, it could discuss questions affecting peace and security and also could make recommendations. So with that set of ideas we began in that month to draft a resolution for the General Assembly to pass which would set up a framework for General Assembly consideration of a peace and security problem in a situation where the Security Council was unable to act because of the veto. The drafts were pretty well finished and approved along in early September, and I remember going to New York at that time with Mr. Dulles who handled this question in the First Committee of the General Assembly. We had a series of meetings over a few weeks with other delegations to solicit their sponsorship (or at least their support) of the resolution in the General Assembly which eventually became the Uniting for Peace plan.

Debates in the General Assembly (September 20, 1950)

Complaints about the veto were gathering steam and several ambassadors referred to the crippling effects of the veto during the General Debate in September 1950. The Brazilian permanent representative, Ambassador De Freitas Valle (1950), stated: "the right of veto has been abused." Ambassador Belaunde of Peru complained of the "difficulty resulting from the paralyzing effects of the veto" where "the veto has gone far beyond the purpose for which it was devised . . . the veto was not a right but an obligation . . . to seek unanimity." Moreover, he mentioned the apprehension of the Latin American countries towards the veto at the conference in San Francisco. Emphasizing the power of the General Assembly, Ambassador Belaunde (1950) referred to Article 10 of the Charter[2], asserting that "the Assembly's jurisdiction . . . constitutes . . . the legal foundation for any proposal for convening the Assembly in case of emergency to deal with the exigencies of peace when the Council is paralyzed."

In his speech on September 20, 1950, Dean Acheson (A/PV.279), U.S. Secretary of State, openly accused the Soviet Union, stating that, "we have been confronted with many and complex problems, but the main obstacle to peace . . . has been created by the policies of the Soviet Union." The United States delegation put forth a set of recommendations before the General Assembly which included the provision of an emergency session within twenty-four hours' notice (General Assembly A/1373: para. 43–49).

In response to the accusations and the proposals put forth by the United States, Ambassador Vyshinsky of the Soviet Union, in his speech at the UN, targeted the United States and earlier resolutions passed on Korea through the initiative of the United States, stating that "the United States delegation . . . adopted a number of illegal and unjust decisions on the Korean question . . . to camouflage the armed intervention in Korea."[3] A similar attitude was adopted by the Soviet Union towards the Uniting for Peace resolution as well. The Soviet argument was that the UN could not be strengthened by weakening the Security Council which would be the result if the proposals were adopted. The Soviet ambassador referred to the "primary responsibility" given to the Security Council for the maintenance of international peace and security as an "exclusive right." According to him, to address the abuse of the veto would mean liquidating the unanimity clause and to do that properly the Charter would have to be amended, in accordance with Article 109 of the Charter (General Assembly First Committee 1950). The Soviets pointed to Article 24 (1) of the Charter which provides that the Security Council has the "primary responsibility for the maintenance of international peace and security." This primary responsibility is detailed principally in Chapters VI and VII which set out certain explicit powers to be exercised by the Council. Others claimed that the use of the word "primary" implied that other bodies could play secondary roles. The Charter never states that these powers are "exclusive" to the Council.

In a 1991 interview with Canadian diplomat Geoffrey Murray (1991: interview), he stated that Canada was not "too keen on the whole Uniting for Peace procedure – mainly because . . . it irritated the Russians and possibly because we had our own hesitations about its constitutionality in terms of the United Nations Charter."

Discussion in the First Committee of the General Assembly

Once the General Assembly had agreed to include the United States proposal on the agenda it was referred to the First Committee. A joint effort called the "Seven-Power" draft resolution was submitted by Canada, France, Philippines, Turkey, U.K., USA., and Uruguay (Sohn 1956: 4–8).

Section A of the draft resolution A/C.1/576 proposed that the General Assembly could promptly make a recommendation if Security Council action was blocked. Though recommendations of the General Assembly are not binding, past experience on the Korean situation demonstrated that responses to recommendations could be very effective. Fifty-three members had carried out the recommendations. With regard to the question of whether the provisions of section A in the draft Uniting for Peace resolution calling for special sessions of the Assembly were consistent with Article 20 of the Charter,[4] Mr. Younger, the U.K. representative, stated that the General Assembly had the right to determine the time of its sessions and the circumstances in which they should be called. Action by the Security Council was a procedural matter for which an affirmative vote by seven members would suffice (now nine after the Charter amendment in 1965).[5]

Section B of the joint draft resolution called for the establishment of a peace observation mission with the members to be chosen by the General Assembly from among member states other than the so-called "great powers" and examples of Greece and Korea were stated to support the recommendation. Section C of the draft resolution proposed that member countries designate troops drawn from their national militaries to serve under the UN when needed and that a panel of military experts would serve under the authority of the Secretary-General. Under section D of the Seven-Power draft resolution, the Security Council and the General Assembly were to receive reports from a Collective Measures Committee on the whole problem of collective security. Leonard Meeker (1990: interview) who worked on the plan explains how "collective measures" was defined at the time in relation to "collective security."

> Well, it's very much related to collective security. The Charter and the UN organization as a whole were created to support and assure collective security. It was originally supposed that the Security Council would be the organ that would arrange all this, and when it turned out that the Council (because of the veto) would not be able to function in some important cases, then a transfer to the forum was decided upon. The General Assembly (which has in it all of the Members of the UN) would be designed to assure collective security by using the powers which it had—powers of recommendation—and of course, it could take certain preparatory measures in advance through the Collective Measures Committee by setting up a system of contribution of forces by Member States and providing for their suitable military organization.

In the end, the First Committee approved the draft resolution as amended, by 50 votes to 5 (the Soviet Bloc), with 3 abstentions (Argentina, India—which voted in favor of sections A, B, and E only—and Syria) (General Assembly First Committee 1950). The General Assembly adopted Resolution 377 (V) on November 3, 1950, by 52 votes to 5, with 2 abstentions (Syria now voting in favor) (General Assembly First Committee 1950). Under the resolution, a Peace Observation Commission of 14 members was established to be dispatched to troubled areas in order to advise the Assembly of any necessary action. A Collective Measures Committee of 14 members was established in order to coordinate the actions taken by the members on the recommendations of the Assembly.

Additional legal arguments

The International Court of Justice (ICJ) in the "Certain Expenses of the United Nations" case (1962) in a majority opinion advised that the Security

Council had "primary" but not "exclusive" authority, and that "whilst the taking of enforcement action was the exclusive prerogative of the Security Council under Chapter VII this did not prevent the Assembly from making recommendations under Articles 10 and 14."[6]

The Charter provides for a certain interaction between the Council and the Assembly. It is the General Assembly which elects the Security Council's ten non-permanent members as stated in Articles 23(1) and 18(2).[7] Under Article 10, the General Assembly is given the right to discuss any issues falling within the realm of the Charter, which is essentially a very wide range of issues. Moreover, Article 5 and Article 6 of the Charter[8] show that the General Assembly and the Security Council work in tandem with each other with regard to suspension and expulsion of defaulting members. Under Articles 15(1) and 24(3), "the Security Council shall submit annual and, when necessary, special reports to the General Assembly for its consideration,"[9] thus emphasizing the substantial role of the General Assembly.

Though Article 11(1) limits the General Assembly's involvement to general principles, 11(2) along with Article 14 together provide a positive mandate for the General Assembly to assume a secondary role through discussions on issues of international peace and security. Furthermore, Articles 10, 11(2), 14, and 18(2) allow the General Assembly to make recommendations to the Security Council and even non-members.[10]

The Australian delegate stated in the First Committee in 1950 that the Uniting for Peace resolution "did not confer upon the General Assembly a competence which it did not have under the Charter,"[11] thus emphasizing the legitimate basis for the resolution and addressing the challenging arguments of the Soviet Union that termed the resolution a violation of the UN Charter. This implies that something similar to the resolution was envisaged when the Charter was drafted. Some believe that the Uniting for Peace resolution was never required since Article 12(2) already provides that issues can be brought by the Security Council to the General assembly. Article 12(2) states that the "Secretary-General" with the "consent of the Security Council" can refer a matter to the General Assembly. Yet, the provision does not define "consent" which was left open to interpretation. The Uniting for Peace resolution simply clarifies that consent process.

Using the resolution on Korea

The prerequisite for adopting the Uniting for Peace resolution and shifting authority to the Assembly is that the Security Council must have failed "to exercise its primary responsibility for the maintenance of international peace and security." In addition, in order to follow strictly the legal provisions in the Charter, the Council must not be seized of the matter. The Assembly is forbidden to take up an issue for recommendation if the Council is already engaged in that matter. While some scholars claim that the Uniting for Peace plan was not used on Korea, in fact, the procedure was used in January and

February 1951, soon after the Uniting for Peace resolution was passed in November 1950. The resolution 377 (V) was not written into the documents directly, but the procedure was executed according to plan. At this time Communist China had entered the war in Korea and the West was eager to condemn the action, but the Soviets would not go along. Therefore, on January 31, 1951, the Security Council passed resolution 90 (1951) which states: "The Security Council: Resolves to remove the item 'Complaint of aggression upon the Republic of Korea' from the list of matters of which the Council is seized."

With that legal obstacle out of the way, the General Assembly could move to take up the issue and on February 1, 1951, the General Assembly adopted GA resolution 498 titled: "498 (V). Intervention of the Central People's Government of the People's Republic of China in Korea." The resolution called upon the People's Republic of China to withdraw from Korea. It affirmed "the determination of the United Nations to continue its action in Korea to meet the aggression," and called upon all states to assist the UN. The resolution also requested: "a Committee composed of the members of the Collective Measures Committee as a matter of urgency to consider additional measures to be employed to meet this aggression and to report thereon to the General Assembly." In this manner, the General Assembly took up the authority on peace and security.

Suez

Though the Uniting for Peace strategy was executed during the Korean War, the first time the resolution was invoked by name was in response to the 1956 Suez crisis, when under resolution 377 (V) the General Assembly called for an Emergency Special Session. Following the nationalization of the Suez Canal Company, Israel, in collusion with France and the United Kingdom, invaded Egypt. Egyptian leader Gamal Abdel Nasser had forbidden Israel from using the Canal once it was nationalized, a move which Israel considered an act of war. France and Britain in an attempt to regain the Canal convinced Israel to make the first move, promising to "come to the rescue" of Egypt by imposing their forces between the warring parties. When the Security Council attempted to take action under the UN Charter to end the aggression, the British and the French as permanent members exercised their veto. In response, nonpermanent Council member Yugoslavia, with the full support of U.S. President Dwight D. Eisenhower, invoked the Uniting for Peace resolution transferring the Suez question to the General Assembly on October 31. The first emergency special session of the General Assembly was convened on November 7–10, 1956. The General Assembly demanded the immediate withdrawal of Israel from the Sinai and French and British troops from the north and authorized the first ever deployment of *armed* UN peacekeepers. These first UN peacekeeping troops were sent into Egypt to monitor a buffer zone between Egyptian and Israeli forces as the French and British withdrew. This was the first application of the Uniting for Peace resolution that resulted in UN-led, armed military action. This time the Soviets were pleased to see the British and French at the other end of the stick.

Other instances of the use of the Uniting for Peace resolution

At the same time as Suez in 1956, Uniting for Peace was used by the United States to pressure the Soviet Union to cease its intervention in Hungary. The Soviet Union had used its veto to prevent the passage of a resolution in the Security Council calling on the Soviet Union not to intervene in the Hungarian uprising. On November 4, 1956, the Hungarian question was referred to the General Assembly and the Soviet Union was called upon to cease its intervention, with the withdrawal of all "foreign forces." Additionally, the General Assembly called on the UNHCR to provide assistance. As history shows, the Soviets simply ignored the Assembly's demands.

Two years later, the General Assembly was called into emergency session by the Security Council on August 8–12, 1958, under the Uniting for Peace Resolution on the crisis in Lebanon, citing the Council's lack of unanimity among the permanent members. UNOGIL, the UN Observation Group in Lebanon, was created in 1958 to send 600 peacekeeping observers to the Syrian–Lebanese border to report on the alleged infiltration of arms and personnel into Lebanon from Syria.

On September 17, 1960, following a Soviet veto in the Security Council over the extent and nature of United Nations' Operation in the Congo (ONUC), the case of the Congo was referred to the General Assembly in an emergency session on September 17–19, 1960.

In a letter dated June 13, 1967, the Soviet Union itself requested the Secretary-General to convene an emergency special session of the General Assembly in order to debate the 1967 war in the Middle East. Because the Soviets had never recognized the Uniting for Peace resolution, they requested the special session of the General Assembly under Article 11 of the UN Charter which states that the General Assembly may discuss any questions related to international peace and security. Council calls for a ceasefire had been ignored and the situation was in crisis. Ninety-eight member states, more than the required majority under Uniting for Peace, agreed to take up the issue, even though the U.S. voted against it, claiming the Security Council was still considering the matter. The General Assembly session debate continued from June 17 through July 5, 1967, but outside the explicit framework of the Uniting for Peace resolution (*United Nations Yearbook* 1967: 191). Ultimately a ceasefire was reached and Security Council resolution 242 was passed.

Further GA special sessions followed. Regarding the India/Pakistan conflict, on December 6, 1971, the East Pakistan (now Bangladesh) question was referred to the General Assembly under the Uniting for Peace resolution. Several years later, the General Assembly held an emergency special session, on January 10–14, 1980, on the issue of the Soviet invasion of Afghanistan. On July 22–9, 1980, a special session was held on the Israeli invasion of Lebanon, and this session was continued again on several dates in 1982. The General Assembly passed a resolution in a session on September 3–14, 1981, under Uniting for Peace, calling for sanctions on South Africa because of its continued occupation of South West Africa, now Namibia. Again in January/February 1982, under Uniting for Peace a session was held to address the Occupied Territories in the Middle East.

Two other events happened in the 1980s that resulted in the General Assembly taking up a matter on international peace and security when the Security Council was blocked by a permanent-member veto. In October 1983, the United States joined by some Caribbean nations militarily intervened in Grenada, following a period of internal unrest. Hundreds of Cuban advisors were in the country, and the tense political nature of events, in the eyes of U.S. policy-makers, conveyed a sense of Cuban ideological expansionism (*United Nations Yearbook* 1983: 211–17). At the request of Nicaragua, the Security Council considered the situation in a meeting from October 25–8. A draft resolution (S/16077/Rev.1.) called for the withdrawal of foreign troops but was vetoed by the United States in a vote that took place on October 28. On October 31, Nicaragua requested that the General Assembly take up the matter under "rule 15 of the rules of procedure of the General Assembly." Attached to the ambassador's letter to the Secretary-General making the request was an explanatory memorandum with several items:

4. The examination of this question by the Security Council on 25, 26, 27, and 28 October 1983 unequivocally showed that the majority of the Members of the Organization rejected the military invasion of Grenada and demanded the immediate and unconditional withdrawal of all foreign troops from its territory.

5. The General Assembly should, therefore, adopt the draft resolution submitted by Guyana, Nicaragua and Zimbabwe to the Security Council which the Council failed to adopt because of the negative vote of one of its permanent members and which is now introduced in a revised form.

(United Nations General Assembly A/38/245)

On November 2, 1983, the General Assembly adopted resolution A/38/7, condemning the Grenada invasion and calling for the removal of foreign troops. Nicaragua (a friend to the Soviets who never recognized the Uniting for Peace resolution) did not call on 377 (V) A, but used General Assembly rules of procedure. Nevertheless, the purpose was the same: to circumvent the veto.

Again drawing on "rule 15 of the rules of procedure of the General Assembly" (not Uniting for Peace due to Soviet objections to the measure), the permanent representatives of Cuba and Nicaragua, on December 21, 1989, requested that an item entitled the "Grave situation in Panama" be added immediately to the agenda of the General Assembly (United Nations General Assembly A/44/906). On December 15, 1989, General Manuel Noriega had declared war on the United States. The U.S. had asked him to step down as president when he did not win re-election. As a result, on December 20, the U.S. sent in military troops and in a few days had captured Noriega, removing him from the country. Nicaragua asked for a meeting of the Security Council on the issue of Panama, accusing the U.S. of an act of aggression by invading Panama. On December 23, the Security Council put to a vote a draft resolution strongly deploring the U.S. intervention and demanding immediate withdrawal. However, the measure was vetoed by three permanent members: France, the United Kingdom, and the United States. The U.S. claimed its purpose was to defend democracy in Panama. On December 29, 1989, the General Assembly adopted resolution 240, deploring the intervention in Panama and calling for an immediate withdrawal and respect for Panama's sovereignty (*United Nations Yearbook* 1989: 172–6).

In 1997, the Uniting for Peace resolution was once again revived and the "Tenth Emergency Special Session" was convened to handle the ongoing conflict in the Middle East. Rather than open a new session on the Middle East conflict every time there is a new event, the Tenth Emergency Special Session, under resolution 377 (V) A, is simply reopened when the majority of the General Assembly asks the president of the General Assembly to resume the session. The Assembly's Tenth Emergency Special Session was first held in 1997 after the Security Council in two separate meetings failed to adopt a draft resolution on a new Israeli settlement south of East Jerusalem. Using the "Uniting for Peace" formula, a special emergency session of the General Assembly was convened in April and again in July and November of 1997. The same tenth session resumed in 1998 (March 17), 1999 (February 5 and 9), 2000 (October 18 and 20), 2001 (December 20), 2002 (May 7 and August 5, and 2003 (October 20–1). The discussions, often ending in long statements with no action, demonstrated the frustration of the Assembly on the inability to find a peaceful solution to the Israeli–Palestinian conflict, but they were equally unable to produce any results. Unfortunately, by turning Uniting for Peace into yet another forum for rhetorical debate, the once useful strategy was threatening to become essentially useless.

The contemporary context

The Uniting for Peace resolution was designed, ironically, by the United States, for conditions where the use of the veto by one or more of the permanent five had paralyzed the Council. However, in 1999, when a humanitarian crisis erupted in Kosovo and Yugoslavia was accused of carrying out mass killings, neither the Security Council nor the General Assembly were consulted. Without UN authorization, NATO forces engaged in a series of bombing attacks in an attempt to force Yugoslavia to remove its troops and Serb-supported militias from Kosovo. The U.S. and Europe had anticipated a Russian veto and never brought it to a vote in the Security Council. A de facto, rather backhanded, approval of NATO action became apparent when the Council refused to pass a condemnation of the NATO initiative, twelve countries voting against the condemnation. Nevertheless, a lack of "disapproval" does not offer legal authorization for the use of force. Council members could have invoked the Uniting for Peace resolution but that was not done. Why not? Perhaps it was determined that there was not enough time to engage in debate or perhaps members did not trust that the Assembly would authorize NATO action. It is also possible that the West is now in the same position that the Soviet Union was in during the early years, in essence not having control over the Assembly and what it might do. Therefore, perhaps protecting the right of the veto in the long run has become more precious. The U.S., who had been the early instigator of the resolution, has lost much of its influence in the Assembly and cannot guarantee an outcome to its liking. Paul Heinbecker (2004: interview) who was the Canadian ambassador to the UN and on the Council at the time of Kosovo explains what happened:

> As it happens, Canada had the chair of the Security Council in February 1999 . . . And we raised the issue of the "Uniting for Peace resolution" informally three times. We were warned off each time that we raised it; we should not bring this to the Assembly. In the first instance, we came to the conclusion that there were no doubts the Russians would veto in the Council. And if the Russians did then the Chinese would likely follow suit . . . But in the circumstances, then we thought we might go for a Uniting for Peace resolution. But we didn't do that. There were two reasons: one was we thought that the Yugoslavs, who were founding members of the Non-Aligned Movement, probably had enough chits out there or enough sympathy that it could have taken time and we might have gotten a watered-down resolution. Meanwhile people were dying. There was another angle that people have lost sight of and that is the P-5 didn't want it . . . Because none of them wants to deprecate the value of a veto.

Conditions for invoking the Uniting for Peace resolution emerged again in 2003 with regard to Iraq. Iraq had refused to allow UN inspectors to return to finish their work of removing weapons of mass destruction. No inspections had been carried out from the end of 1998 through 2002. Despite the fact that the UN had destroyed most or possibly all the weapons, there were still unanswered questions and the Council had been unable to get a full and complete report when the inspections were aborted. By 2002, the U.S. was ready to take more forceful action but others on the Council disagreed. The stalemate in the Council pitted the United States, the United Kingdom, and Spain on one side calling for the use of force and France and Germany on the other, with France threatening to use the veto against a U.S. resolution. Russia proposed various different solutions, with still no agreement. There was clearly a lack of unanimity in the Council and it could be interpreted that the Council was unable to act.

Others might say that the Council was fulfilling its role exactly as the founders had anticipated by not approving an action that was considered flawed. The U.S. once again could have taken the issue to the General Assembly but most likely there would not have been the nine needed votes in the Council to do so nor a majority in the Assembly to approve it. Finally, the decision by the United States and United Kingdom with the support of Spain to proceed with the use of force without a further resolution directly meant that the Security Council had failed to achieve unanimity among the major powers nor general consensus.

Nongovernmental organizations and others throughout the world called for a resolution to prevent a U.S.-led attack on Iraq. The Arab Group at the United Nations with 22 members, and the Organization of Islamic Conference (OIC) with 57 members, had resolved to introduce a resolution to convene an emergency meeting of the General Assembly, demanding an immediate end to the U.S. invasion of Iraq. They appeared intent on demonstrating an overwhelming international opposition to the U.S.-led action and discussing ways to bring about a withdrawal of all foreign troops from Iraq. The Non-Aligned Movement with 115 nations, and several other governments, including Russia, China, Indonesia, and Jamaica, had also expressed their support for an emergency United Nations General Assembly session, under the Uniting for Peace resolution. However, neither UN Secretary-General Kofi Annan nor the President of the General Assembly ever received a request from any nation to convene such an emergency session, as would be required.

Had the resolution been invoked, the General Assembly could have called upon Iraq to adhere to the resolutions of the Security Council and allow for complete access to its weapons facilities by the UN inspectors. The condemnation of the use of force against Iraq by a large majority in the General Assembly might have offered such a demanding moral authority that it could have prevented the U.S.-led attacks; but in hindsight this was unlikely.

Security Council resolution 1441, passed in the fall of 2002, represented international support for a tougher stance on Iraqi disarmament, and the U.S. used that resolution and the 1991 ceasefire resolution 687 to justify its legal support for the use of force. But the vast majority of UN members were not supportive of such action. The U.S. may have succeeded in building a legal defense, although Kofi Annan and others have declared the 2003 war in Iraq illegal under international law and the UN Charter. Legal or not, strategically the U.S. has blundered in Iraq in a way the founders of the UN had hoped would never happen. The alliance of the major powers was supposed to be held firm by the unanimity clause, but the U.S. failed to build that consensus. The U.S. was caught under-forced and with no concept for building the peace.

UN authorization could have minimized the bitterness toward American forces in Iraq and would have made it much easier to recruit peacekeepers from around the world to help share the burden.

A recent use of the Uniting for Peace resolution took place in the fall/winter of 2003. Israel had undertaken to build a wall to protect itself from suicide bombing attacks which had been increasing at an alarming rate. Parts of the wall had encroached into the Occupied Territories, cutting off Palestinians from sections of their land and from access to towns, water, and other necessities. The Security Council had introduced a resolution on October 14, 2003 to condemn the wall, but the U.S. vetoed the provision, saying that such a statement should also include language condemning the killing of innocent Israeli citizens. Several other drafts on the issue of the wall were also vetoed. Under a provision in the Uniting for Peace resolution that allows the members of the General Assembly to take a decision that the Security Council is unable to act, in this case due to the veto, the General Assembly took up the issue. The 10th Emergency Special Session established under Uniting for Peace 377 (V) A was resumed by the president of the General Assembly, Mr. Julian Robert Hunte (Saint Lucia) at the request of a majority of the members. The session was resumed on October 20-1 and again on December 3, 2003. The resulting General Assembly resolution passed on December 8 (A/RES/ES-10/14) requested an Advisory Opinion of the International Court of Justice on the legal status of the Wall on the Occupied Territories. The Court accepted the request and by July 2004 issued a majority decision (14–1) declaring the "Wall on the Occupied Territories" to be illegal (International Court of Justice 2004). The decision, however, failed to say anything about the parts of the wall built within the State of Israel, those sections presumably considered legal. Nevertheless, the process of the ICJ taking the request and hearing the arguments resulted in the simultaneous action of the Israeli Supreme Court itself taking up the issue and declaring parts of the wall illegal. As a result, some parts of the wall were moved. While Israel refused to formally recognize the decision of the ICJ, the process did have some positive consequences on the ground.

Conclusion

In conclusion, while most people outside the UN are completely unaware of it, the Uniting for Peace resolution is still functioning. It is alive and breathing, but is it well? The Advisory Opinion of the ICJ seemed to have had some impact on the construction of the wall which has been altered in anticipation of the ruling by Israel's own Supreme Court. So, the General Assembly's action could be interpreted as having an impact. Nevertheless, using the Uniting for Peace resolution to ignite yet another talkathon is counter-productive, as the seemingly unending tenth emergency session has demonstrated. Without the backing of at least a few of the major powers and most particularly the United States, it is unlikely that member states would be capable of implementing General Assembly resolutions other than requests for an Advisory Opinion which do not require troops and economic resources.

A current challenge facing the UN is the humanitarian crisis in the western region of Sudan, Darfur. The U.S. Congress and former Secretary of State Colin Powell have declared the crisis "genocide" as did former Secretary-General Kofi Annan. The African Union sent peacekeeping observers to the region but the violence carried out by government-backed militia groups called the Janjaweed continued: burning villages, killing, and raping innocent villagers, many of whom fled to neighboring Chad, while others faced starvation, atrocities, and murder. Hundreds of experts visited Darfur during the period 2003 to early 2007, returning with horrific assessments of the crisis. Neither the Council nor the Assembly have taken strong action other than condemning the situation and calling for a ceasefire. The Council imposed a series of limited sanctions, but because they did not include sanctions on the sale of oil or other meaningful limits, no leverage has been achieved. Thousands more are dying with no solution on the horizon. The African Union and the UN are trying to mediate a solution, but again the AU has few resources and Sudan has continued to visibly assist the Janjaweed even though they flatly deny it. The UN Security Council in 2006 approved sending UN peacekeeping troops to assist the AU in Darfur, but this has become complex and Sudan has refused to give consent to the deployment.

There are a number of obstacles blocking any UN action. On the Security Council, both Russia and China are reluctant to intervene in a sovereign nation without the consent of the Sudanese government. Both Russia and China have their own internal problems: Russia with Chechnya, and China with Tibet and Taiwan. China also purchases much of its oil from Sudan. While there was much talk about humanitarian intervention after the tragedy in Rwanda, events in Kosovo in 1999 when NATO took action without UN authority and the war in Iraq in 2003–5 again undertaken against Security Council protests, member states are extremely reluctant to violate the sanctity of sovereignty. The paradigm shift from the notion of "national security" to the concept of the sovereign person or "human security" has not yet taken place in the minds of government leaders who have their own personal agendas. This can also be said for the General Assembly. No one seems to be coming forward, most particularly the Arab states that are remaining loyal to Arab leaders in Khartoum, which just recently hosted the annual meeting of the AU. If member states garnered the will to take the issue out of the Council to avoid a veto by China or Russia, they could do so, but what then? What country would lead the action and provide the manpower and resources? With the U.S. tied down in Iraq and the U.K. still taking criticism at home for its role in Iraq and even its rather small but pivotal role in Sierra Leone, there does not appear to be a likely candidate. Ultimately, using the Uniting for Peace resolution is a strategic tool for finding a forum for action. But when there is no will to act, it is useless.

The Charter was drafted in the 1940s, and even at that time political realities were in the process of change, as we entered the cold war. The Uniting for Peace resolution filled in the gaps of Article 12(2) which had limited provisions for a potential lack of unanimity among Security Council members resulting in an abuse of the veto. Thus, the Uniting for Peace resolution was a landmark in terms of "revealing a latent potential" in the Charter itself and "setting it on a firm foundation, in a sense re-legitimizing, enhancing and supporting what was already there" (Reicher 1963). The drafters of the resolution and the members at the time knew that legitimate authority must be based on a clear set of rules. Even if the authority of the General Assembly existed in the Charter, Uniting for Peace laid out a set of rules to temporarily move authority out of the Council. It therefore acknowledges the authority of the Council, preserving its power, and only borrowing the authority under stress when the Council is unable to act.

In order to be invoked, all the prerequisites need to be met. In present times the nature of conflict has altered to a large extent. Civil war, genocide, and crimes against humanity have emerged to take over the spotlight from heretofore interstate wars. Like Darfur, this presents a dilemma for member states who must choose between higher order values of sovereignty on the one hand and guaranteeing the protection of human rights and human security on the other.

Nevertheless, when there is the will among the UN members, the General Assembly represents the consensus of 192 countries which is representative of a universal moral authority. From a legal perspective, though General Assembly recommendations are not binding, they convey "great moral force." The Uniting for Peace resolution was conceived as an instrument to take action in resolving conflict and acts of aggression. Recently in practice it has not managed to be used to its best potential as it was once used in the 1956 Suez crisis or in the Congo in the 1960s. Yet, it should be reconsidered as a useful strategy. The expectations placed on the United Nations to become the protector of human rights is becoming a kind of litmus test for the legitimacy of the organization. If the UN cannot do that or is unwilling to take the risks of playing that role, then should other regional organizations be legally authorized to take action in the face of a universal vacuum of will? Can the General Assembly fill the vacuum of leadership when the Security Council fails?

In 1949, the General Assembly, in resolution 290, called "upon the five permanent members of the Security Council . . . to broaden progressively their cooperation and to exercise restraint in the use of the veto in order to make the Security Council a more effective instrument for maintaining peace." A few months later the General Assembly, in answer to its own frustration, passed Uniting for Peace. All these years later, is the Uniting for Peace resolution alive? The answer is: yes, it is breathing, but is it well? Barely; it is clearly not thriving. Yet, the Uniting for Peace resolution should be viewed with a renewed perspective in order to increase the effectiveness of the United Nations in combating the challenges posed by threats to the peace in an increasingly complex world and when narrow state interests threaten UN inaction.

Notes

1 For example, see details of cablegrams sent by Glasheen.
2 UN Charter Article 10, "The General Assembly may discuss any questions or any matters within the scope of the present Charter or relating to the powers and functions of any organs provided for in the present Charter, and, except as provided in Article 12, may make recommendations to the Members of the United Nations or to the Security Councilor to both on any such questions or matters."
3 United Nations General Assembly A/1456 and A/1481. See the speech by Mr. Vyshinsky (Union of Soviet Socialist Republic).
4 UN Charter Article 20, "The General Assembly shall meet in regular annual sessions and in such special sessions as occasion may require. Special sessions shall be convoked by the Secretary-General at the request of the Security Councilor of a majority of the Members of the United Nations."
5 The Amendments to Articles 23, 27, and 61 of the Charter were adopted by the General Assembly on December 17, 1963 and came into force on 31 August 1965. The amendment to Article 23 enlarges the membership of the Security Council-from eleven to fifteen. The amended Article 27 provides that decisions of the Security Council on procedural matters shall be made by an affirmative vote of nine members (formerly seven) and on all other matters by an affirmative vote of nine members (formerly seven), including the concurring votes of the five permanent members of the Security Council.
6 UN Charter Article 14, "Subject to the provisions of Article 12, the General Assembly may recommend measures for the peaceful adjustment of any situation, regardless of origin, which it deems likely to impair the general welfare or friendly relations among nations, including situations resulting from a violation of the provisions of the present Charter setting forth the Purposes and Principles of the United Nations."
7 UN Charter Article 23(1), "The Security Council shall consist of fifteen Members of the United Nations . . . The General Assembly shall elect ten other Members of the United Nations to be non-permanent members of the Security Council."
   UN Charter Article 18(2), "Decisions of the General Assembly on important questions shall be made by a two-thirds majority of the members present and voting. These questions shall include, recommendations with respect to the maintenance of international peace and security, the election of the non-permanent members of the Security Council . . . the admission of new Members to the United Nations, the suspension of the rights and privileges of membership, the expulsion of Members . . ."
8 UN Charter Article 5, "A Member of the United Nations against which preventive or enforcement action has been taken by the Security Council may be suspended from the exercise of the rights and privileges of membership by the General Assembly upon the recommendation of the Security Council. The exercise of these rights and privileges may be restored by the Security Council."
   UN Charter Article 6, "A Member of the United Nations which has persistently violated the Principles contained in the present Charter may be expelled from the Organization by the General Assembly upon the recommendation of the Security Council."
9 UN Charter Article 15(1), "The General Assembly shall receive and consider annual and special reports from the Security Council; these reports shall include an account of the measures that the Security Council has decided upon or taken to maintain international peace and security."
10 See UN Charter Articles 11(1), (2), (3), (4) and Article 35 (1) where any member can bring a dispute to either the Security Councilor the General Assembly and (2).
11 See UN Charter Article 14.

Table 9.1 Instances of transfer of authority from the Security Council to the General Assembly

	Topic and document(s)	Date of session	Convened by	Security Council resolution, date, and votes
1	**Northern Greece** Creation of UNSCOB by GA- A/ 109	October 21, 1947	**Security Council**	Security Council moved the issue to the GA-S/555, September 15, 1947
2	**Korea** Calling for China to remove its forces, A/498 (V).	February 1, 1951	**General Assembly**	S/RES/90 (1951). No longer seized of the matter Voting unanimous
3	**Suez** A/3354 (GAOR, 1st Emergency Special Session (ESS), Suppl. No. 1)	November 1–10, 1956	**Security Council**	S/RES/119, October 31, 1956 Adopted by 7 votes to 2 (France, U.K.) with 2 abstentions (Australia and Belgium)
4	**Hungary** A/3355 (GAOR, 2nd ESS, Suppl. No. 1)	November 4–10, 1956	**Security Council**	S/RES/120, November 4, 1956 Adopted by 10 votes to 1 (USSR) at the 754th meeting
5	**Lebanon** A/3905 (GAOR, 3rd ESS, Suppl. No. 1)	August 8–21, 1958	**Security Council**	S/RES/129, August 7, 1958 Adopted unanimously at the 838th meeting
6	**Congo question** A/4510 (GAOR, 4th ESS, Suppl. No. 1)	September 17–19, 1960	**Security Council**	S/RES/157, September 17, 1960 Adopted by 8 votes to 2 (Poland and USSR) with 1 abstention (France)
7	**Middle East 1967 War** A/6798 (GAOR, 5th ESS, Suppl. No. 1)	June 17– September 18, 1967	**USSR**	Letter from USSR (A/ 6717); under Article 11 of the Charter
8	**India/Pakistan** A/2832 (26th GA Session)	December 16, 1971	**Security Council**	S/RES/303, December 6, 1971 Adopted by 11 votes to 0 with 4 abstentions
9	**Afghanistan** *(Soviet invasion)* A/ES-6/7 (GAOR, 6th ESS, Suppl. No. 1), Press Release GA/6172	January 10–14, 1980	**Security Council**	S/RES/462, January 9, 1980 Adopted by 12 votes to 2 (Germany, USSR) with 1 abstention (Zambia) *(Continued Overleaf)*

Table 9.1 Continued

	Topic and document(s)	*Date of session*	*Convened by*	*Security Council resolution, date, and votes*
10	**Palestine (Israeli withdrawal)** A/ES-7/14 + Add.1 + Add.1/Corr.1 (GAOR, 7th ESS, Suppl. No. 1), Press Release GA/6245 + Add.1–4	July 22–9, 1980 April 20–8, 1982 June 25–6, 1982 August 16–19, 1982 September 24, 1982	**Senegal (Chairman, Palestinian Rights Committee)**	Letter from Senegal (A/ES-7/1), A/37/205-S/14990 Convened pursuant to the Uniting for Peace Resolution
11	**South West Africa/ Namibia** (*sanctions on South Africa*) A/ES-8/13 (GAOR, 8th ESS, Suppl. No. 1), Press Release GA/6414	September 3–14, 1981	**Zimbabwe**	Letter from Zimbabwe (A/ES-8/1) Convened pursuant to the Uniting for Peace Resolution
12	**Occupied Arab territories** A/ES-9/7 (GAOR, 9th ESS, Suppl. No. 1), Press Release GA/6560	January 29– February 5, 1982	**Security Council**	S/RES/500, January 28, 1982 Adopted by 13 votes to none, with 2 abstentions (U.K and U.S) at the 2330th meeting
13	**Grenada** On the issue of U.S. intervention: GA res. A/38/7	November 2, 1983	**General Assembly**	Draft resolution vetoed by U.S., S/16077/Rev.1 Nicaragua request GA meet under rule 15
14	**Panama** Intervention of U.S. to remove Manuel Noriega; GA res. A/44/240	December 29, 1989	**General Assembly**	Draft resolution on December 23, vetoed by France, U.K., and U.S.; letter by Cuba and Nicaragua request GA meeting under rule 15
15	**Occupied East Jerusalem and the rest of the Occupied Palestinian territory** (10th Emergency Session) A/ES-10/5 A/ES-10/L.1 + Add.1 A/ES-10/L.2/ Rev.1 A/ES-10/L.3 + Add.1 A/ES-10/L.4/ Rev.1+ Rev.1/Add.1 A/ES-10/L.5/ Rev.1*	April 24–5, 1997 July 15, 1997 November 13, 1997 March 17, 1998 February 5, 8 and 9, 1999 October 18 and 20, 2000 December 20, 2001 May 7, 2002	**Qatar**	Letter from Qatar Convened pursuant to the Uniting for Peace Resolution

Topic and document(s)	Date of session	Convened by	Security Council resolution, date, and votes
A/ES-10/L.6 A/58/ES-10/L.13 A/58/ES-10/L.16 [Add.1] A/58/ES-10/ L.17 [Add.1] A/RES/ ES-10/2–11	August 5, 2002 September 19, 2003 October 20–1, 2003 December 3, 2003		
16 **Israeli security wall** *(resumption of 10th ES)* Resolution passed on the wall—A/RES/ 58/3 Request to the ICJ for an Advisory Opinion A/RES/ES-10/14	October 21, 2003; December 3 and 8, 2003	**General Assembly**	Vetoed Security Council draft resolution S/2003/980, October 14, 2003

Source: Adapted from a United Nations Department of Public Information table with additions by the authors.

Part IV

Conclusion

10 Conclusion

Assessing the Council's authority

Bruce Cronin and Ian Hurd

In late 2004, a high-level panel on UN reform appointed by United Nations Secretary General Kofi Annan issued a report that advocated the most radical reorganization of political relations among states since the UN was founded in 1945 (United Nations 2004). As Anne Marie Slaughter (2005: 620) argues, this report seeks nothing less than revising the 1945 consensus underlying the UN Charter, by posing a challenge to the post-World War II concepts of sovereignty, responsibility, and collective security. "Membership in the United Nations is no longer a validation of sovereign status and a shield against unwanted meddling in a state's domestic jurisdiction," Slaughter (2005: 627) holds. "It is rather the right and capacity to participate in the United Nations itself, working in concert with other nations to sit in judgment and take action against threats to human security whenever and wherever they arise." The "new security consensus" advanced in the report "embraces an expanded global solidarity" requiring UN action in alleviating "disease, hunger, illiteracy, environmental degradation, internal conflict, systematic human rights violations, weapons proliferation, and terrorism."

In this sense, this restructuring proposal envisions not only an enhanced role for the Security Council in areas of international politics that go well beyond those foreseen by the organization's framers. It also advocates a fundamental redefinition of the relationship between the Council, the membership of the UN, and by extension, the international community as a whole. Whether the underlying premise of the report—that an enlarged *role* for the Council is synonymous with expanded *authority* for that body— reflects current political reality, is one of the main issues addressed in this volume.

We opened *The UN Security Council and the Politics of International Authority* with a set of theoretical and practical questions pertaining to the interaction between the Council, international authority, and legitimacy. In this final chapter, we will revisit these questions and other issues raised in the Introduction and Chapter 2 in light of the discussions and empirical observations advanced in Chapters 3–9.

Increased role/increased authority

The preceding chapters confirmed the common view that the Council has dramatically increased its role in international affairs well beyond its original task of maintaining international peace and security. Traditionally, international security has been defined as maintaining the territorial integrity and political independence of the member states. Yet as Chapters 3–8 discussed, the Council has become deeply involved in prosecuting war crimes, promoting human rights, alleviating humanitarian emergencies, protecting civilian populations within sovereign states, and challenging political violence initiated by non-state actors. In and of itself, this finding alone would be somewhat banal; there is little doubt that the Council has become a significant player in an increasingly wider range of political issues throughout the world. The more significant question concerns whether an increase in the Council's *role* in international affairs means a corresponding increase in its *authority*. If, as Ian Hurd maintains in Chapter 2, authority is a relationship among actors in which one group is recognized by all parties as having both the right and the competence to make binding decisions for the rest of the community, evidence of increased authority requires more than simply an increase in activity.

Therefore, the authors addressed the broader relationship between action and authority. Based on the discussions in the preceding chapters, we generally conclude that the increased role of the Council has indeed also meant an increase in its authority, although there may not be unanimous agreement on this point. We based this conclusion on several factors.

First, the Council has not only expanded the scope of its involvement into new areas of international politics without first obtaining formal approval from the membership. It has also imposed greater obligations on the member states to adopt new domestic policies on terrorism (Chapters 5 and 7), arrest and extradite international war crimes suspects (Chapters 4 and 6), ban the practice of ethnic cleansing (Chapter 4), restrict economic activities with states involved in gross human rights abuses (Chapter 7), cooperate with UN peacekeepers and non-governmental organizations involved in providing humanitarian assistance to their citizens (Chapter 8), and permit international supervision of domestic conflicts (Chapter 4). Although some of these actions raised controversy when they were adopted, few states directly challenged the *right* of the Council to undertake them, and those that did remained in the minority. Moreover, as demonstrated in the previous chapters, these obligations have remained intact even after the issues that gave rise to them were resolved. The ability to create new obligations for others to follow is a clear indication of a relationship between a superior and a subordinate, an essential element of authority.

More specifically, in each of the preceding cases, the obligations created by the Council were aimed at inducing the member states to adopt policies that many may not have otherwise done on their own. As Ian Johnstone pointed out in Chapter 5, in passing resolution 1373, the Council required states to adopt measures drawn from the International Convention for the Suppression of the Financing of Terrorism, despite the fact that the treaty was not yet in force and that only 43 of the 192 member states had even signed (much less ratified) the agreement.[1] Similarly, in creating the international criminal tribunals for the former Yugoslavia, Rwanda, East Timor, and Sierra Leone, the Council required all states to cooperate with the court even though there was no agreement or treaty to this effect. The requirements included arresting and extraditing suspects to The Hague, regardless of whether a particular state's domestic laws permitted the government to do so. Perhaps the most intrusive obligation imposed by the Council was its demand that all parties to the internal conflict within Bosnia take a number of specific measures to protect the population of selected cities and provide unlimited freedom of movement to an external military force (UNPROFOR). It is not the act of issuing these mandatory declarations that offers evidence of increased authority, but, rather, the fact the most member states accepted the *right* of the Council to do so.

Second, the Council created these obligations without relying on coercion, making them a legal requirement rather than a dictate from the world's most powerful states. Nowhere in any of the resolutions discussed in the previous chapters were there implied or explicit threats against those who failed to accept the new obligations, nor did the resolutions mobilize any of the Council's coercive resources that it had available to it in Chapter VII of the UN Charter.[2] In fact, as Johnstone pointed out in Chapter 5, the members of the Council did not expect resolution 1373 to be enforced, but, rather, relied on the member states to voluntarily "buy in" to the anti-terrorism regime. In this sense, the Council expected the member states to accept these obligations because it said so. Similarly, the mandate that all states cooperate with the international criminal tribunals was issued by the Council without the threat of economic, diplomatic or military sanctions. The members of the Council assumed that the relevant states (apart from Serbia, which was the main target of the tribunals) would comply. Even the (ultimately unsuccessful) creation of safe zones within Bosnia was an assertion of Council authority rather than a Chapter VII military action.

Although the success of these actions was mixed, the lack of compliance by specific states does not undermine the authority (that is, the right) of the Council to issue its directives, any more than violation of domestic laws by criminals nullifies the authority of the legislature to pass laws declaring certain acts to be crimes. Certainly widespread defiance by the member states would severely diminish the credibility of the Council (and ultimately render its authority irrelevant); however, in the cases studied in this volume, there is little evidence of significant opposition. In the most egregious case, the establishment of safe zones in Bosnia, defiance was limited to the main protagonist, the Serbian paramilitaries. Although the Council was not able to achieve consensus on enforcement measures, it was the establishment of these zones by the Council that provided NATO with the legal justification to take military action—Operation Deliberate Force—in defense of the Council's mandates (NATO 2002). In an indirect sense, then, the zones did enable the subsequent intervention by NATO that ultimately ended the Serbian campaign of ethnic cleansing.

Defining the scope of the Council's authority

If the Council has indeed increased its authority within both the United Nations and the broader international community, this raises the logical question of who decides when, how, and to what extent the Council can assume greater decision-making power over the member states. In the preceding chapters, all of the authors found that it is the Council itself that ultimately determines the extent of its own legal authority, but that it only does so within the framework of the goals, procedures, norms, and the Charter of the United Nations. In a broader sense, we also found that the Council is keenly attuned to the limits imposed by international law and the political dynamics that exist within the broader international community. The means through which they make these determinations include *deliberation, precedent, delegation*, and *consensus*.

Deliberation

In explaining how the Council could expand its authority to include legislative action, Johnstone demonstrated how the quality of its deliberations—that is, the use of argumentation, justification, and appeals to reasons that reach beyond narrow self-interest—provide a method through which that body can determine whether and how to move into areas that was never envisioned by either the Charter or the political bodies of the United Nations. By removing the discussion a step away from a conversation defined by a clash of self-interests, the Council has often been able to act as a collective body that accepts the responsibility for security management and a sense of "common good" for the the collectivity of states. In this sense, the *process* through which the Council discusses and debates specific issues makes it possible for it to consider its limits and prerogatives.

This is not to say that Council deliberations reflect an ideal deliberative setting. As Johnstone acknowledges, legislating by the Council has qualities of hegemonic law in action. By this he means a situation in which the powerful states short-circuit the normal law-making process to write rules that serve their interests, while benefiting from the legitimation that working through the Council brings. At the same time, most political leaders have accepted the Council as representing an "interpretive community" with the authority and competence to make judgments concerning issues related to international peace and security.[3] Moreover, the theory of deliberative democracy does not require that all agree with the outcome of the deliberations, only that the decision be preceded by the opportunity for the relevant participants to express their views within accepted procedures. This condition appears to be satisfied, at least in most of the cases discussed in the preceding chapters. Therefore, although the members of the Council obviously promote their own individual interests during the meetings, the body itself has adopted a common discourse (that is, the language of non-aggression, human rights, and humanitarian action), guided by a common goal ("the maintenance of international peace and security"), and a detailed justification for each of its actions that are based on a set of common principles.[4]

Precedent

In addition to relying on deliberation to determine the extent of their collective authority, we also found that the Council makes use of precedent. While the concept of precedent is usually reserved for legal arguments within a hierarchical law system, *political* precedent also provides a potent mechanism for determining whether a particular course of action is acceptable to the general community. In the case of the Council, several of the contributors examined the degree to which the Council draws from past decisions to determine current courses of action and justify expanding the scope of their activities. Sandholtz argued that following precedent legitimizes a political action by demonstrating that like cases are judged alike and that judgments are not just predilections or random events. When the Security Council initiates an action that states may view as overstepping its authority, the existence of even a single precedent is enough to challenge the argument that a particular course of action cannot be taken, inasmuch as it already has been. We saw in Chapter 7 how precedents established by the Council can build on each other and institutionalize expansions of authority. Although many scholars and political leaders viewed Nuremberg as "victor's justice," the trials still provided a precedent for submitting individual political leaders to international criminal jurisdiction, thereby making it easier for the Council to justify the practice when they decided to establish international criminal trials for the Balkans. This in turn formed both a precedent and a point of reference for the Council's discussions concerning Rwanda, East Timor, Sierra Leone, and Cambodia. In this sense, the Council was able to expand its authority by drawing from past experiences, when similar actions were met either with general approval or at least with a bare minimum of disapproval from the member states.

Cronin, Andreopolis, and Graubart found similar uses of precedent. In establishing safe zones within Bosnia and Herzegovina in 1993 and Rwanda in 1994, the Council drew from a precedent established by the U.S. and Britain in 1991. While the 1991 Iraqi safe havens were not specifically authorized by the Council, the fact that they were implemented in the aftermath of a UN-sponsored Chapter VII action—and that most observers considered them to be successful—helped to justify the use of this newly discovered mechanism for extending the Council's authority to maintain international peace and security. As with the case of the international criminal tribunals, the establishment of safety zones in Bosnia and Herzegovina made it easier for the Council to establish them in Rwanda a year later. Much of the debate and discussion over the propriety of creating the zones had already occurred previously, and—as Sandholtz pointed out—it became difficult to claim that the Council was not authorized to take this action since they had already done so. Building from this, the Council established safety zones again in March of 1994, in order to protect the transportation of provisions and relief workers in the war-torn southern region of Sudan.

The Council also drew from precedent when it began to expand its definition of international peace and security to include the protection of human rights and the provision of humanitarian assistance during the 1990s. As Andreapolis argues, since the founders of the UN did not foresee this role when they drafted the Charter a half century earlier, the Council built upon precedents established during the cold war in its dealings with South Africa and Rhodesia. From this, they increased their authority to become involved in domestic conflicts in Somalia, Angola, and the Balkans. Graubart also found the Council's use of precedent to be an important mechanism for redefining its authority in establishing peacekeeping operations. Although cold war peacekeeping was strictly based on the consent of the conflicting parties, after the end of the East–West conflict, the Council began to either initiate or authorize more intrusive types of interventionary actions under the broad peacekeeping label. They did so even though its actions were not always based on the consent of the parties and often went well beyond simply keeping warring factions apart (as traditional peacekeeping did). Moreover, Graubart also found that the recent practice of "subcontracting" peacekeeping/building to coalitions of states aided by humanitarian nongovernmental organizations (NGOs) also built upon prior precedents. There is nothing in either the UN Charter or in the original design of the organization that permits the Council to act as an authorizing body for interventions either by other international organizations, individual states, or coalitions of states. As Voeten argues, the idea of "subcontracting" the task of maintaining peace and security emerged over time, but by now such subcontracting has become routine. Similarly, the Council's use of NGOs to provide relief and reconstruction services has become a common aspect of virtually all nation-building and peacekeeping operations.

At the same time, precedent has also worked to diffuse the Council's authority. As both Voeten and Krasno and Das explain, the initial decision by the Council to authorize the General Assembly to become involved in security matters through the Uniting for Peace resolution has in effect given that body the ability to encroach on what most people assume to be the province of the Council. While the Uniting for Peace procedure has only been evoked ten times, it remains part of the Assembly's toolbox of options.

Delegation

Probably the most obvious mechanism for the Council to determine the scope of its authority is for the P5 to consider exactly what powers the member states have implicitly and explicitly delegated to it. As Voeten pointed out, states have specifically granted to the Council discretion over two areas, decisions on whether *particular* uses of force are appropriate and the *types* of responses the Council can consider when threats to international peace and security emerge. As history has taught us, these areas are very broad and subject to a wide variety of interpretations, as evidenced by the many types of situations that the Council has labeled a "threat or breach of the peace." Yet, as Voeten has pointed out, since the Council cannot actually enforce its decisions—at least not directly—it needs to create situations in which the member states find it in their interests to comply. In part, this goes to the heart of our discussion on legitimacy, which we will address in the next section. However, in general this means that the Council must act within what it believes to be the boundaries that the non-Council states accept as legitimate exercises of authority.

Consensus

How are these boundaries set? The preceding chapters demonstrated that Council decisions are guided at least in part by the principles, goals, procedures, and norms of the United Nations in particular and the broader international community in general. In total, these goals and principles constitute the normative environment through which the Council operates at a particular point in time. Cronin found that the Council can expand its authority in those areas in which there is a consensus within the international community as to what constitutes a legal obligation in a particular area of international politics. Drawing from a wide variety of sources—including peremptory norms, General Assembly resolutions, law-making treaties, customary international law, and the charters of international organizations—he found that the Council has become an arbiter of what constitutes a legal consensus and acts based on this finding. In this sense, the process through which the Council determines the existence of a consensus acts as a mechanism for defining both the limit and scope of its legal authority.

In this vein, Cronin, Sandholtz, Graubart, and Andreopolis all agree that contemporary norms concerning limitations on internal state violence have enabled the Council to expand into the previously excluded areas of human rights, humanitarian intervention, criminal prosecution, and nation-building. Based on these emerging norms, the Council has reconceptualized systematic human rights violations, ethnic cleansing, genocide, refugee flows, and even massive starvation as threats to international peace and security. In another normative environment, the Council would have been neither able nor most likely interested in making such determinations.

Most of the authors also agree that the normative frameworks that dominate during a particular period provide both a grammar and set of principles upon which the Council can draw, either to determine their policies or to justify those that they already decided to pursue. As George Andreopoulos observed, the rise of human rights norms after World War II enabled the Council to redefine the parameters of the domestic jurisdiction clause of the Charter (Article 2(7)). Internal acts that would have been previously considered purely domestic matters have become not only a concern to the Council but also the target of their actions. In this vein, the way in which the Council defines "threat or breach of the peace" and "international peace and security" depends largely on contemporary normative frameworks. For example, Nuremberg could serve as precedent in the discourses surrounding the establishment of the international criminal tribunals during the 1990s only because the normative context was favorable to such an interpretation. International norms against gross human rights violations and grave breaches of the laws of war were clear and widely accepted. The international community was thus predisposed by its normative commitments to accept some mechanism for imposing accountability on perpetrators.

Legitimacy

Underlying all of these issues is the question of legitimacy; that is, the degree to which the UN membership recognizes the Council as having both the right and the competence to act on behalf of the international community in addressing issues related to international peace and security. Since legitimacy entails a shared belief about the appropriateness of an organization or actor's capabilities, this raises the further question of whether states consider the Council to be the proper body to address the increasing variety of new issues that it has confronted over the past decades. Over the past half century, a variety of regional and global organizations have emerged, giving states a wide choice of forums through which to address an increasing number of complex international issues. Technically, there is no hierarchy of organizations under international law; each organization theoretically has equal status in relation to its members. If, however, states endow the Council with a special status by seeing it as the most *appropriate* organization to address issues of peace and security, its ability to maintain its position depends on the perpetuation of its legitimacy.[5]

We posited in the Introduction that the scope and quality of the Security Council's authority expands and contracts proportionately with the degree of legitimacy that it gains from the membership. This section will discuss the extent to which this hypothesis is supported by the cases discussed in the preceding chapters.

Legitimacy is important for establishing, building, and maintaining *any* form of authority in the international system, inasmuch as the system itself is defined precisely by the *absence* of formal hierarchy among states.[6] Yet the preceding chapters suggest that legitimacy is particularly important for the Council. The disjuncture between authority and accountability has created a democratic deficit within the organization inasmuch as there is no system of checks and balances in the UN system and the Council is not a representative body of the organization. Yet at the same time, since its resolutions carry a legal obligation, it holds a unique position in international politics. For this reason, the degree of Council legitimacy is crucial for determining the scope and quality of its authority. In order to approach this question, it is useful to review whether the cases discussed in the preceding chapters have effectively demonstrated that the Council has achieved at least one of the three types of legitimacy introduced in the Introduction: procedural, purposive, or performance.

As discussed in the first chapter, *procedural* legitimacy requires that the grant of authority to an institution be consistent with its existing rules and decision-making procedures. So long as the institution conforms to these rules and procedures, it can expand into new areas without violating its trust. Johnstone confirmed that the Council had established its right to "legislate" by first engaging in extensive deliberations not only among the P5 and E10, but at times with other states who shared an interest in the outcome of particular decisions. Although most UN observers recognize that Council decisions are made primarily by the P5, Johnstone argued that legitimacy in the Council does not require democracy in making the final decision, but rather transparency and inclusion during the deliberative process. Therefore, it is the quality of their deliberations (that is, appeals to organizational principles), their attention to procedure (as articulated in the Provisional Rules of Procedure) and the increasing transparency of the decision-making process (beginning with the new procedures adopted at the 1991 Security Council Summit) that have increased its procedural legitimacy in the eyes of the membership. This has enabled that body to expand its authority into new areas without sparking a revolt from the membership.

Cronin and Sandholtz examined the degree to which the Council's *purposive* legitimacy has strengthened its authority to take action in areas that go well beyond its mandate. As defined in the Introduction, purposive legitimacy suggests that the purposes served by an institution are seen by the relevant actors as consistent with the broader norms and values of international society. Cronin argued that the Council was able to expand the scope of its authority into new areas of international life without the explicit consent of the United Nations membership because its actions furthered goals that were generally accepted by the international community. Specifically, he demonstrated that since there was a broad consensus that international law prohibits the exercise of "excess violence" by the state, Council actions aimed at challenging these practices were accepted by the membership, even though this required an expansion of its legal and political authority within the UN. Clearly, its performance legitimacy strengthened its ability to do so. Similarly, Sandholtz found that since the creation of tribunals to prosecute those accused of major war crimes and crimes against humanity furthers well-established international human rights norms, the Council's actions were viewed by the UN membership as legitimate. This in turn enabled that body to expand its authority into the area of judicial action.

Krasno and Das took the opposite approach to performance legitimacy in investigating how the Council's authority can *diminish* when it fails to act consistently with the norms and the expectations of the membership. They argue that because the Council is given the primary authority to address threats or breaches of the peace, its legitimacy is reduced when it fails to act when such threats or breaches occur. This shows in practice the importance for the legitimation of "effectiveness" in achieving social purposes, as discussed in Chapter 1. The Uniting for Peace resolution both recognized and facilitated a transfer of authority from the Security Council to the General Assembly.

Change in the Security Council

What can all of this teach us about the probable direction of change within the Security Council, in particular, in the relationship between the Council and the broader UN membership? Organizational change could take place along at least three dimensions—in formal structure, in operating procedure, and in the substance of the organization. This section will discuss change in the Council in light of the findings from preceding chapters.

Formal structure

Change in the formal structure of the Council is by its nature much more easily identifiable than changes in the other two dimensions. It has happened only once, with the addition of four new non-permanent seats by an agreement reached in 1963 that took effect in 1965 (see Luck 2003). The timing of this change suggests that the procedural legitimation of its authority during the period of decolonization was a function of increased participation by the smaller states. The end of the cold war and the corresponding increase in Council activity provided an impetus for another important set of changes. Since 1995, the General Assembly has had an Open Ended Working Group (OEWG) active on the issue of Council reform. The fruits of these efforts have not included agreement on the main issues (the distribution and powers of possible new seats on the Council) but it has identified the main cleavages that divide the factions and so has helped to define the parameters of the debate. This proved to be useful information to the Secretary-General's High-Level Panel in 2004, the report of which has become the foundation on which a possible expansion of the Council might be built in the coming years. The High-Level Panel took advantage of the prior deliberations when it considered the range of possible expansion choices, and narrowed its proposals accordingly.

Although there has to date been only one formal change to the Council, there are still interesting connections between the composition of Council membership and the general issue of Council power and authority. The logic behind the expansion, together with the extensive discussions in the OEWG and elsewhere, is based on an assumption that by managing the membership question we can gain leverage over the Council's legitimacy (Hurd 2008). Most proposals for expanding the Council rely on the hypothesis that an increase in its size (and thus participation by the general membership) will lead to a corresponding increase in its legitimacy (and thus its authority and power). This may well be true, but the causal claims that are implicit within it have not been tested and are very rarely even directly explained by the proponents of expansion.[7]

One version of this claim is that the Council's legitimacy is harmed by the growing gap between the distribution of Council permanent seats and the distribution of power in the world system. Both defenders and critics of the Council share this premise.[8] Adding Germany and Japan as permanent or semi-permanent members is thus seen as a necessary step to stop the erosion of Council authority. A distinct version—drawing on analogous logic but a different empirical claim—is that the over-representation of rich, Northern states among permanent members reduces the Council's legitimacy in the eyes of the rest of the world, or at least the rest of the world's governments. On this view, the future of the Council depends on making it more representative of the General Assembly, or of the world's population. The argument about "representativeness" is often blended with one about "diversity," although these are conceptually separate. The "diversity" view claims that the Council gains legitimacy to the extent that it reflects the full range of views embodied by the General Assembly, and so membership changes should be designed to maximize its diversity even if that means over-representing some marginal views.

Each of these views is founded on a different hypothesis about how legitimacy is created or earned by organizations, but all are based on the assumption that formal membership is important for legitimation. This assumption is often criticized in the fields of organizational studies and management, at least as it applies to the legitimacy of business firms. In these cases, there is little evidence to support the view that membership is the most important contributor to organizational legitimacy—although the matter is clearly complex and resists mono-causal explanations.[9] In the case of the UN, the important question is the degree to which the smaller state would cooperate in implementing Council actions (such as peacekeeping and extraditing war criminals) if it perceives that Council to be primarily a great power club. As discussed above, Johnstone found that transparency is more important for the Council's legitimacy than its membership. If his conclusions are correct, then the debate over enlarging the Council may be less important than the one over its accessibility and openness (Hurd 1997).

A separate question arises as well, namely whether changes in membership are likely to improve or exacerbate the problems for which the Council is most often criticized. Russett (1997), for instance, suggests that the trade-off between effectiveness and size in the Council is one of the central dilemmas that must be faced by the planners of Council reform. This implies a more complex relationship between membership and legitimacy than is imagined in the arguments above. If adding members reduces effectiveness (presumably because it could add new vetoes and would certainly add clashing interests) then the claim that the Council's power would be increased by increasing its legitimacy through adding new members may not hold. Instead, in this view, representativeness, legitimacy, and effectiveness are separate and potentially competing values. Not all good things go together. More generally, we might wonder whether the values of democracy are appropriate to the Security Council. If democratizing the Council means a trade-off with its effectiveness, then there needs to be a critical comparison between the costs and benefits implicit in democratization. It is not enough to assume that a more "democratic" Council is preferable to the status quo; this needs to be considered through analysis. Changes in Council membership will have unpredictable effects on Council authority.

Procedures

As with the determination of what constitutes a threat or breach of the peace, the Council is the master of its own operating procedures and these have evolved considerably over the years. This is true of both the formal "Rules of Procedure" envisioned in Article 30 of the Charter and the informal practices that have grown up around the Council. Both kinds of procedural change have had a significant effect on the deliberative process at the Council and thus on its authority. Certainly it impacts on the question of procedural legitimacy, as discussed in the Introduction.

Among the informal procedures of the Council that are designed to increase its procedural legitimacy, the most significant might be the growth in the use of small-group consultations prior to official Council meetings. At these unofficial meetings of a subset of both Council and potentially non-council states, the members can arrange important substantive decisions. These have been thoroughly discussed elsewhere (Bailey and Daws 1998: ch. 2), but we focus on them here only to highlight their potential connection to change in the authority of the Council. Deliberative theories of legitimation argue that states will be more likely to accept the Council as authoritative if there are clear mechanisms for the other states to present their views. This was confirmed by Johnstone's study in Chapter 5. While the P5 will always retain their crucial decision-making influence, the legitimacy of their special status could be enhanced to the extent they involve those states that have a direct interest in the outcome of a particular issue. Both the Charter and the Council's rules of procedure enshrine this principle, but the practice of secret, informal consultations among a few permanent members may undermine it. There is evidence that the leading members of the Council are conscious of these issues and have at least considered steps to bolster their legitimacy in this area. Since the early 1990s the Council has made significant changes in the way it discusses issues and reports these discussions to the general membership. It began to increase the number of open meetings held prior to the official votes and now regularly publishes its program of work for the month in advance of even its closed meetings. In addition, beginning in 1994, the Council decided to have its president give informal oral briefings to non-members on the broad outlines of its internal consultations (See Hulton 2004: 246; Hurd 1997; Bailey and Daws 1998).

Substance

It is frequently noted that the Council's interpretation of its substantive powers has changed over time. Given the Council's authority over the terms of its mandate, there has been a good deal of discussion—both in this volume and elsewhere—about the flexibility of the Council's interpretation of the phrase "threat to international peace and security." Was it appropriate to so characterize Libya's handling of the Lockerbie suspects? Was it appropriate to *not* so characterize Cuba's nuclear missiles in 1962? As we discussed in the sections above, the legal question is easily handled: the Council under Article 39 of the Charter determines for itself what constitutes a threat to or breach of international peace and security, and there is no clear legal mandate for any other organization, notably the International Court of Justice, to perform a review of these determinations. So, what the Council says is a threat *is* by definition a threat.

Developments in the set of "threats" identified by the Council are perhaps the clearest existing evidence for the argument that there has been significant change in the substance of the Council's work since 1945. These developments press outward the scope of the authority claimed by the Council, reaching into new conceptual territory including refugee flows, humanitarian crises, and international finance. In the area of domestic conflicts, for instance, Sutterlin (2003: 85) argues—and Andreopoulos confirms in Chapter 6—"it is increasingly accepted, albeit conditionally at times, that intrastate conflict, if it threatens unconscionable loss of life and property, is of legitimate concern to the United Nations." If this is the case, then the plain meaning of Article 2(7) on matters "essentially within the jurisdiction" of a state is no longer the operative understanding of a limit on UN activities. The domain of authority of the Council is therefore broader than one would believe from a reading of the Charter's text. Ruth Wedgewood (2003) has made this into a more general claim about the importance for international security of "successive adaptations" of the Charter that allow "alternative methods of decision-making" to those formally set out in the Charter. Her interpretation remains highly contentious in that it appears to endorse whatever decision procedure allows the strong powers to do what they please, and so undercuts the contribution of formal rules. At the same time, it is useful in highlighting the history of informal adaptations in both the procedures and substance of Council decision-making.

Implications for the Council reform debate [10]

Among the competing proposals for reforming the UN Security Council, one theme is a near-constant: that the Council's legitimacy is in peril unless the body can be reformed to account for recent changes in world politics. This consensus is driven by a number of developments: geopolitical changes (in the distribution of military and economic power), systemic changes after decolonization (which multiplied the number of UN members), and normative changes (in the value given to diversity, equity, and representation). The result, summarized by the *New York Times*, is that the Security Council "is indisputably out of date." Hoge 2004. Most arguments in favor of Council expansion identify the gap between the structures of Council membership and contemporary international realities as a problem because it is a threat to the *legitimacy* of the Council. The gap is an objective fact, but the link to legitimacy is what gives it its political salience and has made it a controversial matter in world politics.

By far the most common malady identified at the Council is that the membership of the Council contains such inequalities that it threatens to delegitimize the Council as a whole. The High Level Panel said that "the effectiveness of the global collective security system . . . depends ultimately not only on the legality of decisions but on common perceptions of their legitimacy" (United Nations 2004: 57) and that the anachronistic structure of membership rules "diminishes support for Security Council decisions" (United Nations 2004: 66).

In addition to the composition of the membership, as discussed in the above section, many UN observers argue that the inequalities inherent in the structure of Council membership are a drag on the legitimacy of the Council. The distinctions between permanent and non-permanent members, and the different formal and informal powers of each group keep it from achieving the maximum potential level of legitimacy that might in principle be available to an international organization. Second, this lack of legitimacy is then said to reduce the effectiveness of the Council as a whole. Without legitimacy, a society must rely on other tools to maintain order, notably coercion and inducement (Hurd 1999). This is particularly problematic for the Security Council, which cannot reliably use coercion to exert compliance with its decisions and it has no resources to use as inducements.[11] A Council without legitimacy would therefore have few tools with which to win states' support and so would quickly lose power, influence, and effectiveness in world politics.

Many Council reform proposals interpose the concept of deliberation between the formal membership of the Council and the legitimacy of its outputs. In this view—and in the view of Ian Johnstone in Chapter 5—deliberation is the source of legitimacy for international organizations.

Opening up the Council's membership is a means to increasing its deliberative qualities. The existing deliberative process at the Council includes some formal rights of participation for non-members.

The Charter requires that the Council invite parties to a dispute to participate in its deliberations on the dispute (Article 32) and allows that the Council may invite any state whose interests it considers "specially affected" by the issue at hand (Article 31). In practice, the latter provision is used by non-members to request a seat in the deliberation. According to Bailey and Daws (1998: 623, n.128), such requests are "seldom opposed." It is almost automatic that a non-member state can add its voice to the *formal* deliberations of the Council when it wants to. Because the deliberative model is mainly concerned with the breadth of information flowing into the process rather than the formal status of the speakers, this goes some distance toward satisfying a purely deliberative model of legitimation in that it opens the channel for states to express their views in the Council without distinction between members of the Council and non-members.

States that are accepted into the process under Article 31 already have the opportunity to contribute to the deliberation. Therefore, the potential increase in deliberation from adding new members must be quite small.

This conclusion may have to be amended based on changes in the Council's practice of informal consultations that we discuss above (Hulton 2004; Luck 2005). The issue depends on whether we see the many informal processes as extensions of Council deliberations or as circumvention of them.[12] If Council members have access to these informal sessions greater than non-members, then becoming a member might increase one's participation in the broader deliberative process. It is plausible that this might be true, though it probably depends on the state in question. Large states may already participate in informal consultations even as non-members and so would not produce a net increase in deliberation if they were given formal Council seats (Hurd 1997). Small non-member states are unlikely to be invited to informal sessions except in unusual circumstances—but even as formal members of the Council they might find themselves excluded from informal sessions too. The power of the informal process at present is precisely that it allows the dominant states on the Council to choose from among the members and non-members only those whose contribution to deliberation they feel is valuable to them. It erases the distinction between member and non-member for the deliberation (Prantl 2005; Hurd 1997) but enhances the hierarchy of power between them.

Summing it up

The UN Charter defines the legal structure of the Security Council but the Council's practical influence depends on the construction and reconstruction of its political authority. Its authority is a product of the legitimation of the Council, and the essays in this volume trace the sources, effects, and implications of the authority relationship between states and the Council. While much of IR scholarship takes as its starting premise that states exist in an anarchic realm devoid of political authority, the essays here have shown that the Council is often in a position of authority relative to states. We have seen how the authority of the Council is fragmentary, contested, and problematic, but also how it shapes state decision-making, international law, and the international system more broadly. By showing that political authority can exist between an international organization and the states that make it up, this volume opens a path for future research into the complex politics and history involved in constituting, challenging, and understanding international authority around the Council and elsewhere.

Notes

1 A list of signatories in late 2000 (a year prior to the adoption of 1373) can be found at www.state.gov/s/ct/rls/crt/2000/2463.htm.
2 See resolutions 819, 824, 836, 827, 955, 1373, and 1540.
3 On the Security Council as an interpretive community, see Johnstone 1991 and 2003.
4 See, for example, the resolutions discussed in the previous chapters, including 819, 824, 836, 827, 955, 1373, and 1540.
5 This is analogous to Great Powers needing to be seen as legitimate in order to retain their privileged status as Great Powers. See Cronin 2003; Simpson 2004; Hurd 2007b.
6 Cf. Simpson 2004, who characterizes the unequal legal systems created by strong states as formal, legal hierarchies in the international system, see Hurd 2007a.
7 "Expansion skeptics" tend to pay more attention to the internal logic of these arguments. See Weiss 2003.
8 Compare, for instance, the report of the High-Level Panel (United Nations 2004) and Glennon 2003. See also Weiss 2003.
9 For causal studies of the contributors to legitimation in firms see Kostova 1999; Massey 2001; Deephouse 1996. For studies in social groups, see the essays in Jost and Major 2001. For an excellent theoretical overview, see Zelditch 2001.
10 This section draws on Hurd 2008.
11 This is true of material resources, since the Council must rely on *ad hoc* contributions from states, but if we consider legal authority or the power to legitimate as "resources" then we could see some independent power in the Council.
12 Prantl (2005: 561) sees "informal groups" as "narrowing the participatory gap." The increase in participation is not necessarily in conflict with the conclusion that informal processes increase the power of the permanent members, since power and participation address separate issues.

References and interviews

Abbott, Kenneth and Duncan Snidal (1998) "Why States Act through Formal International Organizations." *Journal of Conflict Resolution*, 42 (1).

Abbott, Kenneth and Duncan Snidal (2002) "Values and Interests: International Legalization in the Fight Against Corruption." *Journal of Legal Studies*, 31 (1).

Abbott, Kenneth W., Robert O. Keohane, Andrew Moravcsik, Anne-Marie Slaughter, and Duncan Snidal (2000) "The Concept of Legalization." *International Organization*, 54 (3).

Adler, Emmanuel and Michael Barnett (1998) "A Framework for the Study of Security Communities." In Emmanuel Adler and Michael Barnett (eds.), *Security Communities*. Cambridge: Cambridge University Press.

"Agreement Between the United Nations and the Government of Sierra Leone on the Establishment of a Special Court for Sierra Leone" (2002) January 16. Available at www.sc-sl.org/scsl-agreement.html. Accessed April 3, 2007.

Ahmedani, Miriam, Meghan Stewart, Brianne McGonigle, Lissie Rushing, Anne Heindel, and Leslie Thompson (2006a) "Updates from the International Criminal Courts." *Human Rights Brief*, 13 (3).

Ahmedani, Miriam, Anne Heindel, Jeffrey Forbes, Robin Murphy, and Leslie Thompson (2006b) "Updates from the International Criminal Courts." *Human Rights Brief*, 13 (2).

Akram, Ambassador (2004) Interview conducted on July 21.

Albin, Cecelia (2001) *Justice and Fairness in International Negotiations*. Cambridge: Cambridge University Press.

Alger, Chadwick (2003) "Evolving Roles of NGOs in Member State Decision-making in the UN System." *Journal of Human Rights*, 2 (3).

Alvarez, Jose (1996) "Judging the Security Council." *American Journal of International Law*, 90 (1).

Alvarez, Jose (2001) "Constitutional Interpretation in International Organizations." In Jean-Marc Coicaud and Veijo Heiskanen (eds.), *The Legitimacy of International Organizations*, 104–54. Tokyo: United Nations University Press.

Alvarez, Jose (2003) "Hegemonic International Law Revisited." *American Journal of International Law*, 97 (4).

Alvarez, Jose (2005) *International Organizations as Law-makers*. Oxford: Oxford University Press.

Amnesty International (1998) "International Criminal Tribunal for Rwanda: Trials and Tribulations." AI Index IOR 40/003/1998. Amnesty International.

Amnesty International (2001) "East Timor: Justice Past, Present and Future." AI Index ASA 57/001/2001. Amnesty International. Available at web.amnesty.org/library/pdf/ASA570012001ENGLISH/$File/ASA5700101.pdf

Amnesty International (2002) "Rwanda: Gacaca: A Question of Justice." AI Index AFR 47/007/2002. Amnesty International.

Amnesty International (2005a) *Amnesty International Report 2005: Cambodia.* Available at web.amnesty.org/report2005/khm-summary-eng

Amnesty International (2005b) *Amnesty International Report 2005: Timor-Leste.* Amnesty International. Available at web.amnesty.org/report2005/tmp-summary-eng

Amnesty International (2005c) "International Criminal Tribunal for Rwanda: Trials and Tribulations." Available at web.amnesty.org/library/Index/ENGIOR 400031998?open&of=ENG-RWA. Accessed May 26, 2005.

Amnesty International (2005d) "Rwanda: Gacaca: A Question of Justice." Available at web.amnesty.org/library/Index/ENGAFR470072002?open&of=ENG-RWA. Accessed May 26, 2005.

Andreopoulos, George J. (2002) "Introduction: A Half Century after the Universal Declaration." In George J. Andreopoulos (ed.), *Concepts and Strategies in International Human Rights.* New York: Peter Lang.

Andreopoulos, George J. (2005) "The Impact of the War on Terror on the Accountability of Armed Groups." In Howard Hensel (ed.), *The Law of Armed Conflict: Constraints on the Contemporary Use of Military Force.* Aldershot: Ashgate.

Andreopoulos, George J. (2007) "The Human Rights/Humanitarian Framework in the Age of Terror," *Journal for Human Rights.* Menschenrechte und Terrorismus, no. 1, Wochenschauverlag Schwalbach/Ts.

Andreopoulos, George J. (unpublished) "Pathways to Intervention: The Changing Nature of Threats."

Andreopoulos, George J., Zehra F. Kabasakal Arat, and Peter Juviler (eds.) (2006) *Non-state Actors in the Human Rights Universe,* 141–63. Bloomfield, CT: Kumarian Press.

Anghie, Antony (2005) *Imperialism, Sovereignty and the Making of International Law.* Cambridge: Cambridge University Press.

Annan, Kofi (1999) "Two Concepts of Sovereignty." *The Economist,* September 18.

Annan, Kofi (2002) Interview. *BBC News,* September 10, vews.bbc.co.uk/2.hi/middle_east/2250948.stm.

Arend, Anthony (1999) *Legal Rules and International Society.* Oxford: Oxford University Press.

Arend, Anthony, Robert Beck, and Robert Vander Lugt (1996) *International Rules: Approaches from International Law and International Relations.* New York: Oxford University Press.

Arendt, Hannah (1958) "What Was Authority?" *NOMOS I.* Cambridge, MA: Cambridge University Press.

Arendt, Hannah (1997) *Between Past and Future.* New York: Penguin Books.

Ashley, Richard (1998) "Untying the Sovereign State: A Double Reading of the Anarchy Problematique." *Millennium,* 17 (2).

Avni, Benny (2004) "WMD Proliferation Resolution Passes." *New York Sun,* April 29, 7.

Bailey, Sydney D. and Sam Daws (1998) *The Procedure of the UN Security Council.* 3rd edn. Oxford: Oxford University Press.

Baker, James A. III (1995) *The Politics of Diplomacy: Revolution, War and Peace 1989–1992*. New York: Putnam's Sons.

Barker, J. Craig (2001) *International Law and International Relations*. New York: Continuum Press.

Barnett, Michael (1997) "Bringing in the New World Order: Liberalism, Legitimacy, and the United Nations." *World Politics*, 49 (4).

Barnett, Michael (2001) "Authority, Intervention, and the Outer Limits of International Relations Theory." In Thomas Callaghy, Ronald Kassimir, and Robert Latham (eds.), *Intervention and Transnationalism in Africa*. Cambridge: Cambridge University Press.

Barnett, Michael (2002) *Eyewitness to a Genocide: The United Nations and Rwanda*. Ithaca, NY: Cornell University Press.

Barnett, Michael and Raymond Duvall (2004) *Power in Global Governance*. Cambridge: Cambridge University Press.

Barnett, Michael and Martha Finnemore (1999) "The Politics, Power, and Pathologies of International Organizations." *International Organization*, 53 (4).

Barnett, Michael and Martha Finnemore (2004) *Rules for the World: International Organizations in Global Politics*. Ithaca: Cornell University Press.

Bass, Gary Jonathan (2000) *Stay the Hand of Vengeance: The Politics of War Crimes Tribunals*. Princeton, NJ: Princeton University Press.

Bassiouni, M. Cherif (1996) "International Crimes: *Jus Cogens* and *Obligatio Erga Omnes*." *Law and Contemporary Problems*, 59.

Belaunde, Ambassador (1950) Speech given at the General Assembly Fifth Session, September 20.

Benhabib, Seyla (1996) "Toward a Deliberative Model of Democratic Legitimacy." In Seyla Benhabib (ed.), *Democracy and Difference: Contesting the Boundaries of the Political*. Princeton, NJ: Princeton University Press.

Bennett, A. LeRoy (1995) *International Organizations: Principles and Issues*. Englewood Cliffs, NJ: Prentice Hall.

Bennett, Andrew, Joseph Lepgold, and Danny Unger (1994) "Burden-sharing in the Persian Gulf War." *International Organization*, 48 (1).

Benvenisti, Eyal (2004) *The International Law of Occupation*. Princeton, NJ: Princeton University Press.

Berger, Mark (2006) "From Nation-building to State-building: The Geopolitics of Development, the Nation-state System and the Changing Global Order." *Third World Quarterly*, 27 (1).

Bertodano, Sylvia de (2004) "East Timor: Trials and Tribulations." In Cesare P. R. Romano, André Nollkaemper, and Jann K. Kleffner (eds.), *Internationalized Criminal Courts and Tribunals*. Oxford: Oxford University Press.

Betts, Richard K. (1992) "Systems of Peace or Causes of War?" *International Security*, 17 (1).

Bianchi, Andrea (2007) "Assessing the Effectiveness of the UN Security Council's Anti-terrorism Measures: The Quest for Legitimacy and Cohesion," *European Journal of International Law* 17 (5).

Biddiss, Michael (2004) "From the Nuremberg Charter to the Rome Statute: A Historical Analysis of the Limits of International Criminal Accountability." In Ramesh Thakur and Peter Malcontent (eds.), *From Sovereign Impunity to International Accountability: The Search for Justice in a World of States*. New York: United Nations University Press.

Biersteker, Thomas (1992) "The 'Triumph' of Neoclassical Economics in the Developing World: Policy Convergence and Bases of Governance in the International Economic Order." In James Rosenau and Ernst-Otto Czempiel (eds.), *Governance without Government: Order and Change in World Politics*. Cambridge: Cambridge University Press.

Biersteker, Thomas (2007) "The UN's Counter-terrorism Efforts: Lessons for UNSCR 1540." In Olivia Bosch and Peter van Ham (eds.), *Global Non-proliferation and Counter-terrorism*. Washington, DC: Brookings Press, Chatham House, and Clingendael.

Bjola, Corneliu (2005) "Legitimating the use of Force in International Politics: A Communicative Action Perspective." *European Journal Of International Relations*, 11 (2).

Blokker, Niels (2000) "Is the Authorization Authorized? Powers and Practice of the UN Security Council to Authorize the Use of Force by 'Coalitions of the Able and Willing'." *European Journal of International Law*, 11 (3).

Blum, Yehuda (1993) *Eroding the United Nations Charter*. New York: Springer.

Bodansky, Daniel (1999) "The Legitimacy of International Governance: A Coming Challenge for International Environmental Law?" *American Journal of International Law*, 93 (3).

Bohman, James (1999) "International Regimes and Democratic Governance: Political Equality and Influence in Global Institutions." *International Affairs*, 75 (3).

Bolton, Patrick and Mathias Dewatripont (2005) *Contract Theory*. Cambridge, MA: MIT Press.

Bosch, Olivia and Peter Van Ham (2007a) "UNSCR 1540: Its Future and Contribution to Gobal Non-proliferation and Counter-terrorism." In Olivia Bosch and Peter van Ham (eds.), *Global Non-proliferation and Counter-terrorism*. Washington, DC: Brookings Press, Chatham House, and Clingendael.

Bosch, Olivia and Peter Van Ham (eds.) (2007b) *Global Non-proliferation and Counter-terrorism*. Washington, DC: Brookings Press, Chatham House, and Clingendael.

Bourantonis, Dimitris and Ritsa A. Panagiotou (2004) "Russia's Attitude towards the Reform of the United Nations Security Council, 1990–2000." *Journal of Communist Studies and Transition Politics*, 20 (4).

Bowett, Derek William (1964) *United Nations Forces: A Legal Study of United Nations Practice*. London: David Davies Memorial Institute.

Bowman, Herbert D. (2004) "Letting the Big Fish Get Away: The United Nations Justice Effort in East Timor." *Emory International Law Review*, 18 (1).

Bradol, Jean-Herve (2004) "Introduction: The Sacrificial International Order and Humanitarian Action." In Fabrice Weissman (ed.), *In the Shadow of "Just Wars": Violence, Politics and Humanitarian Action*. Ithaca, NY: Cornell University Press.

Brauman, Rony and Pierre Salignon (2004) "Iraq: In Search of a 'Humanitarian Crisis'." In Fabrice Weissman (ed.), *In the Shadow of "Just Wars": Violence, Politics and Humanitarian Action*. Ithaca, NY: Cornell University Press.

Brett, Rachel (1995) "The Role and Limits of Human Rights NGOs at the United Nations." *Political Studies*, 43.

Brierly, J. L. (1936) *The Law of Nations: An Introduction to the International Law of Peace*. Oxford : Clarendon Press.

Brooks, Stephen and William Wohlforth (2005) "International Relations Theory and the Case against Unilateralism." *Perspectives on Politics*, 3 (3).

Buchanan, Allen (2003) *Justice, Legitimacy, and Self-determination: Moral Foundations for International Law*. Oxford: Oxford University Press.

Buchanan, Allen and Robert Keohane (2004) "The Preventive Use of Force: A Cosmopolitan Institutional Proposal." *Ethics and International Affairs*, 18 (1).

Bull, Hedley (1977) *The Anarchical Society: A Study of Order in World Politics*. New York: Columbia University Press.

Buzan, Barry, Charles Jones, and Richard Little (1993) *The Logic of Anarchy: Neo-realism to Structural Realism*. New York: Columbia University Press.

Byers, Michael (1999) *Custom, Power and the Power of Rules: International Relations and Customary International Law*. Cambridge: Cambridge University Press.

Byers, Michael (2005) *War Law: Understanding International Law and Armed Conflict*. London: Grove Press.

Calas, Francoise and Pierre Salignon (2004) "Afghanistan: From 'Militant Monks' to Crusaders." In Fabrice Weissman (ed.), *In the Shadow of "Just Wars": Violence, Politics and Humanitarian Action*. Ithaca, NY: Cornell University Press.

Camilleri, Joseph (2002) "Peace Operations: The Road Ahead." In Esref Asku and Joseph Camilleri (eds.), *Democratizing Global Governance*. New York: Palgrave Macmillan Press.

Cantaloube, Thomas and Henri Vernet (2004) *Chirac contre Bush: l'Autre Guerre*. Paris: Jean-Claude Lattes.

Caplan, Richard (2004) "International Authority and State Building: The Case of Bosnia and Herzegovina." *Global Governance*, 10 (1).

Carr, E. H. (1946) *The Twenty Years' Crisis, 1919–1939: An Introduction to the Study of International Relations*. London: Macmillan.

Carrideo, Davide (2004) Permanent Mission of Spain. Interview conducted on July 20.

Cassese, Antonio (2004) "The Role of Internationalized Courts and Tribunals in the Fight Against International Criminality." In Cesare P. R. Romano, André Noll-kaemper, and Jann K. Kleffner (eds.), *Internationalized Criminal Courts and Tribunals*, 3–13. Oxford: Oxford University Press.

Center on Global Counter-Terrorism Cooperation (2006) *Reports on Standards and Best Practices for Improving States Implementation of UN SC Counter-terrorism Mandates*. September.

Chandler, David (2001) "The Road to Military Humanitarianism: How the Human Rights NGOs Shaped a New Humanitarian Agenda." *Human Rights Quarterly*, 23.

Chandler, David (2006) *From Kosovo to Kabul And Beyond*, new edn. London: Pluto Press.

Cherian, John (2003) *Frontline*, 20 (15), July 19–August 1.

Chesterman, Simon (2001) *Just War or Just Peace?: Humanitarian Intervention and International Law*. Oxford: Oxford University Press.

Chicago Council on Foreign Relations (2004) *The Hall of Mirrors: Perceptions and Misperceptions in the Congressional Foreign Policy Process*. Chicago: Chicago Council on Foreign Relations.

Chinkin, Christine (2003) "Gender, Human Rights, and Peace Agreements." *Ohio State Journal of Dispute Resolution*, 18.

Chong, Dennis (2000) *Rational Lives: Norms and Values in Politics and Society*. Chicago: University of Chicago Press.

Christopher, Warren (1998) *In the Stream of History: Shaping Foreign Policy for a New Era*. Stanford, CA: Stanford University Press

Claude, Inis (1967) *The Changing United Nations*. New York: Random House.

Claude, Inis (1984) *Swords in to Plowshares: The Problems and Progress of International Organization*, 4th edn. New York: McGraw-Hill.

Cobban, Helena (2006) "International Courts." *Foreign Policy*, 153.

Cogan, Charles (2003) *French Negotiating Behavior: Dealing with La Grande Nation.* Washington, DC: Institute of Peace.

Cohen, David (2002) *Seeking Justice on the Cheap: Is the East Timor Tribunal Really a Model for the Future? Asia-Pacific Issues*, no. 61. Honolulu: East–West Center. Available at www.eastwestcenter.org/stored/pdfs/api061.pdf

Cohen, David (2006a) " 'Justice on the Cheap' Revisited: The Failure of the Serious Crimes Trials in East Timor." *Analysis from the East–West Center*, no. 80. East–West Center. Available at www.eastwestcenter.org/stored/pdfs/api080.pdf. Accessed April 2, 2007.

Cohen, David (2006b) "Indifference and Accountability: The United Nations and the Politics of International Justice in East Timor." *East–West Center Reports*, no. 9. East–West Center. Available at www.eastwestcenter.org/res-rp-publication details.asp?pub_ID=2005. Accessed April 2, 2007.

Cohen, Joshua (1997) "Procedure and Substance in Deliberative Democracy." In James Bohman and William Rehg (eds.), *Deliberative Democracy: Essays on Reason and Politics.* Cambridge, MA: MIT Press.

Coicaud, Jean-Marc (2001) "Conclusion: International Organizations, the Evolution of International Politics, and Legitimacy." In Jean-Marc Coicaud and Veijo Heiskanen (eds.), *The Legitimacy of International Organizations.* Tokyo: United Nations University Press.

Coicaud, Jean-Marc and Veijo Heiskanen (eds.) (2001) *The Legitimacy of International Organizations.* New York: United Nations University Press.

Corneliu, Bjola (2005) "Legitimating the Use of Force in International Politics: A Communicative Action Perspective." *European Journal of International Relations*, 11 (2).

Cortright, David, George Lopez, Alistair Millar, and Linda Gerber (2004) "An Action Agenda for Enhancing the UN Program on Counter-terrorism." Fourth Freedom Forum and Joan Kroc Institute for International Peace Studies, University of Notre Dame.

Court of First Instance of the European Communities (2006a) Case T-315/01, *Yassin Abdullah Kadi v. Council of the European Union and Commission of the European Communities*, http//europa.eu.int/eur-lex/lex/LexUriServ/LexUriServ. do? uri=CEL. Accessed August 16, 2006.

Court of First Instance of the European Communities (2006b) Case T-306/01, Ahmed Ali Yusuf and Al Barakaat International Foundation v. Council of the European Union and Commission of the European Communities, http//curia. europa.eu/jurisp/cgi-bin/gettext.pl?where=&lang=en&nu. Accessed August 16, 2006.

Cox, Robert (1986) "Social Forces, States and World Orders: Beyond International Relations Theory." In Robert Keohane (ed.), *Neorealism and its Critics.* New York: Columbia University Press.

Crawford, Neta (2002) *Argument and Change in World Politics: Ethics, Decolonization, and Humanitarian Intervention.* Cambridge: Cambridge University Press.

Cronin, Bruce (2003) *Institutions for the Common Good: International Protection Regimes in International Society.* Cambridge: Cambridge University Press.

Cunningham, Frank (2002) *Theories of Democracy: A Critical Introduction.* New York: Routledge.

Cutler, A. Claire A. (2002) "Private International Regimes and Interfirm Cooperation." In Rodney Bruce Hall and Thomas J. Biersteker (eds.), *The Emergence of Private Authority in Global Governance.* Cambridge: Cambridge University Press.

Dahl, Robert (1998) *On Democracy.* New Haven: Yale University Press.

D'Amato, Anthony A. (1971) *The Concept of Custom in International Law.* Ithaca, NY: Cornell University Press.

Datan, Merav (2005) "Security Council Resolution 1540: WMD and Non-state Trafficking." *Disarmament Diplomacy,* 79 (April/May).

Davis, Jeffrey W. (2002) "Two Wrongs Do Make a Right: The International Criminal Tribunal for the Former Yugoslavia was Established Illegally—But it Was the Right Thing to Do. So Who Cares?" *North Carolina Journal of International Law and Commercial Regulation,* 28.

De Freitas Valle, C. (1950) Speech given at the General Assembly Fifth Session, September 20.

De Waal, Alex (1997) *Famine Crimes: Politics & the Disaster Relief Industry in Africa.* London: International African Institute.

De Wet, Erika and Andre Noellkaemper (eds.) (2003) *Review of the Security Council by Member States.* Antwerp: Intersentia.

Deephouse, David L. (1996) "Does Isomorphism Legitimate?" *Academy of Management Journal,* 39 (4).

Department of State Bulletin (1976) Vol. 74, no. 1909, January 26.

Diehl, Paul (1993) *International Peacekeeping.* Baltimore, MD: Johns Hopkins University Press.

Diehl, Paul (2002) *The Politics of Global Governance: International Organizations in an Interdependent World.* Boulder, CO: Lynn Rienner.

Douzinas, Costas (2000) *The End of Human Rights.* Oxford: Oxford University Press.

Drezner, Daniel (2000) "Bargaining, Enforcement, and Multilateral Sanctions: When Is Cooperation Counterproductive?" *International Organization,* 54 (1).

Dryzek, John (1999) "Transnational Democracy." *Journal of Political Philosophy,* 7 (1).

Duffield, Mark (1997) "NGO Relief in War Zones: Towards an Analysis of the New Aid Paradigm." *Third World Quarterly,* 18 (3).

Duffy, Helen (2005) *The "War on Terror" and the Framework of International Law.* Cambridge: Cambridge University Press.

Durch, William (1993) *The Evolution of UN Peacekeeping: Case Studies and Comparative Analysis.* New York: St. Martin's Press.

Eckstein, Harry (1973) "Authority Patterns: A Structural Basis for Political Inquiry." *American Political Science Review,* 67 (4).

Eichengreen, Barry and Peter B. Kenen (1994) "Managing the World Economy under the Bretton Woods System: An Overview." In Peter B. Kenen (ed.), *Managing the World Economy: Fifty Years after Bretton Woods.* Washington, DC: Institute for International Economics.

Elman, Colin (2005) "Explanatory Typologies in Qualitative Studies of International Politics." *International Organization,* 59 (2).

Elster, Jon (1998) "Introduction." In Jon Elster and Adam Przeworski (eds.), *Deliberative Democracy.* New York: Cambridge University Press.

Eriksen, Erik Oddvar (2000) "Deliberative Supranationalism in the EU." In Erik

Eriksen and John Erik Fossum (eds.), *Democracy in the European Union: Integration through Deliberation?* London: Routledge.

Eriksen, Erik Oddvar and John Erik Fossum (eds.) (2000) *Democracy in the European Union: Integration through Deliberation?* London: Routledge.

Etcheson, Craig (2004) "The Politics of Genocide Justice in Cambodia." In Cesare P. R. Romano, André Nollkaemper, and Jann K. Kleffner (eds.), *Internationalized Criminal Courts and Tribunals*, 181–205. Oxford: Oxford University Press.

Falk, Richard (2002) "The Challenges of Humane Governance." In George J. Andreopoulos (ed.), *Concepts and Strategies in International Human Rights*. New York: Peter Lang.

Farer, Tom (2002) "Beyond the Charter Frame: Unilateralism or Condominium Frame?" *American Journal of International Law*, 96 (2).

Farer, Tom (2003) "Humanitarian Intervention before and after 9/11: Legality and Legitimacy." In J. L. Holzgrefe and Robert Keohane (eds.), *Humanitarian Intervention. Ethical, Legal and Political Dilemmas*. Cambridge: Cambridge University Press.

Farley, Maggie (2005) "U.N. Divided Over Proposal to Expand Security Council." *Los Angeles Times*. Home Edition. May 13. Available at www.latimes.com/news/nationworld/world/la-fg-unreform13may13,1,411951.story

Fassbender, Bardo (2000) "*Quis judicabit?* The Security Council, Its Powers and Its Legal Control." *European Journal of International Law*, 11(1).

Fearon, James D. (1995) "Rationalist Explanations for War." *International Organization*, 49 (3).

Fearon, James D. (1998) "Bargaining, Enforcement, and International Cooperation." *International Organization*, 52 (2).

Fearon, James D. and David Laitin (2004) "Neotrusteeship and the Problem of Weak States." *International Security*, 28 (4).

Ferguson, Niall (2004) *Colossus: The Price of America's Empire*. New York: Penguin Books.

Filkins, Dexter (2003) "Turkish Deputies Refuse to Accept American Troops." *New York Times*, March 2, p. A1.

Finkelstein, Lawrence (1990) Yale–UN Oral History Interview, November 23. Yale University Archives and Manuscripts Library, New Haven, CT; and the UN Dag Hammarskjold Library.

Finnemore, Martha and Kathryn Sikkink (1998) "International Norm Dynamics and Political Change." *International Organization*, 52 (4).

Fodor, Neil (1990) *The Warsaw Treaty Organization: A Political and Organizational Analysis*. Basingstoke: Macmillan.

Franck, Thomas M. (1990) *The Power of Legitimacy among Nations*. New York: Oxford University Press.

Franck, Thomas M. (1992) "The Powers of Appreciation: Who Is the Ultimate Guardian of UN Legality?" *American Journal Of International Law*, 86.

Franck, Thomas M. (2002) *Recourse to Force: State Action Against Threats and Armed Attacks*. Cambridge: Cambridge University Press.

Franck, Thomas M. (2003) "What Happens Now? The United Nations after Iraq." *American Journal of International Law*, 97 (3).

Frederking, Brian (2003) "Constructing Post-cold War Collective Security." *American Political Science Review*, 97 (3).

Friedman, Richard B. (1990) "On the Concept of Authority in Political Philosophy." In Joseph Raz (ed.), *Authority*. New York: New York University Press.

Gaer, Felice (2003) "Implementing International Human Rights Norms: UN Human Rights Treaty Bodies and NGOs." *Journal of Human Rights*, 2 (3).

General Assembly First Committee (1950) Discussion in the First Committee of the General Assembly, October 9–19, GAOR, V, First C.

Gibson, James L. and Gregory A. Caldeira (1998) "Changes in the Legitimacy of the European Court of Justice: A Post-Maastrict Analysis." *British Journal of Political Science*, 28.

Gidley, Ruth (2004) "Aid Agencies Discuss Security in Dangerous New Era." *Alert-Net*, March 30.

Gilpin, Robert (1981) *War and Change in World Politics*. Cambridge: Cambridge University Press.

Glasheen (1948) Cablegram 71, Salonika, July 24, http://www.info.dfat.gov.au/info/historical/HistDocs.nsf/2ecf3135305dccd7ca256b5d007c2afc/c6b98fe19f327e7dca256cd900161569?OpenDocument. Accessed October 9, 2007.

Glennon, Michael (2001) *Limits of Law, Prerogatives of Power: Interventionism after Kosovo*. New York: Palgrave.

Glennon, Michael (2003) "Why the Security Council Failed." *Foreign Affairs*, 82.

Goldstein, Judith, Miles Kahler, Robert Keohane, and Anne-Marie Slaughter (eds.) (2000) "Legalization and World Politics." Special issue of *International Organization*, 54 (3).

Gordenker, Leon and Thomas Weiss (1996) "Pluralizing Global Governance: Analytical Approaches and Dimensions." In Thomas Weiss and Leon Gordenker (eds.), *NGOs, the UN, and Global Governance*. Boulder, CO: Lynne Rienner.

Gordenker, Leon and Thomas Weiss (1997) "Devolving Responsibilities: A Framework for Analysing NGOs and Services." *Third World Quarterly*, 18 (3).

Gordon, Michael R. (1999) "U.S. Urges NATO Plan to Block Yugoslavia's Oil Shipment by Sea But France Questions Legality of Action." *New York Times*, April 19.

Gowlland-Debbas, Vera (2000) "The Functions of the United Nations Security Council in the International Legal System." In Michael Byers (ed.), *The Role of Law in International Relations and International Law*. Oxford: Oxford University Press.

Grant, Ruth W. and Robert O. Keohane (2005) "Accountability and Abuses of Power in World Politics." *American Political Science Review*, 99 (1).

Graubart, Jonathan (2004) " 'Legalizing' Politics, 'Politicizing' Law: Transnational Activism and International Law." *International Politics*, 41 (3).

Gray, Christine (2004) *International Law and the Use of Force*, 2nd edn. Oxford: Oxford University Press.

Grewe, Wilhelm G. (2000) *The Epochs of International Law*. Michael Byers, trans. and rev. New York: Walter de Gruyter.

Gruber, Lloyd (2000) *Ruling the World: Power Politics and the Rise of Supranational Institutions*. Princeton, NJ: Princeton University Press.

Guilhermo, Luis (2004) Permanent Mission of Brazil. Interview conducted on July 21.

Gutherie, Peter (2004) "Security Council Sanctions and the Protection of Individual Rights." *New York University Annual Survey of American Law*, 60.

Gutmann, Amy and Dennis Thompson (2004) *Why Deliberative Democracy?* Princeton, NJ: Princeton University Press.

Habermas, Jürgen (1972) *Legitimation Crisis*. Boston, MA: Beacon Press.

Habermas, Jürgen (1998) *Between Facts and Norms: Contributions to a Discourse Theory of Law and Democracy*. William Rehg, trans. Cambridge, MA: MIT Press.

Habermas, Jürgen (2001) "Why Europe Needs a Constitution." *New Left Review*, 11.

Haggard, Stephan (1995) *Developing Nations and the Politics of Global Integration*. Washington, DC: Brookings Institute.

Hall, Rodney Bruce (1999) *National Collective Identity: Social Constructs and International Systems*. New York: Columbia University Press.

Hall, Rodney Bruce and Thomas J. Biersteker (eds.) (2002) *The Emergence of Private Authority in Global Governance*. Cambridge: Cambridge University Press.

Happold, Matthew (2003) "Security Council Resolution 1373 and the Constitution of the UN." *Leiden Journal of International Law*, 16 (3).

Harper, Keith (1994) "Does the UN Security Council Have the Competence to Act as Court and Legislature?" *International Law and Politics*, 27.

Hart, H.L.A. (1990) "Commands and Authoritative Legal Reasons." In J. Raz (ed.), *Authority*. New York: New York University Press.

Hart, H.L.A. (1994) *The Concept of Law*, 2nd edn. Oxford: Oxford University Press.

Hawkins, Darren G., David A. Lake, Daniel L. Nielson, and Michael J. Tierney (eds.) (2006) *Delegation and Agency in International Organizations*. Cambridge: Cambridge University Press.

Heinbecker, Paul (2004) Yale–UN Oral History Interview on November 8. Yale University Manuscripts and Archives Library and the UN Dag Hammarsjkold Library.

Held, David (1996) *Models of Democracy*, 2nd edn. Stanford, CA: Stanford University Press.

Held, David and Anthony McGrew (2002) *Governing Globalization: Power, Authority, and Global Governance*. Cambridge: Polity Press.

Henkin, Louis (1995) *International Law: Politics and Values*. The Hague: Martinus Nijhoff.

Hensel, Howard M. (ed.) (2005) *The Law of Armed Conflict*. Aldershot: Ashgate.

Hewson, Martin and Timothy Sinclair (1999) *Approaches to Global Governance Theory*. Albany, NY: State University of New York Press.

High Commissioner for Human Rights (2002) *Note to the Chair of the Counter-terrorism Committee: A Human Rights Perspective on Counter-terrorist Measures*. www.un.org/Docs/sc/committees/1373/ohchr1.htm

High Commissioner for Human Rights on Human Security and Terrorism (2002) March 20, www.hrea.org/lists/hr-headlines/markup/msg00274

Hilderbrand, Robert (1990) *Dumbarton Oaks: The Origins of the United Nations and the Search for Postwar Security*. Chapel Hill, NC: University of North Carolina Press.

Hoffmann, Stanley (1998) *World Disorders: Troubled Peace in the Post-cold War Era*. Lanham, MD: Rowman & Littlefield.

Hoge, Warren (2004) "U.N. Tackles Issue of Imbalance of Power." *New York Times*, November 28.

Holzgrefe, J. L. and Robert O. Keohane (eds.) (2003) *Humanitarian Intervention: Ethical, Legal, and Political Dilemmas*. Cambridge: Cambridge University Press.

Howse, Robert (2001) "The Legitimacy of the World Trade Organization." In Jean-Marc Coicaud and Veijo Heiskanen (eds.), *The Legitimacy of International Organizations*. Tokyo: United Nations University Press.

Hulton, Susan (2004) "Council Working Methods and Procedure." In David Malone (ed.), *The UN Security Council: From the Cold War to the 21st Century*. Boulder, CO: Lynne Rienner.

Human Rights Committee (2003) "Human Rights Committee Briefed on Work of Counter-terrorism Committee." Press release HR/CT/630, March 27.

Human Rights Council (2007) *Implementation of General Assembly Resolution 60/251 of 15 March 2006 entitled "Human Rights Council,"* A/HRC/4/26, January 29.

Human Rights Watch (2004) *Hear No Evil, See No Evil: The U.N. Security Council's Approach to Human Rights Violations in the Global Counter-terrorism Effort*. Human Rights Watch Briefing Paper, August 10.

Human Rights Watch (2005a) *World Report 2005: Cambodia*. Human Rights Watch. Available at hrw.org/english/docs/2005/01/13/cambod9804.htm.

Human Rights Watch (2005b) *World Report 2005: Sierra Leone*. Human Rights Watch. Available at hrw.org/english/docs/2004/12/15/sierra9876.htm

Human Rights Watch (2005c) *World Report 2005: East Timor*. Human Rights Watch. Available at hrw.org/english/docs/2005/01/13/eastti9825.htm

Human Rights Watch (2006) "Cambodia: Government Interferes in Khmer Rouge Trial," December 5. Available at hrw.org/english/docs/2006/12/05/cambod 14752.htm. Accessed April 3, 2007.

Hurd, Ian (1997) "Security Council Reform: Informal Membership and Practice." In Bruce Russett (ed.), *The Once and Future Security Council*. New York: St. Martin's Press.

Hurd, Ian (1999) "Legitimacy and Authority in International Politics." *International Organization*, 53 (2).

Hurd, Ian (2002) "Legitimacy, Power, and the Symbolic Life of the Security Council." *Global Governance*, 8 (1).

Hurd, Ian (2005) "The Strategic Use of Liberal Internationalism: Libya and the UN Sanctions, 1999–2003." *International Organization*, 59 (3).

Hurd, Ian (2006) "Unrealizable Expectations: Collective Security, the UN Charter, and Iraq." In Harvey Starr (ed.), *Approaches, Levels, and Methods of Analysis in International Politics*. New York: Palgrave.

Hurd, Ian (2007a) *After Anarchy: Legitimacy and Power in the United Nations Security Council*. Princeton, NJ: Princeton University Press.

Hurd, Ian (2007b) "Breaking and Making Norms: American Revisionism and Crises of Legitimacy." *International Politics*, 44 (2–3).

Hurd, Ian (2008) "Myths of Membership: The Politics of Legitimation in UN Security Council Reform." *Global Governance*, 14 (2).

Hurrell, Andrew (1993) "International Society and the Study of Regimes: A Reflective Approach." In Volker Rittberger (ed.), *Regime Theory and International Relations*. Oxford: Clarendon Press

Ignatieff, Michael (2002) "Is the Human Rights Era Ending?" *The New York Times*, February 5, p. A25.

Ikenberry, John (2001) *After Victory*. Princeton, NJ: Princeton University Press.

Inter-American Commission on Human Rights (2002) Report no. 62/02. Case 12.285, October 22.

International Commission on Intervention and State Sovereignty (2001) *The

Responsibility to Protect: Report of the International Commission on Intervention and State Sovereignty. Available at: www.dfait-maeci.gc.ca/iciss-ciise/report-en.asp

International Council on Human Rights Policy (2002) *Human Rights Crises: NGO Responses to Military Interventions.* Geneva.

International Court of Justice (1971) "Legal Consequences for States of the Continued Presence of South Africa in Namibia (South-West Africa) Notwithstanding Security Council Resolution 276." Advisory Opinion of June 21.

International Court of Justice (1996) "Legality of the Threat or Use of Nuclear Weapons" (Advisory Opinion) 110, *International Law Reports* 163. Also available at www.icj-cij.org/icjwww/icases/iunan/iunanframe.htm

International Court of Justice (2002) Case T-306/01 *R. Abdirisak Aden and Others v. Council of the European Union and Commission of the European Communities.* Proceedings for Interim Measures (2002/C 191/46), *Official Journal of the European Communities,* C 191/26.

International Court of Justice (2004) Legal Consequences of the Construction of a Wall in the Occupied Palestinian Territory (Advisory Opinion) *I.C.J. Reports.* Also available at www.icj-cij.org/icjwww/idocket/imwp/imwpframe.htm

International Criminal Tribunal for Rwanda (1998) "Introduction to the International Criminal Tribunal for Rwanda." United Nations, International Criminal Tribunal for Rwanda. Available at www.un.org/ictr/english/factsheets/ictr.html. Accessed March 29, 2007.

International Criminal Tribunal for Rwanda (2006) *Letter dated 30 November 2006 from the President of the International Criminal Tribunal for the Prosecution of Persons Responsible for Genocide and Other Serious Violations of International Humanitarian Law Committed in the Territory of Rwanda. Completion Strategy of the International Criminal Tribunal for Rwanda.* December 8. United Nations Security Council. S/2006/951. Available at 69.94.11.53/default.htm. Accessed March 28, 2007.

International Criminal Tribunal for Rwanda (2007) "General Information." United Nations, International Criminal Tribunal for Rwanda. Available at 69.94.11.53/ default.htm. Accessed March 2007.

International Criminal Tribunal for the former Yugoslavia (2007a) "ICTY at a Glance: Key Figures of ICTY Cases." United Nations, International Criminal Tribunal for the former Yugoslavia. Last updated February 5, 2007. Available at www.un.org/icty/glance-e/index.htm. Accessed March 28, 2007.

International Criminal Tribunal for the former Yugoslavia (2007b) "ICTY at a Glance: General Information." United Nations International Criminal Tribunal for the former Yugoslavia. Last updated February 7, 2007. Available at www. un.org/icty/glance-e/index.htm. Accessed March 28, 2007.

International Crisis Group (2001) *International Criminal Tribunal for Rwanda: Justice Delayed.* Africa Report no. 30. Nairobi: International Crisis Group. Available at www.crisisgroup.org/library/documents/report_archive/A400442_02102001.pdf

International Crisis Group (2003a) *The Special Court for Sierra Leone: Promises and Pitfalls of a "New Model."* Freetown: International Crisis Group. Available at www.crisisgroup.org/library/documents/report_archive/A401076_04082003.pdf

International Crisis Group (2003b) *Tribunal Penal International pour le Rwanda: Pragmatisme de Rigueur.* Africa Report no. 69. Nairobi: International Crisis Group. Available at www.crisisgroup.org/library/documents/africa/069__ictr_ rwanda.pdf

International Peace Academy (2001) *Refashioning the Dialogue: Regional Perspectives on the Brahimi Report on UN Peace Operations.* www.ipaacademy.org/Publications/Reports/Research/PublRepoReseBrahimi_body. htm. Accessed April 27, 2004.

Izvestia (1999) "Igor Ivanov Rectifies Mistakes of Americans," March 12.

Jackson, Robert (1995) "International Community Beyond the Cold War." In Gene M. Lyons and Michael Mastanduno (eds.), *Beyond Westphalia: State Sovereignty and International Intervention.* Baltimore, MD: Johns Hopkins University Press.

Jakobsen, Peter Viggo (2002) "The Transformation of United Nations Peace Operations in the 1990s: Adding Globalization to the Conventional 'End of the Cold War' Explanation." *Cooperation and Conflict,* 73 (3).

James, Alan (1986) *Sovereign Statehood: The Basis of International Society.* London: Allen and Unwin.

Jepperson, Ronald, Alexander Wendt, and Peter J. Katzenstein (1996) "Norms, Identity and Culture in National Security." In Peter J. Katzenstein (ed.), *The Culture of National Security: Norms and Identity in World Politics.* New York: Columbia University Press.

Joerges, Christian (2002) "Deliberative Supranationalism: Two Defences." *European Law Journal,* 8 (1).

Johnstone, Ian (1991) "Treaty Interpretation: The Authority of Interpretive Communities." *Michigan Journal of International Law,* 12.

Johnstone, Ian (2003) "Security Council Deliberations: The Power of the Better Argument." *European Journal of International Law,* 14 (3).

Johnstone, Ian (2004) "U.S.–UN Relations after Iraq: The End of the World (Order) as We Know it?" *European Journal of International Relations,* 15 (4).

Johnstone, Ian (2005) "Discursive Power in the UN Security Council." *Journal of International Law and International Relations,* 2.

Johnstone, Ian (2006) "The UN Security Council, Counter-terrorism and Human Rights." Paper presented at a conference on "Democracy, Separation of Powers and the Fight against Terrorism," Geneva, November 16–18.

Johnstone, Ian (2008) "Deliberation and Legal Argumentation in International Decision-making." In Hillary Charlesworth and Jean-Marc Coicaud (eds.), *The Faultlines of Legitimacy.* New York: United Nations University Press.

Jorda, Claude (2004) "The Major Hurdles and Accomplishments of the ICTY." *Journal of International Criminal Justice,* 2.

Jost, John T. and Brenda Major (eds.) (2001) *The Psychology of Legitimacy: Emerging Perspectives on Ideology, Justice, and Intergroup Relations.* Cambridge: Cambridge University Press.

Keating, Tom and W. Andy Knight (2004) "Introduction." In Tom Keating and W. Andy Knight (eds.), *Building Sustainable Peace.* Tokyo: United Nations University Press.

Keck, Margaret and Kathryn Sikkink (1998) *Activists Beyond Borders: Advocacy Networks in International Politics.* Ithaca, NY: Cornell University Press.

Kendall, Sara and Michelle Staggs (2005) *From Mandate to Legacy: The Special Court for Sierra Leone as a Model for "Hybrid Justice."* Berkeley: War Crimes Study Center, University of California, Berkeley. Available at ist-socrates.berkeley.edu/~warcrime/SLSC_Report.pdf

Keohane, Robert (1998) "A Functional Theory of Regimes." In Stephen Krasner, *International Regimes.* Ithaca, NY: Cornell University Press.

Keohane, Robert (2002) *Power and Governance in a Partially Globalized World*. London: Routledge.

Khumprakob, Malissa, Tejal Jesrani, and Mario Cava (2004) "Update from the International Criminal Courts." *Human Rights Brief*, 121.

Kirgis, Frederic (1995) "The Security Council's First Fifty Years." *American Journal of International Law*, 89 (3).

Kirgis, Frederic (1999) "Specialized Law-making Processes." In Christopher Joyner (ed.), *The United Nations and International Law*. Cambridge: Cambridge University Press.

Kirkpatrick, Jeane (1984) "U.S. Participation in the United Nations." March 2. Washington, DC: U.S. Dept. of State, Bureau of Public Affairs, Office of Public Communication, Editorial Division.

Kitson, Michael and Jonathan Michie (1995) "Trade and Growth: A Historical Perspective." In Jonathan Michie and John Grieve Smith (eds.), *Managing the Global Economy*. Oxford: Oxford University Press.

Klotz, Audie (1995) *Norms in International Relations. The Struggle against Apartheid*. Ithaca, NY: Cornell University Press.

Knight, W. Andy (2003) "The Responsibility to Protect as an Evolving International Norm." Notes for Canadian Peacebuilding Coordinating Committee Meeting, September 22. Ottawa Conference Centre.

Kooijmans, P. (1993) "The Enlargement of the Concept 'Threat to the Peace'." In Rene-Jean Dupuy (ed.), *The Development of the Role of the Security Council: Peace-keeping and Peace-building*. The Hague: Martinus Nijhoff.

Koremenós, Barbara, Charles Lipson, and Duncan Snidal (2001) "The Rational Design of Institutions." *International Organization*, 55 (4).

Korey, William (1998) *NGOs and the Universal Declaration of Human Rights: "A Curious Grapevine."* New York: St. Martin's Press.

Koskenniemi, Martti (1995) "The Police in the Temple. Order, Justice and the UN: A Dialectical View." *European Journal of International Law*, 6 (3).

Koskenniemi, Martti (1996) "The Place of Law in Collective Security." *Michigan Journal of International Law*, 17.

Koskenneimi, Martti (2005) "International Legislation Today: Limits and Possibilities." *Wisconsin Journal of International Law*, 23.

Kostova, Tatiana (1999) "Organizational Legitimacy under Conditions of Complexity: The Case of the Multinational Enterprise." *Academy of Management Review*, 24 (1).

Krasner, Stephen (1985) *Structural Conflict: The Third World Against Global Liberalism*. Berkeley, CA: University of California Press.

Krasner, Stephen (1991) "Global Communications and National Power: Life on the Pareto Frontier." *World Politics*, 43 (3).

Krasner, Stephen (1999) *Sovereignty. Organized Hypocrisy*. Princeton, NJ: Princeton University Press.

Krasno, Jean (2004a) "Founding of the United Nations: An Evolutionary Process." In Jean Krasno (ed.), *The United Nations: Confronting the Challenges of a Global Society*. Boulder, CO: Lynne Rienner.

Krasno, Jean (2004b) *The United Nations: Confronting the Challenges of a Global Society*. Boulder, CO: Lynne Rienner.

Krasno, Jean and James Sutterlin (2003) *The United Nations and Iraq*. New York: Praeger.

Krauthammer, Charles (1987) "Let it Sink." *The New Republic*, August 24.

Krishnasamy, Kabilan (2003) "The Paradox of India's Peacekeeping." *Contemporary South Asia*, 12 (2).

Kupchan, Charles A. and Clifford A. Kupchan (1991) "Concerts, Collective Security and the Future of Europe." *International Security*, 16 (1).

Kuziemko, Ilyana and Eric Werker (n.d.) "How Much Is a Seat on the Security Council Worth? Foreign Aid and Bribery and the United Nations." Working Paper, Harvard University.

Laitin, David (1998) "Toward a Political Science Discipline: Authority Patterns Revisited." *Comparative Political Studies*, 31 (4).

Lake, David and Robert Powell (1999) *Strategic Choice and International Relations*. Princeton, NJ: Princeton University Press.

Last, Major D. M. (1998) "Early Warning of Violent Conflict: The Role of Multifunctional Observer Missions, the Lester B. Pearson Canadian Peacekeeping Training Centre, January. Available at Columbia International Affairs Online, http://www.ciaonet.org/book/schmeidl/schmeidl09.html

Lauren, Paul Gordon (2003) *The Evolution of International Human Rights: Visions Seen*. Philadelphia, PA: University of Pennsylvania Press.

Lee, Joanne and Richard Price (2004) "International Tribunals and the Criminalization of International Violence." In Richard Price and Mark W. Zacher (eds.), *The United Nations and Global Security*, 123–38. New York: Palgrave Macmillan.

Linton, Suzannah (2001) "Cambodia, East Timor and Sierra Leone: Experiments in International Justice." *Criminal Law Forum*, 12 (2).

Lobel, Jules and Michael Ratner (1999) "Bypassing the Security Council: Ambiguous Authorizations on the Use of Force, Ceasefires and the Iraqi Inspection Regime." *American Journal of International Law* 93, January.

Logan, Marty (2004) "Aid Agency Exit Leaves Nation Further Isolated." *Inter Press Service*, November 6.

Luck, Edward C. (2002) "The United States, International Organizations, and the Quest for Legitimacy." In Stewart Patrick and Shepard Forman (eds.), *Multilateralism and U.S. Foreign Policy*. London: Lynne Rienner.

Luck, Edward (2003) "Reforming the United Nations: Lessons from a History in Progress." Academic Council on the United Nations System (ACUNS) occasional paper.

Luck, Edward (2005) "How Not to Reform the United Nations." *Global Governance*, 11.

Lukes, Steven (1990) "Perspectives on Authority." In Joseph Raz (ed.), *Authority*. New York: New York University Press.

Lynch, Colum (2004) "Weapons Transfers Targeted: UN Security Council Resolutions Seeks Criminalization." *The Washington Post*, April 29, A21.

MacCormick, Neil (1978) *Legal Reasoning and Legal Theory*. Oxford: Oxford University Press.

Maggi, Giovanni, M. Morelli, and M. P. Page. (n.d.) "Self-enforcing Voting in International Organizations." *NBER Working Paper*.

Mahmood, Sohail (2004) Permament Mission of Pakistan to the UN. Interview conducted on July 21.

Mahubani, Kishore (2004) Interview conducted on July 21.

Majone, Giandomenico (2001) "Two Logics of Delegation: Agency and Fiduciary Relations in EU Governance." *European Union Politics*, 2.

Malone, David (1999) *Decision-making at the UN Security Council: The Case of Haiti.* Oxford: Clarendon Press

Malone, David (2004) "Introduction." In David Malone (ed.), *The UN Security Council: From the Cold War to the 21st Century.* Boulder, CO: Lynne Rienner.

March, James, G. and Johan P. Olsen (1998) "The Institutional Dynamics of International Political Orders." *International Organization,* 52 (4).

Martenczuk, Bernd (1999) "The Security Council, the International Court and Judicial Review: What Lessons from Lockerbie?" *European Journal of International Law,* 10 (3).

Martin, Lisa (1992) "Interests, Power, and Multilateralism." *International Organization,* 46 (4).

Martin, Lisa (2003) "Distribution, Information, and Delegation to International Organizations: The Case of IMF Conditionality." Unpublished manuscript, Harvard University, Cambridge, MA.

Martin, Lisa and Beth Simmons (1998) "Theories and Empirical Studies of International Institutions." *International Organization,* 52 (3).

Marx, Karl (1970) "The Eighteenth Brumaire of Louis Bonaparte" (excerpt). In Irving Howe (ed.), *Essential Works of Socialism.* New York: Bantam Books.

Mason, Ann C. (2005) "Constructing Authority Alternatives on the Periphery: Vignettes from Colombia." *International Political Science Review,* 26 (1).

Massey, Joseph Eric (2001) "Managing Organizational Legitimacy: Communication Strategies for Organizations in Crisis." *Journal of Business Communication,* 38 (2).

Matheson, Michael J. (2001) "United Nations Governance of Postconflict Societies." *American Journal of International Law,* 95 (1).

Mazurana, Dyan (2005) "Gender and the Causes and Consequences of Armed Conflict." In Dyan Mazurana, Angela Raven-Roberts, and Jane Parpart (eds.), *Gender, Conflict, and Peacekeeping.* Lanham, MD: Rowman & Littlefield Publishers.

Mazurana, Dyan, Angela Raven-Roberts, Jane Parpart, with Sue Lautze (2005) "Introduction: Gender, Conflict, and Peacekeeping." In Dyan Mazurana, Angela Raven-Roberts, and Jane Parpart (eds.), *Gender, Conflict, and Peacekeeping.* Lanham, MD: Rowman & Littlefield Publishers.

McCormick, Thomas (1989) *America's Half Century: United States Foreign Policy in the Cold War.* Baltimore, MD: Johns Hopkins University Press.

McKay, Freda (2004) Interview conducted on July 20.

Mearsheimer, John (1994/5) "The False Promise of International Institutions." *International Security,* 19 (winter).

Meeker, Leonard (1990) Interview conducted on July 24. Washington, DC.

Meijer, Erniestine E. (2004) "The Extraordinary Chambers in the Courts of Cambodia for Prosecuting Crimes Committed by the Khmer Rouge: Jurisdiction, Organization, and Procedure of an Internationalized Criminal Tribunal." In Cesare P. R. Romano, André Nollkaemper, and Jann K. Kleffner (eds.), *Internationalized Criminal Courts and Tribunals.* Oxford: Oxford University Press.

Meron, Theodor (1998) "Geneva Conventions as Customary Law." In *War Crimes Law Comes of Age: Essays,* 154–74. Oxford: Clarendon Press.

Meron, Theodor (2000) "The Humanization of Humanitarian Law." *American Journal of International Law,* 94 (2).

Millar, Alistair and Eric Rosand (2007) *Allied Against Terrorism: What's Needed to Strengthen Worldwide Commitment.* New York: Century Foundation Press.

Milner, Helen (1991) "The Assumption of Anarchy in International Relations Theory: A Critique." *Review of International Studies*, 17 (1).

Mitzen, Jennifer (2005) "Reading Habermas in Anarchy: Multilateral Diplomacy and Global Public Spheres." *American Political Science Review*, 99 (3).

Moravcsik, Andrew (1993) "Preferences and Power in the UN: A Liberal Intergovernmentalist Approach." *Journal of Common Market Studies*, 31 (4).

Morganthau, Hans (1993) *Politics among Nations: The Struggle for Power and Peace*. Revised by Kenneth W. Thompson. New York: McGraw-Hill.

Morsink, Johannes (1999) *The Universal Declaration of Human Rights. Origins, Drafting and Intent*. Philadelphia: University of Pennsylvania Press.

Mundis, Daryl A. (2005) "The Judicial Effects of the 'Completion Strategies' on the Ad Hoc International Criminal Tribunals." *American Journal of International Law*, 99 (1).

Murphy, Sean D. (1996) *Humanitarian Intervention: The United Nations in an Evolving World Order*. Philadelphia: University of Pennsylvania Press.

Murray, Geoffrey (1991) Interview conducted on January 10. Yale–UN Oral History, Yale Archives Library, New Haven, CT.

Mutua, Makao (2001) "Human Rights and International NGOs: A Critical Evaluation." In Claude Welch (ed.), *NGOs and Human Rights: Promise and Performance*. Philadelphia: University of Pennsylvania Press.

Natsios, Andrew (1996) "NGOs and the UN System in Complex Humanitarian Emergencies: Conflict or Cooperation?" In Thomas Weiss and Leon Gordenker (eds.), *NGOs, the UN, and Global Governance*. Boulder, CO: Lynne Rienner.

NGO Working Group on Women, Peace, and Security (2004) "Four Years On: An Alternative Report and Progress Check on the Implementation of Security Council Resolution 1325." Available at www.peacewomen.org/un/sc/

Nielson, Daniel, and Michael Tierney (2003) "Delegation to International Organizations: Agency Theory and World Bank Environmental Reform." *International Organization*, 57 (2).

North Atlantic Treaty Organization (2002) "Operation Deliberate Force." Allied Forces Southern Europe. AFSouth Fact Sheet. December 16.

O'Brien, Paul (2004) "Politicized Humanitarianism: A Response to Nicolas de Torrente." *Harvard Human Rights Journal*, 17.

O'Brien, Robert, Anne Marie Goetz, Jan Aart Scholte, and Marc Williams (2000) *Contesting Global Governance: Multilateral Economic Institutions*. Cambridge: Cambridge University Press.

Oppenheim, Lassa (1908) "The Science of International Law: Its Task and Method." *American Journal of International Law*, 2.

Orford, Anne (2003) *Reading Humanitarian Intervention. Human Rights and the Use of Force in International Law*. Cambridge: Cambridge University Press.

Oxman, Bernard (1991) "The Duty to Respect Generally Accepted Standards." *NYU Journal of International Law and Politics*, 24.

Paris, Roland (2004) *At War's End: Building Peace after Civil Conflicts*. Cambridge: Cambridge University Press.

Pasqualucci, Jo M. (2003) *The Practice and Procedure of the Inter-American Court of Human Rights*. Cambridge: Cambridge University Press.

Paul, James (2003) "The Arria Formula," www.globalpolicy.org/security/mtgsetc/arria.htm. Accessed July 5, 2004.

Paul, James (2004) "Working with Nongovernmental Organizations." In David

Malone (ed.), *The UN Security Council: From the Cold War to the 21st Century.* Boulder, CO: Lynne Rienner.

Payne, Rodger and Nayef Samhat (2004) *Democratizing Global Politics: Discourse Norms, International Regimes, and Political Community.* Albany, NY: SUNY Press.

Pérez de Cuéllar, Javier (1997) *Pilgrimage for Peace: A Secretary-General's Memoir.* New York: St. Martin's Press.

Philpott, Daniel (1999) "Westphalia, Authority, and International Studies." *Political Studies,* 47 (3).

Piccirilli, Kara (2004) Project Associate for Peace Women: A Project of the Women's International League for Peace and Freedom. Interview conducted on July 20. New York City.

Plunkett, Mark (2003) "Rebuilding the Rule of Law." In William Maley, Charles Sampford, and Ramesh Thakur (eds.), *From Civil Strife to Civil Society: Civil and Military Responses in Disrupted States.* Tokyo: United Nations University Press.

Pollack, Mark. A (1997) "Delegation, Agency, and Agenda Setting in the UN." *International Organization,* 51 (1).

Prantl, Jochen (2005) "Informal Groups of States and the UN Security Council." *International Organization,* 59 (3).

Prosecutor v. Dusko Tadic a/k/a "Dule" (1995) International Criminal Tribunal for the former Yugoslavia. Decision on the Defence Motion for Interlocutory Appeal on Jurisdiction. IT-94-1. Also available at www.un.org/icty/tadic/appeal/decision-e/51002.htm. Accessed October 3, 2005.

Prosecutor v. Joseph Kanyabashi (1997) International Criminal Tribunal for Rwanda, Trial Chamber. Decision on the Defence Motion for Jurisdiction. ICTR-96-15-T.

Ragazzi, Mauricio (1997) *The Concept of International Obligations* Erga Omnes. Cambridge: Cambridge University Press.

Rajagopal, Balakrishnan (forthcoming) "Invoking the Rule of Law: International Discourses." In Agnes Hurwitz (ed.), *Rule of Law in Conflict Management: Security, Development and Human Rights in the 21st Century.*

Ramsbotham, Oliver and Tom Woodhouse (1996) *Humanitarian Intervention in Contemporary Conflict: A Reconceptualization.* Cambridge: Polity Press.

Ratner, Steven (2004) "The Security Council and International Law." In David Malone (ed.), *The UN Security Council: From the Cold War to the 21st Century.* Boulder, CO: Lynne Rienner.

Raven-Roberts, Angela (2005) "Gender Mainstreaming in United Nations Peacekeeping Operations: Talking the Talk, Tripping Over the Walk." In Dyan Mazurana, Angela Raven-Roberts, and Jane Parpart (eds.), *Gender, Conflict, and Peacekeeping.* Lanham, MD: Rowman & Littlefield Publishers.

Raz, Joseph (1990) "Authority and Justification." In Joseph Raz (ed.), *Authority.* New York: New York University Press.

Reicher, Harry (1981) "The Uniting for Peace Resolution on the Thirtieth Anniversary of Its Passage." *Columbia Journal of Transnational Law,* 20(1).

Reindorp, Nicola (2002) "Trends and Challenges in the UN Humanitarian System." In Joanna Macrae (ed.), *HPG Report 11, The New Humanitarianism: A Review of Trends in Global Humanitarian Action.* London: Overseas Development Institute.

Reus-Smit, Christian (1999) *The Moral Purpose of the State: Culture, Social Identity, and Institutional Rationality in International Relations.* Princeton, NJ: Princeton University Press.

Richmond, Oliver (2004) "UN Peace Operations and the Dilemmas of the Peacebuilding Consensus." *International Peacekeeping*, 11 (1).

Rieff, David (2004) "Kosovo: The End of an Era?" In Fabrice Weissman (ed.), *In the Shadow of "Just Wars": Violence, Politics and Humanitarian Action.* Ithaca, NY: Cornell University Press.

Risse, Thomas (2000) "Let's Argue!: Communicative Action in World Politics." *International Organization*, 54 (1).

Risse, Thomas and Kathryn Sikkink (1999) "The Socialization of Human Rights Norms into Domestic Practices: Introduction." In Thomas Risse, Stephen Ropp, and Kathryn Sikkink (eds.), *The Power of Principles: International Human Rights Norms and Domestic Change.* Cambridge: Cambridge University Press.

Roberts, Adam (2004) "The Use of Force." In David M. Malone (ed.), *The UN Security Council: From the Cold War to the 21st Century.* Boulder, CO: Lynne Rienner.

Roberts, Adam and Richard Guelff (eds.) (1989) *Documents on the Laws of War.* Oxford: Clarendon Press.

Romano, Cesare P. R (2004) "The Judges and Prosecutors of Internationalized Criminal Courts and Tribunals." In Cesare P. R. Romano, André Nollkaemper, and Jann K. Kleffner (eds.), *Internationalized Criminal Courts and Tribunals*, 235–70. Oxford: Oxford University Press.

Rosand, Eric (2003) "Security Council Resolution 1373, the Counter-terrorism Committee, and the Fight Against Terrorism." *American Journal of International Law*, 97 (2).

Rosand, Eric (2004) "The Security Council's Efforts to Monitor the Implementation of Al Qaeda/Taliban Sanctions." *American Journal of International Law*, 98 (4).

Rosenau, James N. (1992) "The Relocation of Authority in a Shrinking World." *Comparative Politics*, 24 (3).

Rosenau, James N. and Ernst-Otto Czempiel (1992) *Governance without Government: Order and Change in World Politics.* New York: Cambridge University Press.

Rosenberg, Justin (1994) *The Empire of Civil Society: A Critique of the Realist Theory of International Relations.* London: Verso.

Rostow, Nick (2001) U.S. Mission to the UN. Interview conducted on July 19.

Rostow, Nick (2002) "Before and After: The Changed UN Response to Terrorism since September 11th." *Cornell Journal of International Law*, 35 (3).

Rostow, Nick (2004) Interview conducted on July 21.

Rouleau, Nicolas M., Annelies Brock, Daisy Yu, Anne Heindel, Mario Cava, and Tejal Jesrani (2005) "Updates from the International Criminal Courts." *Human Rights Brief*, 12 (2).

Ruggie, John (1983) "International Regimes, Transactions, and Change: Embedded Liberalism in the Postwar Economic Order." In Stephen Krasner (ed.), *International Regimes.* Ithaca, NY: Cornell University Press.

Ruggie, John (1993) "Territoriality and Beyond: Problematizing Modernity in International Relations." *International Organization*, 47 (1).

Russett, Bruce (1997) "Ten Balances for Weighing UN Reform Proposals." In Bruce Russett (ed.), *The Once and Future Security Council.* New York: St. Martin's Press.

Russett, Bruce and John Oneal (2001) *Triangulating Peace: Democracy, Interdependence, and International Organizations.* New York: Norton.

Sabel, Robbie (1997) *Procedure at International Conferences*. Cambridge: Cambridge University Press.

Sandholtz, Wayne (2002) "Humanitarian Intervention: Global Enforcement of Human Rights?" In Alison Brysk (ed.), *Globalization and Human Rights*, 201–25. Berkeley, CA: University of California Press.

Sandholtz, Wayne and Alec Stone Sweet (2004) "Law, Politics, and International Governance." In Christian Reus-Smit (ed.), *The Politics of International Law*, 238–71. Cambridge: Cambridge University Press.

Sarooshi, Danesh (1999) *The United Nations and the Development of Collective Security: The Delegation by the UN Security Council of its Chapter VII Powers*. New York: Oxford University Press.

Schachter, Oscar (1989) "Self-defense and the Rule of Law." *American Journal of International Law*, 83 (2).

Schachter, Oscar (1999) *International Law in Theory and Practice*. The Hague: Kluwer Academic Publishers.

Scheffer, D. J. (1996) "International Judical Intervention." *Foreign Policy*, 102.

Scheuerman, William (1999) *Carl Schmitt: The End of Law*. Lanham, MD: Rowman & Littlefield.

Schlesinger, Stephen C. (2003) *Act of Creation: The Founding of the United Nations*. Boulder, CO: Westview Press.

Schloms, Michael (2002) "Humanitarian NGOs in Peace Process." *International Peacekeeping*, 10 (1).

Schweigman, David (2001) *The Authority of the Security Council under Chapter VII of the UN Charter*. The Hague: Kluwer Law.

Scott, Matthew (2004) UN Representative for World Vision. Interview conducted on July 20. New York City.

Sen, Amartya (2004) *Interdependence and Global Justice*. Lecture delivered at the General Assembly of the United Nations, October 29.

Shany, Yuval (2003) *The Competing Jurisdictions of International Courts and Tribunals*. Oxford: Oxford University Press.

Shapiro, Martin (1971) *Courts: A Comparative and Political Analysis*. Chicago: University of Chicago Press.

Shapiro, Martin (1972) "Toward a Theory of Stare Decisis." *Journal of Legal Studies*, 1.

Sharp, Alan (1991) *The Versailles Settlement: Peacemaking in Paris, 1919*. New York: St. Martin's Press.

Shaw, Malcolm (1997) *International Law*. Cambridge: Cambridge University Press.

Shimizu, Horofumi and Todd Sandler (2002) "Peacekeeping and Burden-sharing, 1994–2000." *Journal of Peace Research*, 39 (6).

Shraga, Daphna (2004) "The Second Generation UN-based Tribunals: A Diversity of Mixed Jurisdictions." In Cesare P. R. Romano, André Nollkaemper, and Jann K. Kleffner (eds.), *Internationalized Criminal Courts and Tribunals*, 15–38. Oxford: Oxford University Press.

Shringla, Harsh (2001) Permanent Mission of India. Interview conducted on July 21.

Simma, Bruno, Hermann Mosler, Albrecht Randelzhofer, Christian Tomuschat, and Rudiger Wolfrum (eds.) (2002) *The Charter of the United Nations: A Commentary*. Oxford: Oxford University Press.

Simon, Herbert A. (1947) *Administrative Behavior*. New York, NY: Macmillan

Simpson, Gerry (2004) *Great Powers and Outlaw States: Unequal Sovereigns in the International Legal Order*. Cambridge: Cambridge University Press.

Sinclair, Timothy J. (1994) "Passing Judgment: Credit Rating Processes as Regulatory Mechanisms of Governance in the Emerging World Order." *Review of International Political Economy*, 1 (1).

Sinclair, Timothy J. (1999) "Bond-rating Agencies and Coordination in the Global Political Economy." In A. Claire Cutler, Virginia Haufler, and Tony Porter (eds.), *Private Authority in International Affairs*. Albany, NY: SUNY Press.

Slaughter, Anne-Marie (2005) "Security, Solidarity, and Sovereignty: The Grand Themes of UN Reform." *American Journal of International Law*, 99 (4).

Slaughter, Anne-Marie, Andrew Tulumello, and Stephen Wood (1998) "International Law and International Relations Theory: A New Generation of Interdisciplinary Scholarship." *American Journal of International Law*, 92 (3).

Smith, Edwin and Thomas Weiss (1997) "UN Task-sharing: Towards or Away From Global Governance?" *Third World Quarterly*, 18 (3).

Smith, Jackie (1997) "Characteristics of the Modern Transnational Social Movement Sector." In Jackie Smith, Charles Chatfield, and Ron Pagnucco (eds.), *Transnational Social Movements and Global Politics: Solidarity Beyond the State*. Syracuse, NY: Syracuse University Press.

Smith, Jackie, Ron Pagnucco, and Charles Chatfield (1997) "Social Movements and World Politics." In Jackie Smith, Charles Chatfield, and Ron Pagnucco (eds.), *Transnational Social Movements and Global Politics: Solidarity Beyond the State*. Syracuse, NY: Syracuse University Press.

Snyder, Jack and Leslie Vinjamuri (2003) "Trials and Errors: Principle and Pragmatism in Strategies of International Justice." *International Security*, 28 (3).

Soederberg, Susanne (2004) "American Empire and 'Excluded States': The Millennium Challenge Account and the Shift to Pre-emptive Development." *Third World Quarterly*, 25 (2).

Sohn, Louis B. (1956) *Cases on United Nations Law, 1956*. Brooklyn, NY: Foundation Press.

Special Court for Sierra Leone (2004) "First Annual Report of the President of the Special Court for Sierra Leone." Available at www.sc-sl.org/specialcourt annualreport2002–2003.pdf. Accessed April 3, 2007.

Special Court for Sierra Leone (2005a) *Special Court for Sierra Leone, Completion Strategy 18 May 2005* (27 May 2005). United Nations General Assembly. A/59/816. Available at www.sc-sl.org/Documents/completionstrategy.pdf. Accessed April 3, 2007.

Special Court for Sierra Leone (2005b) "Second Annual Report of the President of the Special Court for Sierra Leone." Available at www.sc-sl.org/specialcourt annualreport2004–2005.pdf. Accessed April 3, 2007.

Special Court for Sierra Leone (2006) "Third Annual Report of the President of the Special Court for Sierra Leone." Available at www.sc-sl.org/specialcourt annualreport2005–2006.pdf. Accessed April 3, 2007.

Sriram, Chandra Lekha (2006) "Wrong-sizing International Justice? The Hybrid Tribunal in Sierra Leone." *Fordham International Law Journal*, 29.

Statute of the Special Court for Sierra Leone (2002) (16 January). Available at www.sc-sl.org/scsl-statute.html. Accessed April 3, 2007.

Steiner, Henry J. and Philip Alston (2000) *International Human Rights in Context: Law, Politics, Morals*, 2nd edn. Oxford: Oxford University Press.

Stoddard, Abby (2003) "Humanitarian NGOs: Challenges and Trends." In Joanne Macrae and Adele Harmer (eds.), *HPG Report 14, Humanitarian Action and the "Global War on Terror": A Review of Trends and Issues*. London: Overseas Development Institute.

Strange, Susan (1983) *"Cave! hic dragones:* A Critique of Regimes Analysis." In Stephen D. Krasner (ed.), *International Regims*. Ithaca, NY: Cornell University Press.

Stromseth, Jane (2003) "The Security Council's Counter-terrorism Role: Continuity and Innovation." *American Society of International Law Proceedings*, 97.

Sutterlin, James S. (2003) *The United Nations and the Maintenance of International Security: A Challenge to be Met*, 2nd edn. Westport, CT: Praeger.

Sweet, Alec Stone (1999) "Judicialization and the Construction of Governance." *Comparative Political Studies*, 32 (2).

Szasz, Paul (2002) "The Security Council Starts Legislating." *American Journal of International Law*, 96 (4).

Talmon, Stefan (2005) "Note and Comment: The Security Council as World Legislature." *American Journal of International Law*, 99 (1).

Tams, Christian J. (2005) *Enforcing Obligations* Erga Omnes *In International Law*. Cambridge: Cambridge University Press.

Taylor, Charles (1979) "Interpretation and the Science of Man." In Paul Rabinow and William Sullivan (eds.), *Interpretive Social Science: A Reader*. Berkeley: University of California Press.

Tesón, Fernando R. (1997) *Humanitarian Intervention: An Inquiry into Law and Morality*. Irvington-on-Hudson, NY: Transnational Publishers.

Tharoor, Sashi (2003) "Why America Still Needs the United Nations." *Foreign Affairs*, 82 (5).

Thomas, Daniel C. (2001) *The Helsinki Effect: International Norms, Human Rights, and the Demise of Communism*. Princeton: Princeton University Press.

Thompson, Kenneth (1953) "Collective Security Reexamined." *American Political Science Review*, 47 (3).

Thompson, Kenneth (1981) "Power, Force, and Diplomacy." *Review of Politics*, 43 (3).

Tirole, Jean (1999) "Incomplete Contracts: Where Do We Stand?" *Econometrica*, 67 (4).

Torrente, Nicolas (2004) "Humanitarianism Sacrificed: Integration's False Promise." *Ethics and International Affairs*, 18 (2).

Trachtenberg, Mark (1993) "Intervention in Historical Perspective." In Laura W. Reed and Carl Kaysen (eds.), *Emerging Norms of Justified Intervention*. Cambridge, MA: American Academy of Arts and Sciences.

Triepel, Heinrich (1938) *Die hegemonie: ein buch von führenden staaten*. Stuttgart: Verlag von W. Kohlhammer.

True-Frost, Cora (2005) Coordinator for NGO Working Group on Women, Peace, and Security. Interview conducted on March 29. New York City.

Turk, Danilo (2003) "Law and Policy: Security Council's Ability to Innovate." *American Society of International Law Proceedings*, 97.

Tyler, Tom R. (2001) "A Psychological Perspective on the Legitimacy of Institutions and Authorities." In John T. Jost and Brenda Major (eds.), *The Psychology of Legitimacy: Emerging Perspective on Ideology, Justice and Intergroup Relations*. Cambridge: Cambridge University Press.

United Nations (1951) *United Nations Treaty Series.* No. 1021, vol. 78. New York.

United Nations (1993) *Report of The Secretary-General Pursuant to Paragraph 2 Of Security Council Resolution 808.* Presented May 3 (UN Doc S/25704).

United Nations (1999) *Report of the Secretary-General Pursuant to General Assembly Resolution 53/35* (A/54/549).

United Nations (2003) International Covenant on Civil and Political Rights. Concluding Observations of the Human Rights Committee, Philippines. CCPR/CO/79/PHL 01/12.

United Nations (2004) *A More Secure World: Our Shared Responsibility.* Report of the Secretary-General's High-Level Panel on Threats, Challenges and Change. A/59/565. New York: United Nations.

United Nations (2005) *Multilateral Treaty Framework: An Invitation to Universal Participation.* Available at untreaty.un.org/English/TreatyEvent2005/focus2005.pdf. Accessed May 17, 2005.

United Nations General Assembly (2005) *In Larger Freedom: Towards Development, Security and Human Rights For All.* Report of the Secretary-General, A/59/2005, March 21.

United Nations Yearbook (1967) Published by the United Nations, New York.

United Nations Yearbook (1983) Published by the United Nations, New York.

United Nations Yearbook (1989) Published by the United Nations, New York.

United States Congress (2002) Joint Resolution to Authorize the Use of United States Armed Forces Against Iraq, October 2, http//www.whitehouse.gov/news/releases/2002/10/ 20021002-2.html

United States Institute of Peace (2005) *The Imperative for Action: An Update of the Report of the Task Force on American Interests and UN Reform.* Washington, DC: United States Institute of Peace.

Vagts, Detlev (2001) "Hegemonic International Law." *American Journal of International Law*, 95 (4).

van Ham, Peter and Olivia Bosch (2007) "Global Non-proliferation and Counter-terrorism: The Role of Resolution 1540 and Its Implications." in Bosch and van Ham 2007.

Vayrynen, Raimo (1999) *Globalization and Global Governance.* Lanham, MD: Rowman & Littlefield Publishers.

Voeten, Erik (2001) "Outside Options and the Logic of Security Council Action." *American Political Science Review*, 95 (4).

Voeten, Erik (2005) "The Political Origins of the United Nations Security Council's Ability to Legitimize the Use of Force." *International Organization*, 59 (3).

Voeten, Erik (2007) "Why No UN Security Council Reform? Lessons for and from Institutionalist Theory." In Dimitris Bourantonis, Kostas Infantis, and Panayotis Tsakonas (eds.), *Multilateralism and Security Institutions in the Era of Globalization*, 288–305. London: Routledge.

von Glahn, Gerhard (1996) *Law Among Nations.* Boston: Allyn and Bacon.

Walker, Sophie (2007) "British Pushing for SC Climate Debate." *Reuters*, March 8.

Wallensteen, Peter and Patrik Johansson (2004) "Security Council Decisions in Perspective." In David Malone (ed.), *The UN Security Council: From the Cold War to the 21st Century.* Boulder, CO: Lynne Rienner.

Waltz, Kenneth (1986) "Anarchic Orders and Balances of Power." In Robert O. Keohane (ed.), *Neorealism and its Critics.* New York: Columbia University Press.

Waltz, Susan (2002) "Human Rights Standards and the Human Rights Movement in the Global South: The UDHR and Beyond." In George J. Andreopoulos (ed.), *Concepts and Strategies in International Human Rights*, 51–71. New York: Peter Lang.

Waltz, Susan (2004) "Universal Human Rights: The Contribution of Muslim States." *Human Rights Quarterly*, 26 (4).

Ward, Curtis (2003) "Building Capacity to Combat International Terrorism: The Role of the United Nations Security Council." *Journal of Conflict and Security Law*, 8 (2).

Watson Institute for International Studies (2006) *Strengthening Targeted Sanctions Through Fair and Clear Procedures*. White Paper prepared by the Watson Institute Targeted Sanctions Project. Brown University. March 30, watsoninstitute.org/pub/ Strengthening_Targeted_Sanctions.pdf

Weber, Max (1978) *Economy and Society*. Ephraim Fischoff et al., (trans.); Guenther Roth and Claus Wittich (eds.). Berkeley: University of California Press.

Wedgewood, Ruth (2003) "The Fall of Saddam Hussein: Security Council Mandates and Preemptive Self-defense." *American Journal of International Law*, 3 (97).

Weil, Prosper (1983) "Toward Relative Normativity in International Law." *American Journal of International Law*, 77.

Weingast, Barry R. and Mark J. Moran (1983) "Bureaucratic Discretion or Congressional Control? Regulatory Policy-making by the Federal Trade Commission." *Journal of Political Economy*, 91 (5).

Weiss, Cora (2004) President Hague Appeal for Peace. Interview conducted on July 14. New York City.

Weiss, Thomas (1996a) "Collective Spinelessness: UN Actions in the Former Yugoslavia." In Richard H. Ullman (ed.), *The World and Yugoslavia's Wars*. New York: Council on Foreign Relations Press.

Weiss, Thomas (1996b) "Nongovernmental Organizations and Internal Conflict." In Michael Brown (ed.), *The International Dimensions of Internal Conflict*. Cambridge, MA: MIT Press.

Weiss, Thomas (1999a) "Principles, Politics, and Humanitarian Action." *Ethics and International Affairs*, 13.

Weiss, Thomas (1999b) *Military–Civilian Interactions: Intervening in Humanitarian Crises*. Lanham, MD: Rowman & Littlefield Publishers.

Weiss, Thomas (2003) "The Illusion of UN Security Council Reform." *Washington Quarterly*, 26 (4).

Weiss, Thomas (2005) *Military–Civilian Interactions: Humanitarian Crises and the Responsibility to Protect*, 2nd edn. Lanham, MD: Rowman & Littlefield Publishers.

Weissman, Fabrice (2004a) "Sierra Leone: Peace at Any Price." In Fabrice Weissman (ed.), *In the Shadow of "Just Wars": Violence, Politics and Humanitarian Action*. Ithaca, NY: Cornell University Press.

Weissman, Fabrice (ed.) (2004b) *In the Shadow of "Just Wars": Violence, Politics and Humanitarian Action*. Ithaca, NY: Cornell University Press.

Welch, Claude (2001) "Conclusion." In Claude Welch (ed.), *NGOs and Human Rights: Promise and Performance*. Philadelphia, PA: University of Pennsylvania Press.

Wendt, Alexander (1992) "Anarchy Is What States Make of It." *International Organization*, 46 (2).

Wendt, Alexander and Daniel Friedheim (1995) "Hierarchy under Anarchy: Informal Empire and the East German State." *International Organization*, 49 (4).

White, N.D (1997) *Keeping the Peace: The United Nations and the Maintenance of International Peace and Security*. Manchester: Manchester University Press.

Wilkinson, Rorden (2005) *The Global Governance Reader*. London: Routledge.

Wilkinson, Rorden and Stephen Hughes (2002) *Global Governance: Critical Perspectives*. New York: Routledge.

Willetts, Peter (1996) "Consultative Status for NGOs at the United Nations." In Peter Willetts (ed.), *'The Conscience of the World': The Influence of Non-Governmental Organisations in the UN System*. Washington, DC: Brookings Institution.

Williams, Sarah (2004) "The Cambodian Extraordinary Chambers: A Dangerous Precedent for International Justice?" *International & Comparative Law Quarterly*, 53.

Williamson, John (1990) "What Washington Means by Policy Reform." In John Williamson (ed.), *Latin American Adjustment: How Much Has Happened*. Washington, DC: Institute for International Economics.

Wilson, Carolyn (2004) Interview conducted on July 19.

Winter, Eyal (1996) "Voting and Vetoing." *American Political Science Review*, 90 (4).

Wolfers, Arnold (1988) *Discord and Collaboration, Essays on International Politics*. Baltimore, MD: The Johns Hopkins University Press.

Wood, Ellen M. (1981) "The Separation of the Economic and the Political in Capitalism." *New Left Review*, 1 (27).

Wrong, Dennis (1961) "The Oversocialized Conception of Man in Modern Sociology." *American Sociological Review*, 26 (2).

Yergin, Daniel and Joseph Stanislaw (2002) *The Commanding Heights*. New York: Touchstone Press.

Zagaris, Bruce (2007). "International Criminal Courts: Cambodian Special Tribunal Controversy Continues." *International Enforcement Law Reporter*, 232.

Zelditch, Morris Jr. (2001) "Theories of Legitimacy." In John T. Jost and Brenda Major (eds.), *The Psychology of Legitimacy: Emerging Perspectives on Ideology, Justice, and Intergroup Relations*. Cambridge: Cambridge University Press.

Zürn, Michael (2000) "Democratic Governance Beyond the Nation-state: The EU and Other International Institutions." *European Journal of International Relations*, 6 (2).

Index

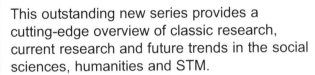

Made in the USA
Middletown, DE
31 August 2017